Kommunikation und Kybernetik in Einzeldarstellungen
Herausgegeben von H. Wolter und W. D. Keidel
Band 2

Structural Linguistics and Human Communication

An Introduction into the Mechanism
of Language and the Methodology
of Linguistics

By

Bertil Malmberg

Professor of Phonetics and Head of the
Department of Phonetics of the Faculty of Arts
University of Lund (Sweden)

With 88 Figures

Second revised edition

Springer-Verlag
Berlin · Heidelberg · New York 1967

© by Springer-Verlag OHG Berlin · Göttingen · Heidelberg 1963
© by Springer-Verlag Berlin · Heidelberg 1967
Printed in Germany

Library of Congress Catalog Card Number 63-12931

Titel-Nr. 6131

TO THE MEMORY

OF

WERNER MEYER-EPPLER

Preface to the first edition

The point of departure of this general survey of modern structural linguistics is the place of language in human relations. Linguistics will consequently be understood as a science of communication. My book is not intended as an elementary handbook. The readers are supposed to be in the first place advanced students of linguistics and phonetics and of neighbouring fields where a real awareness of linguistic methods and problems is essential (such as psychology, phoniatrics, speech therapy, language teaching, communication engineering). The book may, however, be of some value also for the general reader who is interested in language, in language learning, or in communication processes. It might finally serve as an introduction to structural theories and practice for those linguists of traditional orientation who would like to make contact with the new trends in the study of language.

It is self-evident that, under such circumstances, any reader will find certain chapters in this book rather complicated, others irritatingly elementary. This is, however, unavoidable in a work whose aim is to cover a vast field of knowledge and to offer the reader a synthesis of what appears at first sight to be widely disparate facts and phenomena. Many of the facts brought together here may, regarded superficially, seem to have few or no mutual connections. They can, nevertheless, be combined into a wide humanistic and scientific unity within which numerous lines of relationship bind together physical and psychic, individual and social phenomena. It is this synthetic view — which covers such disparate concepts as phonemes and meaning, decibels and linguistic change, literary style and speech disturbances — rather than the mere facts referred to which is, or is meant to be the authors' personal contribution to the problems under discussion. There is no doubt that the presentation of these facts is coloured by the author's own views on language and linguistics. Even if no single idea expressed in this book is new as such, the combination of ideas and viewpoints may at least contain some originality.

My friend and colleague at Bonn, the late WERNER MEYER-EPPLER suggested that I should write a book on structural linguistics for the series "Kybernetik und Kommunikationsforschung in Einzeldarstellungen" when we met at a congress in Paris in 1959. I deeply regret that he was not permitted to supervise my work and to collaborate, as was agreed, on giving it its final form — a collaboration from which I should have greatly profited. I have dedicated my book to his memory.

This preface has also seemed to me to be the place to express my thanks to those to whom I owe my own linguistic and phonetic orientation. I received my basic training in traditional phonetics in Paris under the guidance of PIERRE FOUCHÉ and, not least, of MARGUERITE DURAND to whose memory I do homage on this occasion. Without the stimulating teaching of ANDRÉ MARTINET, whom I met during his first term at the École des Hautes Études, this purely phonetic training would, however, have been of restricted value for future linguistic research. The insight I got under MARTINET's guidance into the then new phonological doctrine became decisive for my work as a linguist and as a phonetician. MARTINET's work has never ceased to be a source of inspiration in my own scientific efforts.

MARTINET's teaching brought me into contact with TRUBETZKOY's works. It was with this background I came to read, in 1941, JAKOBSON's "Kindersprache". It opened a new world to me and determined for ever the direction of my linguistic thinking. Every line in this book bears witness of it. Only many years later did I get the opportunity of meeting ROMAN JAKOBSON and of winning his friendship. My thanks to him are poor.

A little later, during the first years of the war, I got into contact with the Danish school of linguistics, first with VIGGO BRØNDAL's works, and then with LOUIS HJELMSLEV. It would be difficult to express here in a few words what I owe to the Glossematic school and particularly to HJELMSLEV himself. I look upon his "OSG" as one of the most important contributions to linguistic theory since SAUSSURE's "Cours". My personal friendly contacts with HJELMSLEV have been of inestimable value for my own research work. This is true also of my numerous friendly contacts with ELI FISCHER-JØRGENSEN in whom I admire the richness of ideas and the lucid intellectual analyses of complicated phenomena. I owe very much to her, scientifically and personally.

I had the luck to be invited in 1955 to the Haskins Laboratories in New York. My thanks to FRANK COOPER and to my other friends there for this valuable introduction into new analytic and synthetic methods in speech research are profound and sincere.

If the formal approach to language was SAUSSURE's first and nowadays most generally quoted thesis, the social character of human language and its role in the social and cultural context was the other. I owe stimulating ideas in this later direction to the Spanish school of linguistics and particularly to DON RAMÓN MENÉNDEZ PIDAL whose linguistic and historical analyses of the evolution of Castilian are models within this field of research. I shall always remember my visit to DON RAMÓN in

1950, and the kindly way in which he received me in his home. Don Ramón and Louis Hjelmslev are the two extremes between which any linguistic investigation must be carried out, if it is to aim at an exhaustive description of human language. A linguist will find himself closer to one or to the other according to personal taste or to differences in his material. I fully realize the necessity of formalism as a guarantee for scientific accuracy. But I am convinced on the other hand of the importance of extending the structural approach to socio-linguistic and cultural-linguistic relations.

Finally I thank my friend Edward Carney for kindly revising my English and for valuable suggestions, and Kerstin Hadding-Koch who has gone through my manuscript and made numerous important remarks. I also want to thank the staff of the Institute of Phonetics of Lund for their help in the production of this book.

Lund, June 1962

Bertil Malmberg

In the second edition a series of mistakes and misprints have been corrected. Otherwise the text is the same. An index of names quoted in the book has been added.

Lund and Paris, January 1966

B. M.

Contents

Introduction

"... a totality does not consist of things but of relationships" (HJELMSLEV, *Prolegomena to a Theory of Language*, 2nd ed., p. 23).

It would be a commonplace to say that language is the most important invention of man. In fact, it is more than that, because man and language are parallel developments. It is consequently of no use arguing about the priority of one or the other. If we say that primitive man invented language or that the invention of language made some intelligent primate into man, we say the same thing. Man is a talking animal; no other animal talks. It will be clear, I suppose, from later chapters that the so - called languages of some animals (bees, etc.) are not languages in the sense in which this concept is taken in structural linguistics (cf. particularly Chap. XI). So we could more suitably say that the making of man and the making of language are identical. *Homo sapiens* is *homo loquens*.

The following survey of the main problems of modern linguistics will show that the analysis of human civilisation and of human social life in all its different forms and on all its levels is to a very large extent also an analysis of human language — of language conventions and of linguistic systems, inasmuch as social and cultural patterns are reflected by language and because there is no other means of knowing about the so-called facts inside and outside ourselves, than through the structuration which is imposed on these facts by language conventions. It would consequently be unsatisfactory to classify linguistics — the study of language — only as a branch of humanities, as is generally done. Linguistics deals with problems which are basic to all sciences, in so far as all scientific research must be deeply concerned with the functions and particularities of the medium through which scientific preliminaries, scientific conclusions, and scientific descriptions must necessarily be expressed.

In our modern world, communication plays a more important part than ever before and, thanks to technical advance, has adopted forms and aspects formerly unknown and undreamt of. This development has raised new problems not only for the study of communication as such but also, and particularly, for the study of our basic means of communication: language. The problems of technical speech transmission and of sound engineering have created a need for solid knowledge about the structure of language among technicians and communication theorists. The translation machines and related technical devices (for transforming speech into written language, and written language into speech, etc.) are essentially applications of analyses made by linguists. The main obstacles to a complete success in these fields are to be found on the linguistic level, not on the technical. Scientists and engineers engaged in communication problems must know what language is, how it is built up, and how it functions. The same is true for the speech therapist and for the different medical specialists who, in their work, meet language disturbances and abnormal linguistic phenomena. That linguistic analysis is a necessary condition for language teaching and language learning is self-evident. Contacts with other civilisations, with other social systems, and all the forms of international collaboration which are being created and developed in the world of today suppose not only an acceptable knowledge of the phonemic, graphic, and grammatical structure of the respective languages, but also, and in the first place, an acquaintance with the semantic structure and with the sets of concepts and ideas which are the expression of these civilisations. Without any knowledge of languages such as Chinese, Japanese, or Thai, no real understanding of these Eastern peoples' thinking, culture, and reactions are possible, and consequently no real human contacts can be established. The same is valid for Indian, African, and Arabic, and for all cultural patterns which are based on other spiritual and social traditions than those of Western civilisation. The same is to a large extent true also of the young generation which is now being educated in the Communist world according to norms and ideals profoundly different from those which have been current in European tradition for centuries. It may even to a certain extent be true of different generations and of different social layers within the cultural groups in question. Language is not only a way of communicating, in a restricted sense, i.e. of transferring signals by means of an ordinary expression code (as is the Morse alphabet). It is a way of thinking, of structuring a content ("Denkform", GLINZ) — and, as a matter of fact, the only way of doing so. "CARNAP has long felt that the questions of philosophy, when real at all, are questions of language" (QUINE).

These remarks may be enough to motivate a presentation of modern linguistic analysis as generally carried out nowadays by most linguists. The methods of analysis differ in detail, it is true, and sometimes also on important theoretical principles, but they start from a common

outlook in that they regard the structure of language as a system —
or a code — of communication the description of which is their main
concern. On the other hand, the mathematical, scientific, technical,
and sociological approaches to language have opened new views on
language itself and revealed the existence of phenomena unnoticed by
traditional linguists. Thus a confrontation of structural linguistics with
the basic problems of information, communication, sound engineering,
and social anthropology may also be of particular interest to those
linguists who have adhered too much to traditional methods of analysis
to be aware of these new aspects of their own science.

There was hardly any scientific study of language in the strict sense
of the word before the beginning of the 19th century. When human
language was first made the object of scientific analysis, by scholars
like JAKOB GRIMM in Germany and RASMUS RASK in Denmark, it was
from a historical and comparative point of view and under the particular
scientific conditions created by romanticism and by the interest this
movement took in past epochs and in remote countries and, a little
later, by the evolutionary approach characteristic of biology from
CHARLES DARWIN onwards. In his famous book "Die Darwinsche
Theorie und die Sprachwissenschaft" (1863), AUGUST SCHLEICHER expressed the opinion that languages, like plants and animals, are born,
grow, age, and die. It was in this scientific climate, and in order to make
the study of language an exact study in the same sense as physics
and mathematics, that the famous Neogrammarian thesis of the
exceptionlessness of sound laws was put forward, first by AUGUST
LESKIEN (in 1876). Though untenable in its extreme form, this thesis
no doubt brought about order and scientific strictness within linguistics.
Fancy and arbitrary constructions were replaced by scientific accuracy.
Evolution was the only scientific aspect of language. Every explanation
in the domain of linguistic research had to be historical: without history
no scientific approach was possible, according to HERMANN PAUL whose
"Prinzipien der Sprachgeschichte" (first edition 1880, 5th 1920) was
the Bible of the Neogrammarian school.
    Linguistics was first developed not as an independent, but as an
auxiliary science. Thorough knowledge of dead and living languages
was needed for many scientific and practical purposes. Historians
of every kind wanted to read old texts and prehistoric inscriptions.
As was pointed out above, any serious inquiry into the civilisation of
foreign peoples supposes a solid knowledge of their languages. The kind
of language science which aims at an interpretation of the content of a
text — old or new — and for which the content is the essential thing,

is nowadays called philology, a term which, on the Continent, has
normally been used, in a somewhat restricted sense, about the science
of interpreting old texts (including paleography which is devoted more
directly to the reading of the texts, the study of the script, of abbreviations, of palimpsests, etc.). Thus philology is opposed to linguistics
through the fact that the linguist is interested in the study of the language
as such (its sounds, its forms, its words, its system, its development),
whereas, to the philologist, the linguistic analysis he has to make in
order to understand his document, is only a necessary means for unveiling the content. Unfortunately, as linguistics has developed out
of philology to which it was long subordinate, the term philology has
often been used also for the study of language itself, particularly for
traditional historical linguistics. In Great Britain, this terminology has
long been current and particularly such expressions as general philology and comparative philology have been used for what, according to continental usage, is linguistics (French "linguistique", German
"Linguistik", or, with a term common to both branches, ,,Sprach-
wissenschaft"). On the other hand, there seems to be a tendency in the
USA to use the term linguistics only when talking about modern
(structural) linguistics, excluding all traditional historical linguistic
research. Neither of these terminologies will be used in this book,
where, in accordance with a fairly well established continental usage,
"linguistics" will refer to any kind of language analysis and description
which has language itself as its object, and "philology" will be reserved
for the study and interpretation of texts and other documents, old or
contemporary.

The early development of linguistics briefly referred to above is
interesting from the point of view of scientific history in general. The
orientation towards change, evolution, and history which put its mark
on 19th century science as a whole and for a long period to come determined the methods and aims of a whole series of humanistic branches
such as literary and aesthetic analysis, social anthropology, and philosophy, saddled linguistics with an approach to language study which
is, in fact, inconsistent with the basic functions of the object itself and
overemphasizes one of its aspects — and a secondary one — to the
detriment of others. For the establishment of linguistics as an autonomous
science it was no doubt unhappy that its early development should
coincide with a period of romanticism and that its final shape should
be determined by evolutionary influences and biological analogies.
RASMUS RASK, the founder of the comparative method, was in fact
a rationalist and put the stress more on establishing strict sound correspondences than on the historical interpretation of these correspondences which, however, became the primary aim of JAKOB GRIMM and

which was to determine the later German tradition. Modern linguistics still has to fight against this tradition. One of the aims of this book is to demonstrate the possibilities, and the necessity, of building up a new linguistics and to show how the foundations of such a science were laid by, among others, the Swiss comparatist FERDINAND DE SAUSSURE, the American LEONARD BLOOMFIELD, the Russians NICOLAI S. TRUBETZKOY and ROMAN JAKOBSON — the latter naturalized American —, the Dane LOUIS HJELMSLEV, and the Frenchman ANDRÉ MARTINET[1].

Modern linguistics, such as it has been worked out in recent years—essentially after World War I — on the basis of FERDINAND DE SAUSSURE's postumous "Cours de linguistique générale" (1916) by a number of European and American scholars is generally called structural linguistics. We do not need to go into the historical relationships of the various modern schools or the question of their originality. It does not matter very much if BLOOMFIELD owes anything to SAUSSURE, or if the Swede ADOLF NOREEN — another of the forerunners of structuralism, or at least of synchronism — is indebted to foreign models or not. It is a fact, however, that different linguists, within and outside Europe, have been trying, for about 30 years, to analyse language from new points of view and that these points of view are similar in many respects. The similarity consists in the common structural approach.

Although some of the concepts of structural linguistics may be, and actually have been understood rather differently by different scholars and schools, it seems quite possible to define, at least roughly, its main content and general orientation and methods. A structure, according to every day usage, is made up of parts or elements having a certain mutual relationship, as opposed to a mere accumulation of mutually independent items. If human language is said to be structured, this should be understood in such a way that any language is built up of so-called discrete elements (i.e. sharply delimited from each other and without any possible gradual passage from one to the other). Language consequently is analysable into minimal independent units, which are restricted in number and the functions of which are determined by their relations to the other units with which they are combined, within a system of communication possibilities (a paradigm), and within a possible speech sequence, the chain (or the syntagm). These are called

---

[1] It will be pointed out later that, contradictory though it may seem in certain respects, a structural approach to the linguistic expression must be supposed to have directed early comparative method and determined the Neogrammarian conception of sound laws.

respectively the paradigmatic, and the syntagmatic relations. The
distinctions made within the paradigm are generally called oppositions,
those made in the syntagm contrasts[1]. If linguistics is called structural,
this consequently implies that its main concern is the description and
analysis of its functional units (its discrete elements) and of the relations
between these. It would be more or less the same thing to say that a
given language is a system of elements and that it has a certain form
which characterizes it and opposes it to other systems which have other
forms. When for instance phonemics is said to be structural, as opposed
to traditional phonetics, this means that the phonemicist starts his
analysis with a study of the relations between the phonetic elements
and of the form of the systems which they build up, reserving
the different characteristics of the purely physical events through
which these elements are manifested for a later stage in the analytic
process. It does not imply, as some people believe, that he neglects the
physical facts. He only orders his material according to a hierarchy
which is adequate for the object analysed ("une hiérarchie des faits
adéquate à l'objet", MARTINET). Examples and details will be given
later.

It should also be pointed out from the very beginning that the
structural approach to language study and language analysis is not,
in any way, so much opposed to the traditional historical point of
view — the study of language change and of the history of different
languages — as has sometimes been pretended. Structural linguistics
is directed not against history as such but against an old-fashioned
atomistic method of linguistic research which studies the development of
isolated elements—a vowel, an accent, a form, a syntactical procedure,
a meaning — along the axis of time (e.g. from Latin to Modern French)
without taking into account that, at any moment in the history of the
language, this element formed part of a structure and was determined,
as regards its functions, by this structure. It is meaningless to talk
about an isolated Old French diphthong *ue* resulting from Latin short *o*
in an open stressed syllable (Lat. *bove* 'ox', Old Fr. *buef*), if nothing
is said about the place of this diphthong within the vowel system of
Old French about e.g. 1100, etc. Structural linguistics, as applied to
linguistic change, is the study of modifications of systems and of changes
in the relationship between linguistic elements. Traditional linguistics
forgot that the study of an isolated element is of no value for the study
of language, because such an element gets its linguistic function — i.e.
becomes an element of language — only thanks to its position within

---

[1] As for the terminological and conceptual difference established here between
opposition and distinction, see also Chap. III.

a given system[1]. It does not make any sense from the point of view of language and of linguistics to speak about an [i], a -ing, or an inverted word order, if these units are not opposed to, say, an [u], an -ed, or a normal word order. A word like *father* has a meaning only if opposed to *mother*, or to *son*, etc. Synchronic (or descriptive) linguistics examines oppositions and identities — two concepts which will have to be treated in detail in following chapters — whereas diachronic (or historical) linguistics is concerned with the changes suffered by the systems (the sets of oppositions etc.) in the course of history. Both aspects of structural linguistics will be taken into consideration in this survey, though the principles of synchronic description will dominate for the simple reason that these have so far been more thoroughly worked out and are more solidly established. For the same reason, expression analysis will be treated in more detail than content analysis. The synchronic basis is a necessary condition for any meaningful scientific analysis of linguistic change. Only after a synchronic description of a language system — within a given linguistic community and a given period of time — has been carried out does the diachronist know the real object of his research. Neither synchronic study nor diachronic study should concern themselves with isolated pieces of language, only with the coherent structures built up by these elements. This — and only this — is the general principle of structural linguistics.

---

[1] It is on the other hand a matter of fact that the comparative method — which was based on the identification of expression elements (just called "letters", later, and already in the second edition of GRIMM's "Deutsche Grammatik", mentioned as "sounds") on the basis of identical function, e.g. Latin *p* in *piscis*, *pater*, *pecu* equals Germanic *f* in Engl. *fish*, *father*, Germ. *Vieh* — implied a functional point of view in the sense that functional identity was supposed to remain unaltered independently of substance and of change of substance. The regular sound correspondences alone, not any kind of physical sound ressemblance, were proofs of genetic relationship. An often quoted, striking example from Indo-European comparative linguistics is Armenian *erku* — Latin *duo* etc., two forms which can be identified, phoneme by phoneme, according to well established laws of correspondence, though they have no substantial (phonetic) ressemblance whatsoever. E. BUYSSENS has tried to explain SAUSSURE's structural and functional approach by his historical comparative and Neogrammarian background. L. HJELMSLEV has in a similar way pointed out the part played by the same formal, "structural" approach in RASMUS RASK's thinking.

Chapter I

Signs and Symbols. The Linguistic Sign

Almost all the basic ideas in structural linguistics can be traced back to FERDINAND DE SAUSSURE's "Cours de linguistique générale". We shall start our survey of the main trends and features of structural linguistic description by discussing the concept of linguistic sign which is essential for understanding not only SAUSSURE's own system but also many of the modern applications of his ideas, and modern structuralism as a whole.

Every day usage is not quite clear concerning such terms as sign and symbol. A sign is often explained as "something that stands for something" (*aliquid stat pro aliquo*). Sometimes "a sign of something" means an indication of something else ("sign of rain, of illness"). Some people define the distinction between sign and symbol by saying that the sign only indicates the presence of something else, whereas the use of a symbol is due to convention. Smoke is a sign indicating the presence of fire. But the smoke which, after the election of a new pope, comes out through the chimney of the Vatican is a symbol, because it can be interpreted correctly only by those who are familiar with the convention in question.

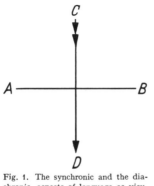

Fig. 1. The synchronic and the diachronic aspects of language as visualized by SAUSSURE in "Cours". *A–B* = synchrony, *C–D* = diachrony

Modern linguistics uses both terms in rather different ways, and in order to cover concepts which can be understood only in the light of the linguistic theory behind them. This is particularly the case with the Saussurean sign ("le signe linguistique"). That is why we shall have to devote some attention to this concept before we go further.

According to SAUSSURE, the sign was a combination of a concept and an acoustic image (Fig. 2). Let us take his own example in English translation. The sign *ox* is a combination of the concept 'ox' — an animal with specific distinctive characteristics — and the sound sequence [ɔks]. In the minds of English-speaking people, these two are so intimately connected that one seems inconceivable without the other. An Englishman, when catching sight of an ox, immediately has the sound sequence [ɔks] "on the tip of his tongue". Inversely, when he hears this sound sequence, the idea of 'ox' immediately comes up in his brain. The sound sequence is the "designans", the concept the "designatum".

To primitive man, the concept and the acoustic image are identical. Many phenomena in folk-lore and primitive thinking get their explanation from this identification (word tabu, etc.). Even modern people's reactions to foreign languages and to unfamiliar words are often determined by the same instinctive feeling. We regard our own words and expressions as the only natural ones and foreign words as odd, ridiculous, or incorrect. Through contact with other languages — by chance, in bilingual surroundings, or by means of deliberate language learning — man discovers, however, that there may be other labels on the objects than those used by himself and that these labels may be equally appropriate. What is *ox* in English, is *bœuf* in French. What is *Pferd* in German, is *horse* in English, *cheval* in French, *caballo* in Spanish. The horse itself is — or, at least, seems to be — the same. Only the "word" is different[1].

Scientific and philosophical analysis has often aimed at getting rid of the "tyranny of words". There is a definite discrepancy between, on the one hand, the primitive interpretation of words and their meaning, and, on the other, the more scientific idea of the arbitrariness of the designations. We shall later see which of these two interpretations of the relationship between words and concepts is the correct one, or at least, the most acceptable, and under what conditions one or the other may be regarded as valid.

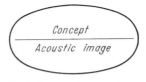

Fig. 2. SAUSSURE's schematic representation of the linguistic sign with its two halves: the concept (content, "designatum"), and the acoustic image (expression, "designans"; which of course may also be e.g. a graphic image). Both have their *form* and their *substance*

In SAUSSURE's French terminology the concept was called the "signifié" and the acoustic image the "signifiant". It is important to notice that both concept and acoustic image are abstractions. The "signifiant" is not the actual sound-wave — not the physical event — but the idea of a sound sequence, an image, or a representation, of such an event. And the "signifié" is not the ox — not a concrete animal — but the idea of an ox, the representation of a class or a category. We may translate SAUSSURE's terms into English by respectively the signified and the signifier. By setting up from the beginning two basic abstractions — signified and signifier — and by opposing them to the concrete physical facts or events they represent or sum up, SAUSSURE anticipated his second fundamental dichotomy: the langue — parole distinction — translated into English as language and speech, a terminology used for instance by the famous British scholar Sir ALAN GARDINER. The language was the abstract, superindividual system, the pattern or the model, and the speech was the concrete individual act of talking or communicating.

---

[1] We shall see in a later chapter that this conception of words as mere labels put on pre-existing concepts or "things" does not hold.

Language is manifested in the concrete world by speech. On the other hand, speech is possible only thanks to the existence of language.

Several comments could be made on this very much discussed and criticized dichotomy which, in fact, needs further gradation in order to correspond to the actual needs of linguistic analysis. We are, however, not going to discuss these problems in detail here. Some of them will be treated in later sections (cf. particularly Chap. IX). It is, however, important to point out already now that for modern communication theory this dichotomy is nothing but one of many well-known cases of a set of possibilities common to a sender and a receiver of a verbal message. The *langue* is, in fact, this "ensemble of possibilities already preseen and provided for" (JAKOBSON) which the communication engineer calls the c o d e, and thanks to which one set of informational units is converted into another set (a grammatical unit into a phonemic or vice versa). The *parole*, i.e. the exchange between interlocutors, is possible only thanks to the *langue*. The attitude of a listener to a piece of unknown language is identical with the attitude of a receiver to a message in an unknown code. The message presupposes the code[1].

Consequently, the sign was not for SAUSSURE the designation of an object or of a concept, as could be supposed according to the normal usage of the word sign. This SAUSSURE called "signifiant". Let us stress once more that the sign was the combination of the concept and the acoustic image into a unit with two halves, like the two sides of a medal (Fig. 2), or according to HJELMSLEV "a two-sided entity, with a Janus-like perspective in two directions". According to SAUSSURE, the sign was a r b i t r a r y, a thesis which has been met with some criticism and has given occasion to much discussion, partly because of misunderstanding of the concept of sign itself. SAUSSURE expressly says that the c o m b i-n a t i o n of the concept and the acoustic image in the signs is arbitrary. The concept 'horse' may be combined with the acoustic image $[hɔ:s]$ into the English sign *horse*. Nothing in the nature of either of the parts of such a sign makes this combination more natural than any other. In French, the "same" concept is combined with the acoustic image $[ʃəval]$ into a sign *cheval*, etc. One is as arbitrary as the other. The signifier $[hɔ:s]$ is a carrier of the "meaning" 'horse' only thanks to convention. The only exception to this rule is the existence in most languages of some sound-imitating words such as *buzz, hush, splash, whistle, whisper, rattle* in English, or the name of the *cuckoo* in many languages (Fr. *coucou*, Lat. *cuculus*, Finnish *käki*, etc.).

There is no need to dwell here on the question of whether the onomatopoeic type of word formation may have played an important part

---

[1] What HERDAN has called "the statistical view of DE SAUSSURE's distinction" will be mentioned in Chap. VII.

at earlier stages in the development of human language[1] and of whether
onomatopoeiae were actually the starting point of speech, as some
scholars believe. Let us just call attention to the fact that in the languages
of today these words are relatively rare and hardly contradict the statement made about the arbitrariness of the sign taken in SAUSSURE's sense.
This is of course still more true about the type of only partly arbitrary
formations ("relativement motivé", according to SAUSSURE) such as
Engl. *rainbow, fox-hunting, blindness* which are evidently not arbitrary
in relation to the single signs on which they are formed. Different languages present, for historical reasons, somewhat different systems in this
respect. Compounds and derivations on the basis of existing word elements are for instance much more common in German or in the Scandinavian languages, where compound and derived words are extremely
common and easily formed, than in French, where word formation and
word derivation is more difficult. The word for 'blind' in French is
aveugle but 'blindness' is *cécité* (a Latin loan-word). English, with its
considerable number of Romance and Classical words is, in this respect,
somewhere between the two extremes.

The Saussurean dichotomy signifier : signified has become basic in
some modern schools of structural linguistics, and particularly in glossematics (the Danish linguist LOUIS HJELMSLEV's theory of language)[2].
It is referred to as a function between two levels: content and expression, which have to be kept apart throughout the linguistic
analysis but the interaction of which in the sign function is at the same
time basic to the structure of all human language. We shall see in a
later chapter the importance of this distinction in language analysis
and its consequences for the setting up of the functional units of a
linguistic system.

Before we can discuss the further consequences of the Saussurean
thesis of the arbitrariness of the sign, we must, however, consider another
of SAUSSURE's statements, the importance of which has also been
fundamental in structural linguistics, i.e. the thesis that language is

---

[1] It is, in any case, a fact that at more primitive stages in the development
of the individual this kind of word formation plays a much more important part
than in normal adult speech. Children use, and often create, onomatopoeic formations to a large extent (saying *laaarge* for *very large*, etc.; cf. Chap. VI). The same
kind of expression also seems to be more frequently used in the languages of many
so-called primitive peoples than in our languages. But it would no doubt be prema-
ture to draw conclusions from this about the origin and early forms of human
language.

[2] Whether this dichotomy is to be regarded as basic or not in linguistic theory
depends on what kind of hierarchic structure language is supposed to be. For those
scholars who look upon language as a single hierarchy — from the phonemes as
the minimal units to syllables, words, sentences, etc. — the Saussurean and glossematic distinction is less important.

form, not substance. This means, to put it briefly, that the linguistic
reality is to be found in the functions and in the mutual relationship
between the linguistic units, not in what they actually are (as physical
events or as meanings). This implies that such elements as phonemes and
morphemes are abstract units defined only through their interrelations.
A vowel phoneme, say Spanish /i/, is defined exclusively by its correlations[1] to the other four vowel phonemes of that language, i.e. only by
being neither /u/, nor /e/, nor /o/, nor /a/, and sometimes also by being
submitted to certain other structural rules or limitations as to its use
(distributional rules). Spanish /i/ is thereby different from, say, English
/i:/, which is opposed to a quite different set of vowel phonemes and
thus must be defined otherwise, among other things by being opposed
(as long or as tense) to the short (lax) /i/, a distinction unknown in
Spanish. Such qualities as tongue or lip position, or formant structure,
have nothing to do with the form, taken in SAUSSURE's sense. In the
same way, a vowel may be defined as an element of expression, capable
of being used alone as a nucleus of a syllable, whereas any element
which has not this capacity is by definition a consonant. No talking
of noise versus tone, or of closed versus open air passage in the mouth
cavity, is involved in such a definition.

SAUSSURE first applied his "formal" approach to linguistic analysis
in his famous solution of a problem of comparative linguistics (1879).
In certain cases, it seemed suitable to reduce the Indo-European long
vowels into sequences of a single vowel + a unit which SAUSSURE symbolized by *A. The advantage of this solution was that the long vowels
were thus eliminated from the system and a striking analogy brought
about between series of ablaut (vowel gradation) which had previously
been regarded as quite different in nature. A series *derk: *dork: *drk
could be parallelized with a series *dheA: *dhoA: *dhA, where *eA has
the same relation to *oA and to *A as *er to *or to *r. This element *A
(the so-called laryngeal), postulated by SAUSSURE, seems to have been
for him a purely abstract unit the phonetic qualities of which he left
out of consideration. Thus the postulated element was defined only
according to its relation to the other elements of the system and to
its position within the syllable (as "une entité oppositive, relative et
négative"). Much later his hypothesis was confirmed by the discovery
of Hittite, an Indo-European language where this element turned out
to have been preserved. For the first time, the term phoneme was used

---

[1] HJELMSLEV establishes a distinction between correlation which is an
either-or function, and relation which is a both-and function. With this terminology a system becomes a correlation hierarchy, a process (a text or an oral message)
a relational hierarchy; in other words, correlations are paradigmatic, relations
syntagmatic (see p. 5).

with reference to an abstract linguistic unit which is not a sound (nor has any other physical substance) but which can be manifested or represented by a sound. It is the same conception which also meets much later in his "Cours" in the form of the "image acoustique"[1]. The problem whether it is possible to define and to describe structurally the functional units of a language only in relational terms, is a problem which we shall also revert to later. The form analysis on the expression level is the concern of phonemics (or phonology), the corresponding analysis of the content belongs to grammar and to semantics, by many scholars referred to under the common heading morphemics (Chap. VIII and IX).

Thus, the whole set of linguistic units, on the expression level as well as on the content level, must be described and defined according to their mutual differences. Two units must be in opposition to each other, or be identical. *Tertium non datur.* The language mechanism is built on this principle ("Le mécanisme linguistique roule tout entier sur des identités et des différences", SAUSSURE[2]). We have already pointed out, as something fundamental, the complex character of both levels. Both expression and content are built up from smaller elements, and are consequently both analysable into smaller, independent units, into discrete elements (cp. above).

When classifying two elements as opposed or identical, the analyser must base his classification on certain qualities, excluding others. This is the principle of relevancy or distinctiveness (cf. Chap. IV and V), in other words the basic idea behind the so – called "Phonological" or "Prague-school", which — in contrast to Glossematics — work on phonetic (i. e. sound) distinctions and base their classification on an analysis of the distinctive function of these differences. The concepts of distinctiveness and of distinctive features are also fundamental in the works of ROMAN JAKOBSON and his collaborators, whereas in more strict accordance with the Saussurean principle, Glossematicians try to give a purely relational description of the linguistic units. The strictly "phonological" analysis is retained so to say on a less abstract level[3], by making the distinctive sound features the basis of the classification. In our analysis of the expression level of language, we shall make this phonological concept of distinctiveness and of distinctive possibilities the starting point of our survey. Linguistic analysis does not differ in this respect from any

---

[1] It should be noticed, however, that in SAUSSURE's "Cours" the word "phoneme" is used to mean a "speech sound".

[2] And still more explicitly: "Tout le mécanisme du langage ... repose sur des oppositions de séquence et sur les différences phoniques et conceptuelles qu'elles impliquent".

[3] The different levels of abstraction in phonemic description will be treated in more detail in Chap. V.

other kind of grouping or categorizing. When we classify a given animal
as a dog, thus identifying the specimen with a certain species, this
means that we leave out of consideration such qualities as the colour,
the size of the ears and the tail, etc. as irrelevant — because different
dogs are very different in respect to those characteristics —, and take
into account only those features which distinguish dogs from cats,
horses, etc. When we interpret the sound-wave emanating from the
mouth of a speaker as a specimen of a known language, we do so by
picking out from the sound complex certain elements which EDWARD
SAPIR called "points in the pattern" and which are important for the
understanding (in its widest sense; cp. Chap. X). We simply overhear
all the rest. We consequently apply the same principle in identifying
an expression unit, or a combination of units (a signifier), and in identifying a content unit (a signified). Certain sound qualities are relevant
in one language, others in another, just as content categories differ from
one language to another. The arbitrariness of the linguistic sign, such as
SAUSSURE understood it, is implied in this arbitrary choice between
different possibilities which a language system has made in order to
distinguish one category from another — one phoneme from another
on the expression level, and one morpheme, one syntactic procedure,
or one semantic unit from another on the content level. The sign is
consequently to be understood as an arbitrarily delimited portion of
an amorphous mass of complex physical events (sound complexes) which,
in an arbitrary way, is combined with an arbitrarily delimited portion
of an equally amorph content mass. The whole structure of language is
thus arbitrary, and due to convention. Neither are any physical (acoustic,
physiological, psychological) facts responsible for the structure of the
expression, nor is the "reality" outside language — i.e. the things and
ideas referred to by language — responsible for the particular form
given to the content in a particular language[1]. Examples will be given
in Chap. VIII. Consequently, language is thesis, not physis. SAUSSURE's
conception of language as an arbitrary form thus actualizes a philosophical discussion which can be traced back to Greek philosophy.

The dichotomy signifier—signified and the combination of both
in the sign function is consequently fundamental in the Saussurean
system as far as this may be reconstructed on the basis of the evidence
given in the "Cours". The same idea is one of the postulates also in
glossematic theory and has been the theoretical motivation for the
commutation test used in many modern linguistic schools as a tool

---

[1] Even though this statement may imply a certain exaggeration — it is for
instance undeniable that the anatomic structure of the vocalic apparatus of man
favours certain types of phonetic distinctions and consequently certain phonemic
structures — it is important to start from the assumption that it is essentially correct.

for establishing invariants. It implies, though this is not always explicitly stated, that any linguistic analysis assumes an analysis from larger
units into smaller ones, and must, sooner or later, arrive at a point
where the parallelism between content and expression (signified and
signifier) ceases and where the elements set up consequently are no
longer signs. HJELMSLEV calls them figurae. Phonemes are therefore
expression figurae, which consequently have no content (for the possibility of content figurae, see also Chap. VIII).

MARTINET has followed up the same idea in a somewhat different way,
or at least with a somewhat different terminology, when talking about the
double articulation of language. The first articulation, according
to MARTINET, refers to the division of bigger linguistic units into smaller
ones (smaller signs) and finally into minimal signs (word-stems, morphemes, endings, or whatever we prefer to call them). To take an example,
a syntagm like *the foxhunter* is composed of *the* + *foxhunter*, the latter
of *fox* + *hunter* and *hunter* finally of *hunt* + *er*. Neither *fox* nor *hunt*,
nor *-er* can be analysed into smaller signs. But according to the principle
of the so-called second articulation, *hunt* may be analysed into the
following expression elements: $/h/ + /ʌ/ + /n/ + /t/$, none of which are
signs and which are all, consequently, void of content. They are figurae.
And equally, *fox* is composed of $/f/ + /ɔ/ + /k/ + /s/$, etc. The first articulation is common to most systems of symbols. A message built on a
system of this type is consequently a series of independent symbols
which are combined into a chain (flag signals e.g.). The expression
analysis of such a message is finished when the simple symbols have
been determined and listed and their mutual relations and possible
distribution established. Any complex message is articulated (in the
etymological sense of this word; Lat. articulus = small limb). But the
essential characteristic of human language is its being subject to a
second articulation, thanks to which man is able to form indefinitely
long messages by using a very limited number of minimal units which
are not signs but which build up signs (not more than about 50 phonemes
and prosodemes in every language). When HJELMSLEV says that the
originality of human language consists in its being not a symbol system
but a system of figurae, he has in mind the same linguistic mechanism
as the one described by MARTINET. The invention of specifically human
language was the invention of this peculiar figura mechanism[1].

---

[1] One of the essential differences between HJELMSLEV and MARTINET is that
the latter, by using the term "double", insists on the expression level being the
only one which is subject to this further articulation below the sign unit, whereas
for HJELMSLEV the parallel structure on both levels — with as a consequence
the existence of content figurae as well as expression figurae — is one
of the basic properties of any linguistic structure meriting this name.

According to MARTINET, effectiveness and economy may, however, not have been the only, or the primary, advantage achieved by means of this particular structure, though an important factor in favour of such a mechanism must have been the fact that the human ear is unable to perceive, and our speech mechanism unable to produce all the different sound effects we should have needed, if every concept (every "content unit") had to be symbolized by one indivisible acoustic quality. MARTINET also stresses the fact that this second articulation of the expression protects the latter from being influenced by the content in the direction of sound imitation and sound symbolism, a tendency which would threaten the principle of the arbitrariness of the sign. The mere fact that every phoneme forms part of a paradigm and so has a controlled physical manifestation, creates an independency between the content and its expression which is one of the principles of human language in its actual form. The second articulation — the figura principle — for evident reasons makes the arbitrariness of the sign an absolute necessity. The same functional principle consequently has two aspects, which both reflect man's struggle for economy in communication. The more complicated the content to be communicated, the greater the necessity to avoid a parallel complication of the set of linguistic units, and the need to get rid of the restrictions laid upon our expression elements by the primitive claim for inherent expressivity (such as is known in certain non linguistic expressive elements, in affective, emphatic, and other linguistic functions, and in many types of "primitive" linguistic structures existing in children's or aphasic's speech or preserved in a specialized vocabulary used for certain purposes in ordinary languages). We shall revert to the question in Chap. XI.

SAUSSURE's definition of language as a semiotic system ("système sémiologique") is also fundamental. The system is the code, a concept without which no act of verbal communication can be exhaustively analysed and totally interpreted. The very concept of code implies social convention. Thus if on the one hand the structure of the code is basic in language, it is on the other hand impossible to isolate the semiotic system from the social context of which it is an essential part. There is consequently no contradistinction between the Saussurean "form" principle from which modern structuralism has originated, and the sociological approach to language which SAUSSURE owed to the French sociological school with which he was so well acquainted (DURKHEIM, LÉVY-BRUHL). This line was followed up by ANTOINE MEILLET. Language is at the same time a social institution and a system of values. These two aspects are not contradictory (FREI, GODEL). On the contrary, they suppose each other.

It is, however, interesting —, and perhaps symptomatic in view of the author's historical and comparative background — that SAUSSURE did not extend his structural approach to diachronic linguistics. On the contrary, he seems to have made a clearcut distinction between synchronic or systemic (structural) on the one hand, diachronic or atomistic on the other ("qui dit grammatical dit synchronique", p. 140, 185). The application of the structural point of view to linguistic change is a post-Saussurean extension of the ideas expressed in the "Cours".

Not all the statements and conclusions made here regarding SAUSSURE's theory of language can be found explicitly in the "Cours", particularly not all the implications and applications of his theses found in later linguistic theory, some of which no doubt go very far beyond the intentions of the author himself. What has been said here about SAUSSURE is, to some extent, an interpretation of his text, but an interpretation which makes some sense and which has been the point of departure of structural linguistics. Whether it is a correct rendering of SAUSSURE's ideas or not[1], it gives linguists a useful tool for analysing appropriately the structure and functions of human language.

Chapter II

The Communication Process

The following survey of the so-called communication process does not aim at a complete treatment of the complicated problem of transferring messages in general, or linguistic messages in particular. The mathematical theory of communication has been explained in numerous handbooks to which we can refer. The purpose of this chapter is simply to give a general theoretical description of the communication process seen from a linguistic point of view and without any mathematical demonstrations.

Let us start from a very simple case of communication between two individuals. One — the sender — conveys a message to another — the receiver. In principle, he can do that in many different ways. He may use cries, or gesture, or mimic. He may attract another person's attention by shouting, by whistling, etc. The receiver may, or may not interpret the message correctly (i.e. in accordance with the sender's intention). If, or to what extent he will "understand" depends on the number of

---

[1] As SAUSSURE's "Cours" is based, not on the author's manuscripts, but on notes taken by some of his students during his courses, it is very difficult to know exactly to what extent the text in the "Cours" represents the ideas of SAUSSURE himself. It is a fact that there is not complete agreement between different chapters in the book.

possibilities he has at his disposal of interpreting the other person's behaviour, and this number will be determined by the context and by the receiver's previous experiences and personal capacity. The interpretation is guesswork, the success of which is a question of probability. The degree of understanding is to a very large extent correlated to the degree of predictability of the elements communicated (i.e. to the amount of redundancy; cp. also Chap. III and V).

Any material means utilized for the transmission of a message from the sender to the receiver may be called a channel, which may have a space dimension (visual or sound messages), a time dimension (e.g. printed letters, grammophone records, tape-recordings, photos), or both, which is the most normal case, no channel having an unlimited speed of propagation and any really temporal channel being capable of spatial replacements. Further it is possible to distinguish between natural channels, where man is the immediate receiver of the message thanks to his perceptual organs (vision, audition, etc.), and artificial or technical channels, where the immediate receiver is a machine (telegraph, grammophone recording device, tape-recorder, etc.) which may be used by man by adding a natural channel, or brought into connection with yet another machine, and so on. In the scientific analysis of communication processes the latter type of channel has more frequently been used to provide examples because of the greater complexity of the natural channels, particularly the difficulty of distinguishing between the brain and the peripheric perceptual organs (Mole). This has led some writers to set up a distinction between communication theory and information theory. On the other hand, cybernetics is the science of "governed" messages (Greek κυβερνήτης 'steersman'), whether the transmission device is natural or artificial. The capacity of any channel is determined by its area and by its number of differential thresholds.

Now let us consider a "normal" linguistic contact, i.e. a situation where a sender chooses to encode his message into a linguistic form[1]. He has to make a choice between alternatives which he takes into consideration to the extent that they are applicable to his situation or to his needs. In some cases, there may be many possibilities to cover these, in other cases perhaps just one or two. In the critical situation where our sender is supposed to be, he chooses, let us say, to pronounce the "word" *murder!* It should be noticed, however, that, in fact, we

---

[1] I do not enter into any discussion here of the question if, or to what extent, such extra-linguistic procedures of communication as those referred to here, may be said to be encoded and structured. I just remind the reader of the fact that e.g. gestures are to a large extent conventional and consequently may be looked upon as a kind of code.

have to do not with a word, but with a whole sentence (a shorter alternative for more "complete" sentences like "there is a murder going on" or "somebody is being murdered", etc.). This short sentence, though superficially it may seem simple, is built up of a whole set of small elements with different functions (of appeal, of emphasis, of emotion, disgust, hatred, fright, etc.), only very imperfectly reflected in the written form (here by the exclamation point), and which, for convenience sake, we disregard for the moment (cp. Chap. IX)[1]. The choice of the sign *murder* already implies a structuration of the message which was evidently not the only possible, but the one which, for some reason, in the given situation may have seemed the most suitable to the sender. This choice implies that the message is formed as a "noun" — as a "nominal sentence" in traditional terminology —, not as a "verb"[2] (*a man is being murdered*, or *somebody is murdering a man*, etc.). This on the "grammatical" level. But it also implies that the message is formed according to a "semantic" code which permits an opposition between, say, 'murder' and 'manslaughter', 'violent robbery', 'killing', etc., and, consequently, also of course opposing it to 'stealing', and to other "crimes". The sign *murder* belongs to a paradigm containing these and lots of other signs among which, in the given situation, it was chosen as the most appropriate. Its amount of information[3] is determined by the number of other possibilities in the paradigm. The information conveyed is restricted e.g. by the fact that the concept of 'murder' covers all possible methods of murdering (shooting, strangling, drowning, etc.). It is more abstract or more general, in a sense, than these terms, but conveys, on the other hand, a piece of information which is not contained in a word like *shooting* (that of deliberate killing). The English code does not admit the transferring of these two data through the same sign. An Englishman must for such a purpose build up a more complicated structure (*a man is shooting another man deliberately*, or — *is murdering* — *by shooting*, etc.)[4].

It is important to stress from the very beginning that this encoding of the message into a given linguistic form concerns the content itself and that it is of no, or little, use talking about "the same content" or the same ideas or concepts differently expressed on different occasions or in different languages. The choice of the sign *murder* consequently implies a certain form given to the message, a form which would have

---

[1] An exempel of analysis of a "short" but linguistically complex utterance will be given in Chap. VIII.

[2] Assuming of course that it is not a command.

[3] Further about this concept in Chap. III.

[4] The semantic structuration will be treated in more detail in Chap. VIII.

2*

been different in any other language. This means that it is not trans-
ferable directly, with the same amount of information — not more
and not less —, into any other language.

By choosing the English sign appropriate for his purpose the sender
has not only chosen a specific content structure but also the expression
structure which, according to the linguistic convention, is necessarily
combined with it, and which, in the communication process, is the carrier
of the information, in our example the phoneme sequence $/\text{'}m\text{ə}{:}d\text{ə}/$.
In fact, this phoneme sequence is the only thing which is actually communicated, from mouth to ear directly through the air, or indirectly
through a channel of some kind in a speech-transmitting device. "Im
'Kanal' fließen nur die Zeichenkörper" (UNGEHEUER). The content
"understood" by the receiver is the result of his interpretation. And
this interpretation necessarily supposes mastery of the code according
to which the message must be deciphered, a code with different levels
(cp. below), but one of which concerns the correspondence established
in the sign function between expression and content.

The linguistic transmission normally takes place either through a
sound-wave generated in the human speech mechanism, or through a
sequence of printed or handwritten figures (letters). In fact, those two
transmitting principles, though different in certain respects, have much
in common. It will be necessary to discuss for a while the relationship
between them and the theoretical problems which are involved therein.

This means that we must first devote some attention to the concepts
of written language and of alphabet. We must first establish a
primary distinction between symbolic (or ideographic) script and
phonemic script (or between content script and expression
script). The symbolic script is of less interest for our present discussion. It implies that any linguistic sign (in the Saussurean sense) is symbolized by a figure which may be — and in most cases originally was —
a picture of the thing symbolized (= 'fish', = 'swallow', etc.).
This principle was used, for example, in the old Egyptian (hieroglyphic) script and in the oldest Chinese alphabet[1]. Soon, however,
the original principle was lost sight of in Egyptian and a picture was
used to denote a quite different concept which happened to be a
homophone or which merely had a similar pronunciation. It is also,
though with modifications which need not be mentioned here, the
principle of the Chinese alphabet (also taken over, but used together

---

[1] The first of the two signs is in fact the original Chinese sign for 'fish', the
second the hieroglyphic sign for 'swallow', which later also came to signify a
stem $w - r$ and thus also e.g. the meaning 'big', a typical instance of a change
from ideographic (content) to expression script.

with a syllabic system, by the Japanese). The ideographic script is consequently based on a principle quite different from the one which characterizes human language. It does not share the double-faced structure of the latter (double articulation, in MARTINET's terms) and consequently does not convey any information about the linguistic expression, with the advantages and disadvantages this may have[1].

The phonemic (or expression) script implies that the linguistic expression is transferred by means of a series of signs which may represent p h o n e m e   s e q u e n c e s (e.g. syllabic script; in Japanese[2]) or, commonly in the languages of Western Civilisation, s i n g l e   p h o n e m e s (p h o n e m e s c r i p t   or, improperly, p h o n e t i c   s c r i p t). The minimal discrete elements of which the sender builds up his message — as sequences of phonemes and as sequences of signs — are encoded directly, through n e r v e   i m-p u l s e s to the muscles of the writing or printing organs, into the corresponding discrete elements of the written chain, i. e. the sequence of letters. In an optimal alphabet, there is a one-to-one correspondence between t h e set of phonemes stored in the brains of the speaker and of the listener and the set of letters equally stored in the brains of both[3]. Even if

---

[1] The principle advantage of such a writing system is, of course, that it may be understood without any knowledge of the code which permits us, in our phonemic systems, to transfer written symbols into phonemes ("sounds") and that, consequently, understanding does not suppose any knowledge of the spoken language. Written Chinese is understood all over the country, though the spoken dialects are not mutually understandable. The principle disadvantage is the enormous number of figures needed and the difficulty of distinguishing between them. Symbolic script is far inferior to spoken language and phonemic script as far as economy and suitability are concerned.

[2] The Japanese syllabic script uses 50 figures, each of them symbolizing one of the 50 possible syllables in the language. It should be noticed that Japanese has no consonant clusters and originally only open syllables (CV). The number of possible phoneme combinations, in comparison with languages like English, German, or Swedish, is consequently extremely restricted. Cf. Chap. VII. The Japanese syllables (according to NOACK) are the following:

a	i	u	e	o	ha	hi	hu	he	ho
ka	ki	ku	ke	ko	ma	mi	mu	me	mo
ssa	ssi	ssu	sse	sso	ja	ji	ju	je	jo
ta	ti	tu	te	to	ra	ri	ru	re	ro
na	ni	nu	ne	no	wa	wi	wu	we	wo

[3] The exceptions from this principle which we have to do with in languages with a non-phonemic spelling (English, French, Swedish) are normally not of a nature to make any serious theoretical difficulties. If, as is the case in many languages, a phoneme has to be rendered graphically by two graphemes (Swedish /ʃ/ as sj or French /ã/ as an), this only means that the written language, by the fact of having a smaller number of units, has to push the analysis of certain units a step further in comparison with the spoken language and that to some of the minimal units of the spoken language correspond complex units in its written form.

this is not so — optimal alphabets are, in fact, rare[1] — the script may permit a translation into spoken language and the spoken language may be transferred into written language, because the spoken unit is to 100% predictable from the written and vice versa. We may know from our acquaintance with the code for instance that /ʃ/ always corresponds to *sj* or *an* to /ã/. However, in neither of the languages quoted this is exactly so, because Swedish /ʃ/ may also be represented by the letters *sk* or *skj* or *stj* or *sch*, etc., and French /ã/ by *en*, sometimes also *em*, *aon*, etc., and on the other hand letter groups like *sk* (in Swedish) or *an*, *en* (in French) often correspond to other (simple or complex) spoken units. When the discrepancy becomes so large as to admit a letter group like *laughed* as the written correspondence of the phoneme sequence /la:ft/, where only the first unit has its (statistically) most probable written counterpart in the conventional spelling, we must look upon the principle of double articulation — of figura analysis — as almost given up, and the written complex as something of principally the same kind as a Chinese character. The pronunciation is no longer predictable from the written form[2]. Even many highly frequent English morphemes can be identified in their written form only thanks to the syntagmatic context (*read* as /ri:d/ or /red/, *bow* as /bou/ or as /bau/, etc.). In many cases, an English written word is consequently half-way between an ideogram and a sequence of figura symbols.

If there is a one-to-one correspondence between written minimal units (letters) and "spoken"[3] ones (phonemes) or not, it remains equally evident that the message, in its written form, is manifested as a sequence of discrete elements[4] and consequently, that if the alphabet and the

---

[1] Among existing European writing systems, Finnish is undoubtedly one of those which come closest to the ideal. Written Spanish is also extremely good, at least as far as standard Castilian is concerned. Another language with a good written form is Czech.

[2] In fact, to anyone who is acquainted with English, the pronunciation in our example is rather easier to guess than could *a priori* be supposed, since *gh* often corresponds to /f/ and the value of -*ed* follows from this. On the other hand, even English-speaking people often hesitate on the pronunciation of names like *Maugham*.

[3] The word "spoken" is used here just to oppose one form of linguistic expression to another. It does not mean that the manifestation of the system through one or the other substance is necessarily of importance for the analysis of the form. We regard "written" language as opposed to "spoken" only in so far as the former differs from the latter, as is almost always the case with ordinary traditional writing systems. But there is no opposition of this kind, in principle, between a "spoken" linguistic sequence and an accurate phonemic transcription of it.

[4] This is of course true, even if in many people's handwriting there is in fact more or less continuity between the different letters and numerous irrelevant details and transition phenomena. But even if the characteristics between the

spelling are as they should be, the message that reaches the receiver is a replica of the form in which the extra-linguistic phenomena to be communicated have been encoded in the sender's brain. The only decoding the receiver has to undertake is the discovery of the rules which, according to the language conventions, determine the relationship between the expression (the letter sequence) and the content, i.e. reestablish the sign starting from one of its halves (in our example the expression part of it). The reverse operation is executed when the speaker "writes down his words". A man who does not know the language, can read the letters but does not know the code according to which he has to establish the signs. However, if the text is written by hand, his interpretation even of the letters, as such meaningless, may be difficult and mistakes in categorizing the variants become numerous. No letter is predictable when the reader does not know the code. This is a case where the interpretation of a written piece of language may show striking analogies with that of a spoken one.

Now let us consider the — at least historically speaking — more normal case when the structured message is finally encoded into a sequence of discrete phonemes which are, in turn, transferred as nerve impulses to the speaking organs and transformed into speech movements (muscular activity), by definition continuous, as is also the sound-wave which results from this muscular activity. The message, according to a new set of rules (i.e. the speech and sound habits, the "articulatory basis"), has been encoded into a continuous wave form which, as a physical event, presents no analogy with the structured sequence of discrete signals from which it was generated. This sound-wave reaches the hearing apparatus of the receiver. The reaction to the acoustic stimuli is a question of pure physiology. All normal ears register the same stimuli in the same way, in complete accordance with the characteristics of the cochlea. Hearing in its physiological sense is not a matter of learning. The infant's hearing mechanism reacts in the same way as that of the adult. We shall have to deal with the characteristics and the possibilities of the ear later (Chap. III and X).

The stimuli registered in the inner ear are transmitted to the brain in order to be interpreted there. This interpretation again supposes a

---

letters are often levelled out and their shape confused, their number is limited and unaltered. Any written letter represents one of a limited set of figures. It is *A* or *B*; no intermediate possibility exists. The printed text renders the original articulated message more accurately than does the handwritten text, since there is less discrepancy between form and substance. The same point of view will of course also permit us to look upon one spoken type of language — one "pronunciation" — as superior to another.

code. Any stimulus, or rather complex of stimuli, must be referred to, i.e. identified with or opposed to, one of the units of the model and "heard" as one of the phonemes of the language. The continuous sound-wave is decoded and perceived as the sequence of discrete elements it was when the message left the sender's brain. If the code is unknown, or if the receiver fails to apply the right code to the stimuli registered, the message is not "understood", i.e. neither the identification of the stimuli as phonemes nor the identification of the phoneme sequences as signs can take place. The application of the wrong code may result in "misunderstanding"[1]. This is what happens when we believe we hear our own language, or another well-known language, spoken in the street in a foreign country, when, in fact, the sound sequence after more careful listening is revealed as completely ununderstandable. This also happens on a higher level when we interpret the words according to a wrong code, e. g. when a Swede interprets the meaning of a Danish word according to the Swedish system (Dan. *rolig* as 'funny' instead of 'quiet'), or an Englishman interprets a phoneme sequence as an English, not as an American sign (for instance Amer. *pavement* as *sidewalk*). Such phenomena suppose a quasi-identity between the code of the sender and that of the receiver, which means that in most cases the application of the receiver's code to the stimuli emanating from the sender actually gives a meaningful message and provokes a fairly adequate reaction on the part of the latter. In a few cases, this procedure fails, and the message is "misunderstood". In fact, however, there is only rarely — if, strictly speaking, ever — complete identity on every point between the two codes (cp. below, Chap. VIII), and concepts such as understanding and interpretation are to be looked upon as relative. A message must be regarded as understood when the receiver's behaviour in relation to the message is quasi-adequate. This restriction is particularly important on the semantic level of language. Disturbances and inadequateness in the interpretation of signs is sometimes spoken of as semantic noise.

---

[1] The consequences of applying a wrong code, and of hesitation about which code to apply, are illustrated by the following example. The author of this book once stood at a bar in a Spanish city together with numerous colleagues of different nationalities, all members of an international congress. Drinks were offered. I heard a voice behind me saying something like ['drai'feri], pronounced with German-like sounds and prosody. What did the man command? Dry sherry or three [glasses of] sherry ("drei Sherry"). The interpretation was of course dependent on the language the man meant to speak and consequently on the code to apply on the sound continuum. The next word the man said gave the cue to the riddle. It was meant to be English, and the man wanted 'dry sherry', in spite of the German character of his sounds.

Communication in the linguistic sense of the word has been established when the acoustic stimuli contained in the sound-wave have been organized in the speaking center of the listener's cortex into a sequence of discrete elements and these elements identified with known linguistic units. This is a more restricted definition of the process of communication than the one ordinarily applied in psychology, though the basic point of view is identical, e.g. when it is said that "communication is the discriminatory response of an organism to a stimulus" (definition given by the psychologist S. S. STEVENS). It is important to stress here the word "discriminatory", which covers a process (discrimination) common to all intelligent and conscious perception and based on the interplay discussed above between opposition and identification (see Introduction, p. 6 and Chap. I, p. 13).

The encoding that takes place in the brain of the sender when the extra-linguistic phenomena are linguistically structured, as well as the decoding which precedes the interpretation of the message in the brain of the receiver (as illustrated in the scheme below), are particular instances of a more general procedure called conceptualization, or concept formation. ALFRED KUHN pointed out recently that this psychological term is equivalent not only to the code formation of information and communication theory, but also to the neurological notion of network formation and to the traditional philosophical (logical) idea of induction. Both concept formation, he stresses, and logical induction depend upon observations of successive items of a given phenomenon. "These successive observations focus upon and isolate those items which are common to all specimens, and push into the background those items which are not." That is in other words the concept of relevancy, which will be discussed in more detail in Chap. VI.

The different stages of encoding and decoding distinguished in our scheme (Fig. 3) are not necessarily consecutive in time and, of course, take place without the speaker being aware of the independency of each of them. The numbers given have nothing to do with time order. It is on the contrary probable that man perceives the auditory stimuli received during speech as gestalts.

The coding of the message is an instance of a much more general phenomenon called quantization in communication theory. An example may illustrate the principle. Suppose a continuous wave has to be transmitted (Fig. 5). It may be quantized into arbitrarily chosen steps as seen in our example. This quantization thus implies that the wave form is not transmitted in its entirety but that it is — with a current scientific term — sampled at arbitrarily chosen, though

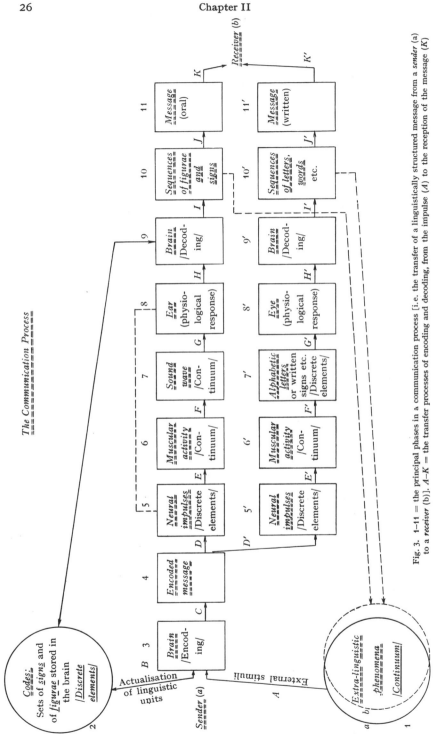

Fig. 3. 1–11 = the principal phases in a communication process [i.e. the transfer of a linguistically structured message from a *sender* (a) to a *receiver* (b)]. *A–K* = the transfer processes of encoding and decoding, from the impulse (*A*) to the reception of the message (*K*)

Commentary. To the *left* the sender (*a*), to the *right* the receiver (*b*). The arrows indicate the direction of the message, and of the relationships. *Above*, the c o d e, i. e. the set of linguistic units, of content and of expression, stored in the brain of both interlocutors (condition for communication). The relations between the code and the two interlocutors are supposed to be the same (though this is a certain simplification). *Below*, the extra-linguistic phenomena to be communicated (with reference to the two interlocutors, 1 *a* and 1 *b*). The arrow from no. 8 back to no. 5 is the so called a u d i t o r y f e e d b a c k, i. e. the guidance of the muscular movements of the speech apparatus through the auditory impulses from one's own speech.

The following phases in the communication chain ought to be particularly pointed out as important and interesting from a linguistic point of view.

The e n c o d i n g of the extra-linguistic c o n t i n u u m into a sequence of (complex and simple) discrete elements implies 1. a structuration, grammatically a n d semantically, of something (i. e. the c o n t e n t) which is neither, being composed of non-linguistic events and facts; 2. the building up of sequences of figurae, pre-existing in the code and subject to pre-established rules of combination (i. e. the e x p r e s s i o n); 3. the combination, according to the prescriptions of the code, of a given content unit with a given sequence of expression units (i. e. the s i g n); 4. the building up of sequences of signs in accordance with the distributional laws of the same code (the s e n t e n c e, and the s e q u e n c e o f s e n t e n c e s). Only in no. 4 do we have a complete m e s s a g e. Communication, however, is not established until the linguistic sequence of discrete elements has been again put into some kind of relationship with an extra-linguistic "reality", i. e. when the content form has been related again to a content substance, which for evident reasons is not always, and hardly ever can be, identical which the one which was present for the sender when he sent his message. This is why this relationship in the scheme is symbolized by a broken line. In fact, there is not complete identity between the speaker's and the listener's codes: they have each their own i d i o l e c t. We simplify by neglecting these differences here. The content substance evoked by the content form is a matter of the receiver's e x p e r i e n c e, just as his (reverse) identification of the expression units (phonemes) on the basis of an expression substance (sounds) is a matter of his experience of the speaker's sound habits. It has therefore seemed convenient to illustrate the sphere of extra-linguistic facts by two circles, only partly covering each other: 1 *a* and *b*.

The transfer of the coded message through nerve impulses implies an encoding into another set of discrete elements, the neurones responding only in a yes-or-no way to the stimuli presented to them. We have to do with a t r a n s p o s i t i o n from one code to another. Through this transfer, the message is broken into its simplest form, a form which is identical as a structure with that of the Teletype Code (see Fig. 10, Chap. III).

Something important takes place when these nerve impulses result in continuous movements of the speech organs. The message, at this new stage, is no longer articulated, no longer structured. Continuity has taken the place of discreteness. The sound-wave is a continuum just as articulations are. The vibrations which reach the ear drum are quite without physical delimitations and can be transferred into a sequence of discrete (linguistic) elements only by means of a d e c o d i n g, which implies that the reference to a code permits a re-interpretation of the continuous sound-wave. The receiver recognizes the acoustic stimuli — i. e. those of them which are picked out as important according to the code — as manifestations of known linguistic units, belonging to the set stored in his brain (f i r s t s u b c o d e). This is the first stage of the decoding. The second is the identification of the phoneme sequences as signs (morphemes, words) and sequences of signs, according to the rules prescribed by the code (s e c o n d s u b c o d e). The interrelations between these signs are in turn interpreted as sentences and sentence sequences according to the distributional rules of the code (t h i r d s u b c o d e).

suitable, intervals[1]. These samples may be transmitted in the form of pulses suitably modulated. This means in turn that the continuous curve, in order to be transmitted through a communication system, has to be quantized into a series of discrete elements. It is a matter of evidence that the first step of encoding referred to above, when the linguistic structure is imposed upon the extra-linguistic continuum, is to the same extent as in the example with the curve a quantization, just as any classification of individuals into groups and categories is one.

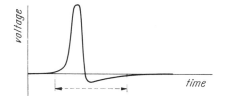

Fig. 4. Schematic representation of a nerve impulse. The nerve knows two, and only two, states; it is *in action or not* ("yes or no"). This implies that one single nerve impulse cannot give any information about the intensity of the stimulus, only about the existence or non-existence of a sufficiently strong stimulus. However, the number of impulses per period of time increases with the intensity of the stimulus. Our nervous system thus transposes intensity into frequency, though only up to a certain limit (of about $1/_{300}$ second), i.e. the minimum distance in time between two stimuli. An increase above this limit does not influence the perceived intensity of the stimulus

A similar quantization, on a physical-perceptual level, takes place when the continuous sound-wave is interpreted as a phoneme sequence, and, of course, when it is transmitted through some speech transmitting device and for that purpose adequately simplified.

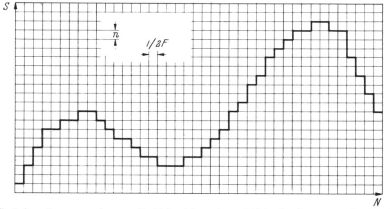

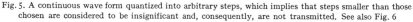

Fig. 5. A continuous wave form quantized into arbitrary steps, which implies that steps smaller than those chosen are considered to be insignificant and, consequently, are not transmitted. See also Fig. 6

---

[1] This is in fact an extremely common procedure and underlies e.g. all conventional indications of measures used in ordinary life. A distance is always given as a determined number of units (a yard, two meters, six miles), which implies an approximation to the nearest step on the scale. Temperature is indicated as a certain number of degrees above or below 0. The distance between 0 and 100 degrees C, for instance, is a continuum and the 100 steps into which it is arbitrarily divided imply a quantization of this continuum. Innumerous other examples of this kind could be given.

D. B. Fry has summarized this part of the communication process as follows: "... the physical input is translated through the neural mechanism into perceptual patterns within the four psychological dimensions of quality, pitch, loudness, and length. These patterns are classified in conformity with habits set up during the process of learning to speak and this completes the part played by perception in speech recognition. The output of the first stage of recognition is a phoneme

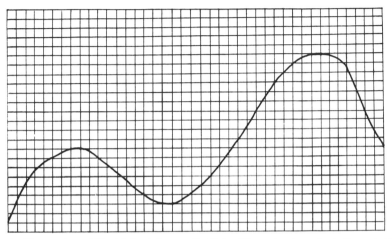

Fig. 6. The wave form of Fig. 5 before being quantized into arbitrary steps (according to Cherry). The horizontal mesh width represents units of time equal to $^1/_2 F$ ($F=$ bandwidth). The vertical mesh width equals the noise level $n \cdot T =$ time. The quantity of information transmitted is proportional to $F\,T \cdot \log$ $(1 + a/n)$ where a is the maximum amplitude

sequence which is transformed in successive stages into morpheme, word, and sentence sequences."

Thus it is possible to set up series of concepts, with their corresponding terms, which on the phoneme level we call (as does Fry) respectively quality, pitch, loudness, and length and to which correspond, mostly in a rather complicated way, the concepts of formant structure (spectrum characteristics, or more exactly the distribution of intensity along the frequency axis of the spectrum), of fundamental frequency, of intensity (along the time axis of the spectrum), and of duration respectively. The relationship between these sets of concepts and between the different levels concerned, will be discussed in several other contexts later, and also the possibility of setting up a corresponding series of content concepts which may be used to describe the content units of language as complexes of minimal elements constantly re-appearing in new combinations (morphemes, "words", etc.).

Chapter III

Preliminary Expression Analysis.
Acoustic and Physiological Variables.
Information

As was pointed out in Chap. I, communication by means of language supposes differences, of sound, or of written or printed figures on the expression level, and differentiated morphological, syntactical or semantic units and combinations on the content level. Communication supposes variation. The transfer medium used for communication must not be predictable to 100%. It has to contain at least some element of surprise. An unvaried and unvariable medium would be predictable both along the time axis (a monotonous sound-wave such as a sinuosidal curve with constant amplitude; Fig. 7), and along the space axis (an

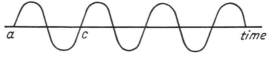

Fig. 7. A sinusoidal curve. The distance a–c = one cycle

undifferentiated visual stimulus, e.g. a straight line or an unlimited repetition of the same printed figure). As the transmission of the message in a restricted sense (physically) is made only through the minimal expression units and through combinations of these — the physical manifestations of which (as sound-waves and as articulatory movements, or as printed or written figures) are the only outside facts actually present in the passage from brain to brain (from 3—8 in our model in Chap. II) —, we shall examine in this special chapter the expression level and try to give a survey of the principal sound differences, and their physiological correlates[1], the principal task of what is traditionally called general phonetics. That is to say that we must start by examining the amount of information of a sound-wave emanating from the speech apparatus of a human being (5—6 in our model). And we do this to begin with without taking into account any differences of distribution between the possible acoustic stimuli. We shall also permit ourselves in this context to talk about our speech mechanism notwithstanding the well-known fact that, originally, man has no speech organ in the same sense as he has a breathing and a digestive apparatus. The so – called organs of speech all have other primary tasks (intake of food, respiration, etc.) and have been

---

[1] A corresponding survey of possible graphic variation would be possible in principle though extremely complicated. It will not be tried here.

adopted secondarily to communication needs. They all still keep their primary functions besides that of speaking. We finally have to take into consideration the reception mechanism (i.e. the human ear) and its particular characteristics.

First, however, a few words about the concept of information [1]. This supposes the presence of a series of alternatives to a given stimulus. The higher the number of alternatives to a given stimulus, the greater its amount of information. Predictability and amount of information are inversely proportional.

In fact, a linguistic message (a word, a sentence) may be said to contain information in a twofold way. It has its "meaning", which is the traditional popular interpretation of the concept. The message "gives us information about something" (cp. Chap. VIII). But information also may imply what we can call here the distinctive information, i.e. the distinctive characteristics which make it possible for the receiver to identify the signs — or more exactly their expression level, for this identification does not necessarily imply understanding of the message (cp. Chap. II, p. 24). Information in this sense has consequently nothing to do with meaning and has no reference to the outside "facts" about which a receiver may be informed through the linguistic message. Only this distinctive information is the object of information theory. This also explains why this theory is applicable in the first place on the expression level of language (cp. hereto Chap. IV, p. 69).

It will in this connection also be necessary to devote a few lines to the question of how a sensorial system, no matter which, reacts to physical stimuli in general. We have to distinguish between the sensibility level, below which the system does not react, the level of saturation, above which the system does not perceive any variations of excitation, and the differential level, i.e. the minimum increase of excitation necessary for the perception of a difference. Consequently, the sensation field between the two extremes, the sensibility level and the saturation level, in order to become measurable, has to be quantized as a series of differential steps (Fig. 6, p. 29). For any variable of physical excitation, there exists consequently a finite number of elements of perception of which the psychologist establishes a repertory. Consequently, as soon as we go over from the physical level to the perceptual, the continuous character of the transmission medium — in our case the sound-wave — is replaced by a repertory of perceptual items, limited in number (though, as we shall see, extremely numerous), i.e. of discrete elements. We introduced in the preceding chapter the

---

[1] As this concept has been treated in detail in other works of a more mathematical orientation, we shall refrain from any kind of advanced mathematical explanations and formulae here.

concept of channel and looked upon the speech transmission as a channel, the capacity of which — in this case as in all others — is described by its area and the number of differential thresholds. The area of the channel, in the speech communication process, is the range of frequencies and of intensities within the boundaries given by our hearing mechanism.

Some of the basic facts within the field of information theory have often been illustrated (e.g. by HERDAN) by a reference to the well-known game of guessing an object by asking questions which may only be answered by "yes" or "no". Let us assume that we have to identify one particular letter in an alphabet of 32 letters (HERDAN's example). If we start by asking if the letter is to be found in the upper half of the 32 letters, and then, depending on the answer, in which of the two appropriate quarters, and so on, we can determine the letter by five successive yes-or-no questions. The number of such questions may be taken as a measure of the information contained in each unit. This information decreases as its probability (i.e. relative frequency) of occurrence increases. HARTLEY had shown (in 1928) that a message of n signs chosen from an "alphabet" of S signs has S^n possibilities and that the quantity, or amount, of information is defined as the logarithm, i.e. $H = N \log S$ [1]. In HERDAN's example, the amount of uncertainty attached to a letter in the given alphabet is never more than 5, since 5 guesses are enough to ascertain the letter. The number of yes-or-no answers may also be referred to as the number of digits, or more accurately binary digits (shorter bits), the unit used in information and communication contexts to measure the information capacity. The number of binary digits is thus a measure of the element of surprise of a unit in the code. This element is the higher, the rarer this unit is according to the receiver's experience. The amount of information (WIENER's term) consequently also becomes a measure of the degree of order — associated with those patterns which are distributed as messages in time. Order favours predictability and consequently reduces the information capacity of each item of a pattern. Disorder on the contrary increases the amount of information of each unit of a pattern, since disorder excludes predictability. Chaos implies chance. The negative of a measure of order, i.e. of information, is a measure of disorder, a negative number which can be made artificially positive by adding a constant quantity, or by starting from some value other than zero. This measure of disorder is known as entropy (a concept taken over from statistical mechanics and now currently used in information theory, sometimes defined as the opposite of information, since the entropy

[1] This was the original form of this theory, which implied the beginning of modern theory of communication. It was based on earlier findings of NYQUIST and KÜPFMÜLLER concerning the so-called band-width.

decrease per symbol is directly proportional to the information recorded)[1], in more popular contexts identified with a general tendency towards chaos. The fundamental distinction on the one hand, the relationships on the other, between information and entropy were defined in clear terms in a recent article by F. TILLMAN and R. ROSWELL RUSSELL. We must content ourselves with this superficial survey of the concepts in question here and for further details refer the reader to the specialized works quoted in the bibliographical notes.

In a binary or dyadic system of the kind referred to here, any number is represented as a sum of powers of 2, thus

$$10 = 1.2^3 + 0.2^2 + 1.2^1 + 0.2^0.$$

The number 10 may therefore be written in positional notation as 1010. 10 in this notation has 4 binary digits, i.e. its information (H') is the logarithm of 10 to the base of 2 (the dyadic logarithm). Information is consequently defined as the dyadic logarithm of the number of alternatives, in our example $32 = 1.2^5 + 0.2^4 + 0.2^3 + 0.2^1 + 0.2^0$. If the dyadic logarithm is represented by ld, r the length of a series (in our example 32), and H' the measure of information about the alphabetic code in terms of the binary code, then

$$H' = (ld\ r),$$

i.e. in our example

$$H' = ld\ 32 = 5,$$

Sign	1st	2nd	3rd	Selections
A	1	1	1	
B	1	1	0	
C	1	0	1	
D	1	0	0	
E	0	1	1	
F	0	1	0	
G	0	0	1	
H	0	0	0	

Fig. 8. An example of binary coding of selections. Three bits of information are required for selection of each unit from among eight equally probable signs ($A---H$). If B is the unit intended, the first question places it within the upper four ($A-D$), the second again within the upper half ($A-B$); the third question gives the right answer (is it A or B?). All according to the formula $2^3 = 8$ ($\log_2 8 = 3$). According to CHERRY

i.e. the number of guesses. Another example of the same kind has been quoted from CHERRY in Fig. 8.

According to HARTLEY's theory, information may also be defined as "instructions to select" (CHERRY). In our two type examples we have assumed (with HERDAN and CHERRY) that the number of signs N in the alphabet (32 and 8 respectively) is an exact power of 2. Even if this is not so the information is still equal to $\log_2 N$ bits per sign selected (Fig. 8), though it will then be a question of an averaging process.

Now let us consider a different case, a message comprising wave forms, not printed or written signs (a continuous phenomenon, not one composed of discrete elements). We mentioned (in Chap. II, p. 2)

---

[1] It should be stressed, however, that "recorded (or bound) information" is not exactly the same as information.

the concepts of sampling and of quantization. The sampling theorem
states that a wave form which has been received through a channel
of finite bandwidth (F cycles per sec) is completely specified by its
amplitudes, at successive time intervals equally spaced by $1/_2 F$ second,
and that these data and the bandwidth F permit a complete reconstruction of the original continuous wave form. The samples define the
wave. The amplitudes, which are physical observations, have to be
quantized (cp. Fig. 7, p. 30), as is done in telecommunication systems
when the successive sample pulses are restricted to their nearest quantal
levels. The wave form thus gets a step-like character (so-called quantization distortion). The steps may be symbolized as $\varDelta s$. The greater
the number of levels (the smaller the $\varDelta s$), the smaller also the distortion
and the greater the precision of transmission (and the rate of transmission of information). Now let us label these levels arbitrarily as
$A - - - H$, according to the following graph:

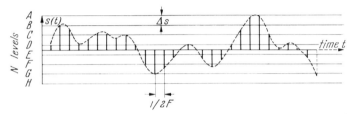

Fig. 9. Band-limited wave form source $s(t)$ (according to CHERRY). The different levels $A\,B\,C\,{-}{-}{-}H$ represent
possible states of this waveform. The successive sample ordinates, here spaced $1/_2 F$ apart, select from these
states. If there are N levels, each sample ordinate contributes $\log_2 N$ bits of information. The steps $= \varDelta s$

The successive selection of the sample ordinates is also a selection of
the corresponding letters (A, B, etc.). We consequently have to do with
a selection closely similar to the one we had in our first and second
examples (a series of discrete signs). The different levels indicated in
our graph as $A\,B{-}{-}{-}H$ consequently represent possible states of
the wave form source. And if there are N such levels or states, each
sample ordinate confers $\log_2 N$ bits of information, in complete accordance with our first examples. If any one of the successive signs selected
by a discrete source does not carry with it any information about its
neighbours in the chain, it is referred to as independent.

For it is important that what has been said so far is valid only
under the condition of equidistribution of the symbols in question, i.e.
without regard to their statistical distribution, or their *a priori* probabilities. If every symbol in a code had the same probability of occurrence,
it would for instance not be possible to guess at missing parts of a
message (say of a fragmentary or a partly illegible text). A code whose
symbols, on the contrary, have unequal probability is said to be

redundant. In fact, there is hardly ever equidistribution of linguistic units, and redundancy consequently becomes an important concept in linguistic description. In fact, almost any linguistic element carries with it at least some information about its neighbours. We shall have to revert to the concept of redundancy later.

If we take the probability of distribution into account — as must consequently be done as soon as linguistically structured messages are concerned —, we obtain a more complicated formula for the measure of information, namely

$$H' = -ld\ 1/r = -ld\ \bar{p}$$

where the amount of information per symbol is the negative dyadic logarithm of the relative frequency $\bar{p}$ per symbol.

In every day terms, the concept of information may consequently be described roughly as follows. The more numerous the alternatives, the richer the information which a stimulus conveys. A Chinese letter is one of about 10 000 possibilities and is consequently very rich in infor-

Fig. 10
International Teletype Code, a binary code for letters

	1	2	3	4	5
A	•	•			
B	•			•	•
C		•	•	•	
D	•		•		
E	•				
F	•		•	•	
G		•		•	•
H			•		•
I		•	•		
J	•	•		•	
K	•	•	•	•	
L		•			•
M			•	•	•
N			•	•	
O				•	•
P		•	•		•
Q	•	•	•		•
R		•		•	
S	•		•		
T					•
U	•	•	•		
V		•	•	•	•
W	•	•			•
X	•		•	•	•
Y	•		•		•
Z	•				•

mation. The amount of information of an English letter is considerably lower, being only one out of 26 possibilities[1]. The red traffic light is one of only three possibilities (red, green, and amber) and consequently has a low amount of information. As the amount of information was the (dyadic) logarithm of the number of alternatives, one possibility out of ten has consequently only half the amount of information contained in one possibility out of 100, and only one third of the amount of information of one out of 1000, under the condition pointed out above of equidistribution of their occurrence. If the occurrence of one symbol is more probable statistically, and so its predictability greater

---

[1] This is obviously why the letters of the Latin alphabet cannot, except for certain very special and limited purposes (in abbreviations, etc.), be used alone as signifiers. A combination of only two letters, however, has an amount of information many times larger (go, no, be).

than that of another, the code is redundant and we can guess certain parts of the message with a reasonable expectation of correctness. In a series XY-, the probability of the missing unit being Z is much higher than of, say, B. This is why any study of linguistic variables and of information possibilities has to start from an analysis of isolated units (mostly words) and from the full forms of these (cp. Chap. IV), i.e. taking into account all the information we need when there is no other cue to the identification of the item than the phonemes alone. This is the situation in which the maximum amount of information of speech sounds has to be utilized. If the context limits the possibilities of choice to just a few acceptable alternatives, the sounds and sound qualities may be to a large extent inferred *a priori* and are consequently redundant to a high degree.

If we leave redundancy out of account for the moment, we can state that the amount of information in a sound-wave depends on the number of possible variations of the wave. We can assume as an average that a normal ear can distinguish 1200 different pitch levels[1]. The degrees of loudness[2] have to be calculated according to the varying sensibility of the ear on different frequency levels (see Fig. 42). The most recent calculations made by specialists in auditory physiology indicate a number of 340000 different acoustic stimuli or sensation quanta[3]. The quantity of information of a sound-wave has for evident reasons to be calculated only according to perceivable variations since it depends on the discrimination possibilities of the human hearing mechanism[4].

We shall see later (Chap. X) that the process of perception is still more complicated than this and that our perception capacity as a whole, and particularly our perception of speech sounds, is far from being a pure matter of physiology. It is to a large extent due to factors such as training (musical training can increase at least a little our discrimination of tones) and acquaintance or unacquaintedness with certain models or patterns. In other words it is strongly determined by redundancy. This makes exact measurements extremely difficult. In any case, the actual amount of information in a sound-wave produced by a human speech organ is consequently many times smaller than the theoretically possible

---

[1] Roughly between a sensibility level at 16 c/s and a saturation level at 16000 c/s, varying according to age, individual differences, etc. (cp. for the linguistically relevant frequencies p. 167).

[2] From an inferior level of 0 db (10^{-16} watts per square centimeter at 1000 c/s) up to 140 db (pain level, $= 0{,}01$ atmospheres). See also p. 61.

[3] It is well-known that children hear higher tones than adults. Frequencies used in speech are seldom lower than $80-85$ c/s.

[4] We leave deliberately out of consideration the possibility of sending messages to machines capable of storing more information than a living being.

number of physical variations and than the maximum discrimination possibilities of the human ear would make us believe *a priori*.

Two basic factors are at work in speech production: the sound source and the filter[1]. In fact, any speech-wave may be specified in terms of these two characteristics. Both imply some kind of modification of an air stream which is in uncomparably most of the cases an expiration but which in exceptional situations may be an inspiration, or, as far as some special speech sounds are concerned, an in- or outgoing airflow brought about through some kind of insucking or outblowing to or from a closed and suddenly opened room in the mouth and pharynx cavities where the air pressure has been either diminished (clicks) or increased (implosives)

Fig. 11. To the right, approximate wave form of the laryngeal tone; to the left, its spectrum

According to the source, speech sounds may be grouped into so-called voiced types, and voiceless types (or noises). A voiced sound has in normal speech its source in the larynx and is a result of the regular opening and closing of the glottis through the vocal cords. In abnormal cases — e.g. after the larynx has been taken away for medical reasons (laryngectomy) — the normal sound source may be replaced by the vibration of some mucous tissue in the pharynx ("oesophagus speech"). The sound-wave generated in the larynx is a periodic (or, in more strictly physical terms, a quasi-periodic) movement. It is a complex wave in which the first partial (the fundamental) dominates and the upper harmonics decrease in amplitude (at a rate of about 12 db per octave in the range 300—2500 c/sec) according to the spectrum in Fig. 11. This so-called laryngeal tone can for evident reasons never be heard in its unmodified form, unless reconstructed artificially. It reaches our ear in a form which is due to the filtering effect of the pharynx, mouth and nose cavities, i.e. of

---

[1] Filtration implies in principle an elimination process through which certain constituents of an original sound-wave are damped and only energy of certain wave-lengths and frequencies are allowed to pass. The channel through which the sound passes is rendered selective to certain frequencies or bands of frequencies. Acoustic filters are divided into three classes: 1. low-frequency pass filters; 2. high-frequency pass filters, and 3. filters of the single-band type. The human vocal tract is a low-frequency pass filter. In a way, filtration and re-inforcement by resonance are opposite aspects of the same phenomenon.

the so-called vocal tract. The vocal tract has more or less the form
of a tube and its resonance effect may be compared with that of tubes
or horns. If we open the mouth and emit a voiced sound without making
any other movements of our speech organs, the result will be a pro-
jection of the resonance properties of this tube on the original spectrum
of the laryngeal tone. It is primarily by means of tongue movements
that the configuration of the vocal tract, and thereby its resonance

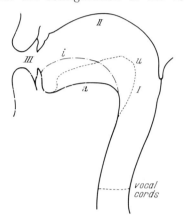

characteristics, are modified. The
upwards movement of the tongue
narrows the tube at a given point,
thus creating two coupled resonators which will act the more independently of each other, the narrower the constriction is. The resonator behind the narrowest point is

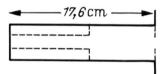

Fig. 12. *Left:* The vocal tract and its principal variables. I–III = the principal resonators. *i, u, a* = tongue
movements for the fundamental vocoids. *Right:* a tube-formed resonator of the length of the human vocal
tract (17,6 cm), closed at one end, open at the other. The vibrating frequencies of such a tube will be at
500 c/s and odd multiples thereof (1500, 2500, 3500, etc.). By means of modifications of the tube, of which
an example is given (dotted line in the picture), the resonances are varied upwards and downwards, thus
causing the formant variation of vocoids. Decrease of the opening lowers the resonance frequency (like
lip rounding in articulatory terms). Extreme lip closure results in a pipe closed at both ends (if the glottis
is supposed to remain closed). The figure to the right according to Fant

the pharynx resonator, or pharynx cavity, the one in front of the
point in question is the mouth resonator, or the mouth cavity.
The Fig. 12 gives schematic illustrations of the principal possibilities.

   Speech sounds which are essentially resonatory modifications of the
laryngeal tone will be called vocoids in this survey, in accordance
with a widespread usage in recent phonetic literature and in order to
distinguish the concept of sound — the physical phenomenon, as articulation or as acoustic timbre — from the vowel which is a linguistic, functional concept (the phoneme). In accordance with this conceptual distinction we use the [ ] signs for vocoids (and contoids), the // signs for phonemes
(see Chap. IV). In many general contexts, however, it may be a question
of taste if one or the other terminology should be used (and the corresponding signs) as the unit under discussion may be at the same time
considered both as a sound and as a linguistic unit.

An example of modification of the larynx tone spectrum brought about by tongue movements is given in Fig. 15 which corresponds roughly to spectrum of the vowel [e] (p. 40).

This spectrum is consequently the result of the effect of the vocal tract on the larynx tone spectrum when the tube has a form approaching

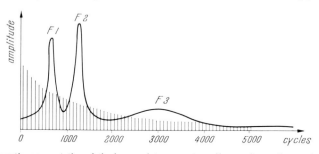

Fig. 13. Schematic representation of the laryngeal tone spectrum (frequencies on the x-axis, intensities on the y-axis) and the filtering effect of the vocal tract (the curve, so-called envelope) in a particular case. $F1$, $F2$ and $F3$ = formants. Partly according to Husson

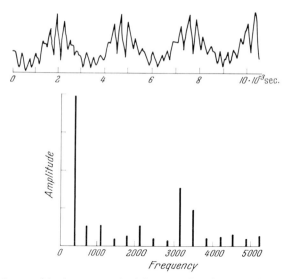

Fig. 14. A complex wave (*above*), as an example of the output through the speech apparatus; and (*below*) the spectrum of the wave after analysis of its components (the partials plotted along the x-axis)

that of [i] in Fig. 12 ([i:] as in Engl. *see*). In the latter case, the narrowing of the passage is extreme — if it goes further, there will arise a constriction noise and the sound effect will be different. In traditional articulatory terms [e] is a half close (high) vocoid. And as the constriction takes place in the front part of the tract — the tongue approaching the hard palate — the vocoid is said to be a front, or a palatal vocoid.

If the constriction point is further backwards ([*u*] in Fig. 12) — the tongue approaching the velum — and the degree of constriction is approximately the same, the result is a c l o s e   b a c k, or v e l a r vocoid [*u:*] (that of Engl. *shoe*).

As a second example we take an extremely low tongue position — an o p e n vocoid —, i.e. approximately the [*a*] in Engl. *father*, where

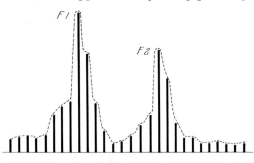

Fig. 15. Spectrum of the vowel [*e:*] (Swedish). On the *x*-axis the frequencies. On the *y*-axis the amplitude Spectrogram obtained by the so-called Siemens Tonfrequenzspektrometer; *on top* its envelope. *F*1 about 350 c/s, *F*2 at 2000 c/s.

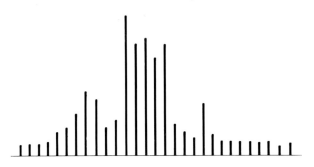

Fig. 16. Spectrum of the vowel [*a*] (Swedish). A typically compact spectrum (cp. p. 44, and Fig. 15)

the raising of the tongue is only slight if any, and takes place in the middle of the mouth cavity, towards the frontier between the hard and the soft palate; see no. (3) in Fig. 12. The spectrum, in this case, will be something like that of Fig. 16.

It goes without saying that the two peaks distinguished in the three figures 13, 15 and 16 (as F 1 and F 2) are the effects of the influence of the vocal tract on the original larynx tone as reflected in the spectrum in Fig. 11. The difference in the so-called e n v e l o p e of the spectrum — the line summarizing its configuration (see Fig. 15) — expresses the resonance effect of the tube in its different forms. The peaks are referred to in phonetics as f o r m a n t s. Vocoids are exhaustively described through their formant patterns (whereas contoids must be described in terms of envelope contours; FANT). The formant frequency equals the position, on the frequency scale, of the highest point of the envelope, i.e. the mid-line of the formant band. According to the well-known physical laws of resonance, that harmonic of the laryngeal tone will be the strongest which comes closest to the formant frequency (in principle the free vibrations of the resonator).

Since the beginning of modern acoustic phonetics it has been customary to talk about formant 2 as mouth formant, and about formant 1 as throat formant, as they were supposed to be due respectively

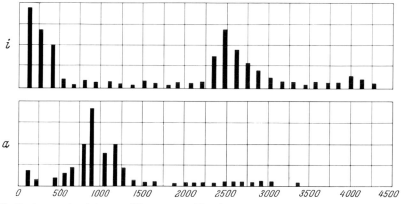

Fig. 17. A comparison between a *diffuse* spectrum [i] and a *compact* spectrum [a]. According to FLETCHER

to the resonance frequency of the mouth and throat cavities. The smaller the mouth cavity, the higher F 2, and vice versa. This is roughly true, but the relationship between vocal tract cavities and formant structure has lately been shown to be far more complicated than has hitherto been supposed. Acousticians nowadays seem to agree on the fact that the whole formant structure of a vocoid, i.e. the whole of the spectrum envelope, is the result of the resonance effect of the resonance tube, and vocal tract, as a whole (cp. Fig. 12). This problem has been studied in detail by the Swedish acoustician GUNNAR FANT. But as it may sometimes be handy to retain this older terminology and talk about mouth formant and throat formant, we shall take the liberty of doing so in this book in cases where it may seem convenient, but it is stressed, in order to avoid misunderstanding, that this is a pedagogical simplification of far more complicated facts.

The spectrum of a sound-wave may be presented in a somewhat different way, if the frequencies are put on the vertical scale and the horizontal scale is used as a time axis. In this case, intensity is either neglected, or expressed by other means. One way of doing it is GEMELLI's method, using a perspective figure, as in Fig. 18 and 19.

In the well-known sound spectrograph produced by the Kay-Electric Company and called Sonagraph — nowadays the most widely used and most convenient apparatus for speech sound analysis — the horizontal axis is the time axis and the vertical one a linear frequency scale.

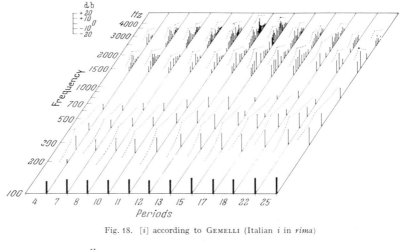

Fig. 18. [i] according to Gemelli (Italian *i* in *rima*)

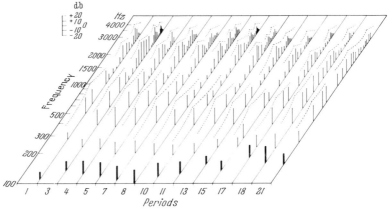

Fig. 19. [a] according to Gemelli (Italian *a* in *pazzo*)

Intensity is roughly reflected by the degree of blacking the paper. Two types of filter are used: narrow at 45 c/s each, and wide at 300 c/s. The first type accordingly permits any partial to appear separately. The second gives a better visual representation of the formants. A so-called cross section gives information of the intensity distribution throughout the sound-wave at a given moment (a spectrum of in principle the same type as in Fig. 14—17). An amplitude display may be added to the spectrogram, indicating the variations of the over-all intensity along the axis of time. To give an idea of the way in which a tone appears in the spectrographic recording, we can show first a few different musical tones (Fig. 20 and 21).

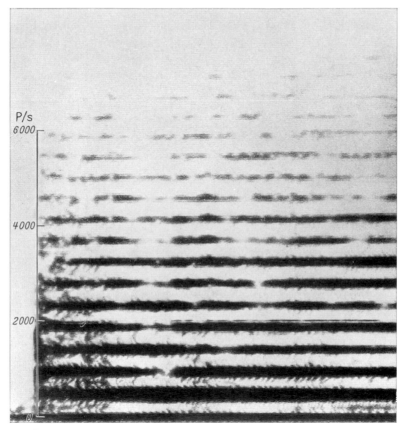

Fig. 20. Spectrum of a piano tone (C′). On the *y*-axis: the frequencies (linear scale); on the *x*-axis: time. Degree of blacking: intensity. The fundamental (first partial) is the first line above the zero-line. Narrow filters

If the partial tones of a wave, instead of being illustrated as in Fig. 13—17, are plotted according to the spectrogram scheme, we accordingly get (for [*i*]) the spectrograms seen in Fig. 22 and 23. The corresponding spectrograms for [*u*] and for [*a*] will have the aspect of Fig. 24—27.

We have by means of these schematic representations given a description of the two basic vocalic[1] distinctions used in linguistic communication systems. We have to do with a distinction between

[1] Vocalic is used with reference to the vocoid as well as to the vowel concept.

a so-called compact spectrum, where the sound energy is concentrated within a domain in the middle of the normal vocoid frequency
range, i.e. with the two formants close to each other and a fairly broad

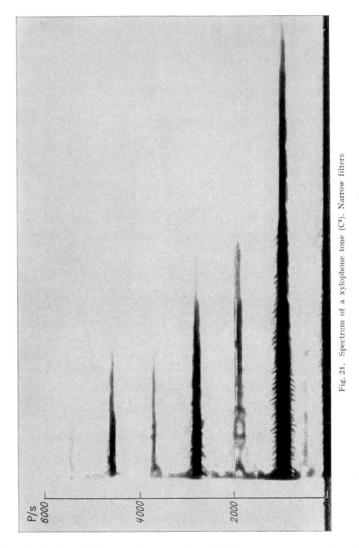

Fig. 21. Spectrum of a xylophone tone (C²). Narrow filters

band of reinforced harmonics; and a diffuse spectrum[1], characterised by two delimited, narrow frequency bands with a clear-cut
distance between them (types [i] and [u]). On the articulatory level it
is a distinction according to tongue height (close — open).

[1] This and the following terms from JAKOBSON-FANT-HALLE.

The more open — the more strictly horn-formed — the vocal tract is, the less justified becomes the correspondence, noted above, between the two formants and the two principal mouth cavities. When the

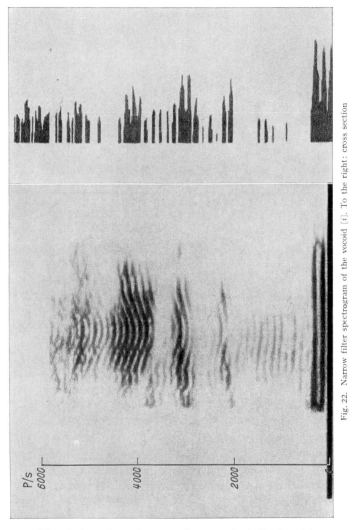

Fig. 22. Narrow filter spectrogram of the vocoid [i]. To the right: cross section

tongue position is low there is no real reason to talk about two resonance cavities. In fact, the two formants tend to fuse into one broad frequency domain. The compact — diffuse distinction is consequently based on a variation of both formants.

On the other hand we have to do with a distinction between a grave and an acute spectrum ([u] as opposed to [i]). The variable

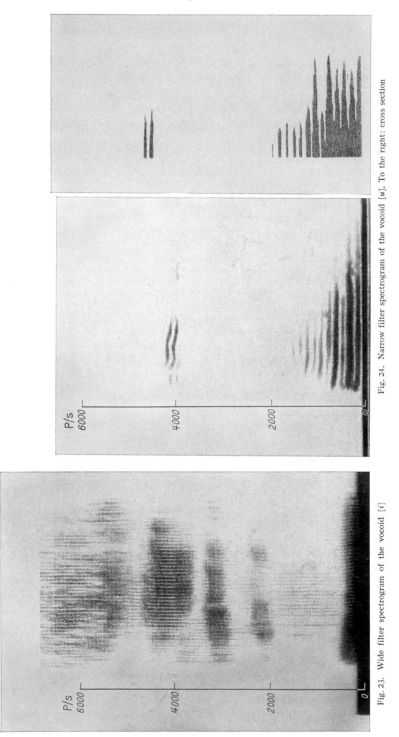

Fig. 24. Narrow filter spectrogram of the vocoid [u]. To the right: cross section

Fig. 23. Wide filter spectrogram of the vocoid [i]

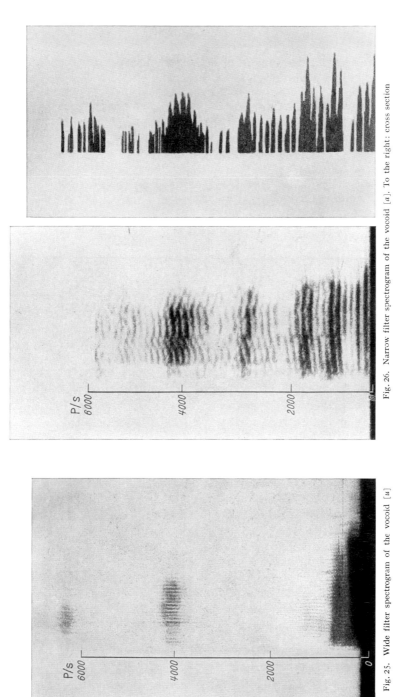

Fig. 26. Narrow filter spectrogram of the vocoid [a]. To the right: cross section

Fig. 25. Wide filter spectrogram of the vocoid [u]

is here formant 2, whose place on the frequency scale is responsible for the traditional articulatory distinction between front and back (palatal and velar) vowels. [i] is the extreme acute, [u] the extreme grave vowel. Theoretically all imaginable spectra intermediate between these extreme limits are possible. The number of types actually utilized in speech is dependent firstly on the discrimination capacity of the human ear (cp. p. 36 and Chap. X), and secondly on linguistic conventions.

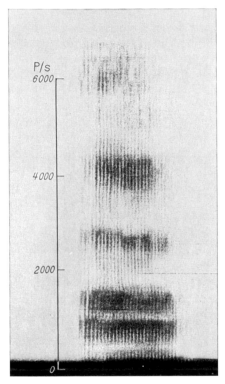

Fig. 27. Wide filter spectrogram of the vocoid [a]

Two more variables must be mentioned, before we have given a complete survey of the distinctive possibilities as far as spectrum modifications are concerned. The opening of the vocal tract, i.e. the lip opening, may be varied according to form and wideness[1]. The frequency of a resonator is lowered, if the opening becomes narrower. Consequently, lip rounding lowers formant 2. It is particularly often used to introduce a variation of the acute type with formant 2 as variable. This is the traditional distinction between rounded (labialized) and unrounded (non labialized) vocoids, e.g. [y] ∼ [i]. The less acute vocoid is said to be flat as opposed to the extremely acute, or plain vowel. The lowering of formant 2 is spoken of as flatting.

Finally, another resonator may be coupled to the vocal tract, i.e. the nose cavity, which may be used to modify its resonator characteristics. The vocoid is said to be nasal or oral according to the presence or absence of nose cavity resonance. Nasality is thought to consist of a

---

[1] It is a matter of fact that the movements of the lower jaw also contribute to the variation of the size of the mouth opening. In speech this factor normally does not work independently of the vertical tongue movements, and its effect on the resonance frequency of the mouth cavity is automatically compensated by the tongue position. If the jaw is lowered, the tongue is lowered too, and the resonance frequency of the mouth remains the same.

certain modification and weakening of the ordinary formants, particularly a weakening of formant 1, and of the addition of a special low
nasal formant (about 250 c/s).

Nasality is only rarely used as a vocalic distinctive feature in a
language system. It is the case in French, in Polish, in a certain sense
in Portuguese, and in a number of dialects and
languages, especially outside Europe.

The three vocoids $[i] - [u] - [a]$ may be looked
upon as three maximally differentiated units, the
extreme points in the two series of distinctions referred
to as basic. We can put them as the corners in a
triangle, as in Fig. 28.

Fig. 28. The three basic vocoids

Any vowel system used in the world's languages is either identical
with this basic system, or is based upon it; i.e. enlarged by the addition
of intermediate types, particularly intermediate degrees of diffuseness
$[e]$, $[\varepsilon]$, etc. in the acute series, $[o]$, $[ɔ]$ etc. in the grave series, or modifications of flatting (labialization): $[y]$, $[ø]$, $[œ]$, or of nasalization:
$[\tilde{\varepsilon}]$, $[\tilde{a}]$, etc.[1].

A vowel system of a more complicated structure may also be presented in the following way, when the vowels (vocoids) are plotted
against each other according to the position of formants 1 and 2 on
the frequency scale, formant 1 on the vertical scale, and formant 2
on the horizontal axis, for instance the German system (long vocoids;
and $/œ/$, $/ɔ/$; cp. below) and the French system:

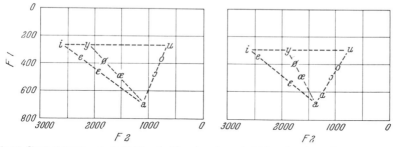

Fig. 29. Chart of German vowels *(left)*, and of French oral vowels *(right)*, plotted according to the positions
of $F1$ (vertical) and $F2$ (horizontal) on the frequency scale. The vowel $[ə]$ has been excluded from the French
chart

A solution put forward by GORDON F. PETERSON to make a three-
dimensional arrangement of vocoids with F3 as the third dimension

[1] The existence, in certain languages, of a triadic system of apparently one
dimension only — $/i/$, $/e/$, $/a/$ —, does not contradict this view, since nothing prevents us from looking upon $/e/$ as diffuse as opposed to $/a/$ and as grave (less acute)
as opposed to $/i/$, thus as another — though less extreme — manifestation of the
grave, diffuse type. Cp. hereto also Chap. IV.

has been criticized by ELI FISCHER-JØRGENSEN as unsuitable, since F3 does not seem to correspond to any perceptional dimension. Synthetic experiments have proved that two formants which are close to each other are heard as one single formant with a frequency in between. This was the reason why some acousticians of the past century only found one formant for back (grave) vowels (HELMHOLTZ).

The above schemes have so far been given only as specimens of possible systems of distinctive vocalic units, not as phoneme systems.

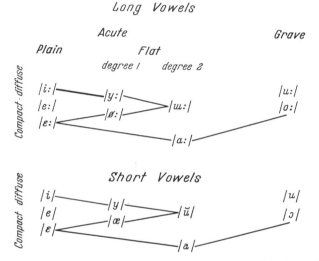

Fig. 30. The Swedish vowel system (according to the author). It should be noticed that the number of degrees of opening (compactness) decreases with increasing flatting

We shall revert in the next chapter to the phoneme concept and to the different methods used in structural expression analysis to determine the number and distinctive qualities of the phonemes of a given phonemic system. We are dealing so far only with possibilities, or potential variables.

The degrees of flatting are not necessarily limited to the two mentioned above ($i-y$, $e-ø$, etc., negative or positive). Swedish has three degrees of flatting: 0 — 1 — 2, i.e. in articulatory terms two degrees of lip articulation, one with lip protrusion and one with lip closure ($i - y - ɯ$)[1]. As the concept of flatting implies a lowering of formant 2, and as the concept of compactness means that F1 and F2 come closer to each other, it is not astonishing to see that, in systems which use flatting as a distinctive feature, the number of degrees in the diffuse—compact (close—open) series, i.e. the number of flat units, is often

_____

[1] The theoretical aspect of this question will be discussed in Chap. VI.

smaller than in the plain series. The Swedish vowel system is instructive in this respect (Fig. 30).

The German system (of long vowels) will be the same, if the [u]-type is left out (Fig. 29).

In the specimens quoted here, the concept of flatting has been exemplified only within the acute (palatal) series. There is, however, a corresponding possibility within the grave (velar) series ($i \sim u$, e.g. Russian i in быть [bit'] 'be').

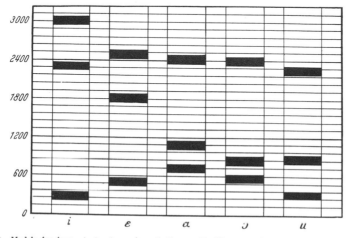

Fig. 31. Models for formant structure of synthetic vocoids ("pattern playback system"; see references in the bibliography), worked out at the Haskins Laboratories, New York (FRANK COOPER et al.). Three formants are taken into consideration, though $F3$ in most cases is essential only for the [i]- and [y]-types

Besides the spectral differences due to the vibration pattern of the vocal cords and to differences of voice quality produced by it (of which we shall speak below; Fig. 38, p. 57), we should mention, in order to make our survey of the distinctive possibilities as complete as possible, two distinctions which imply the introduction of the time factor and the conception of the sound-wave as a linear phenomenon. We have so far considered the acoustic event as a steady-state form, a wave form, or, as analysed and schematized, a spectrum. This implies either that we retain exactly the same conditions of the source and the filter for some time — which may be in practice unfeasable in a living being but can easily be arranged in a speech synthesizer —, or that we pick out a given point in the spectrum — a given period in the wave — and generalize therefrom. A time factor may, however, be introduced among the distinctive possibilities, essentially in two ways, either as a distinctive characteristic of a vowel as opposed to another, i.e. an opposition between short and long (between two or more degrees of duration), or as a distinction between a steady-state vowel with, in principle, unchanged formant structure — a monophthong — and a vowel with changing formant structure (a gradual modification of one, or of both formants within a time period supposed for a given unit; cp. below). This is the definition of a diphthong (a triphthong, etc.).

A change of the formant structure may be either sudden, or slow with gradual differences which may play a part as distinctive elements. We shall have to talk more about formant transitions later. Let us just mention here that such transitions may play a part in communication as carriers of consonantal distinctions. Differences in the rate of formant change may be illustrated by the schematic (synthetic) spectrograms in Fig. 34 a, where (1) represent a stop contoid + a vocoid, (2) a frictionless consonant ("semivowel") + a vowel, and (3) diphthongs (gradual passage from one formant structure to another). Such differences of contoid — vocoid transitions have proved sufficient to serve as cues for the phonemes in question.

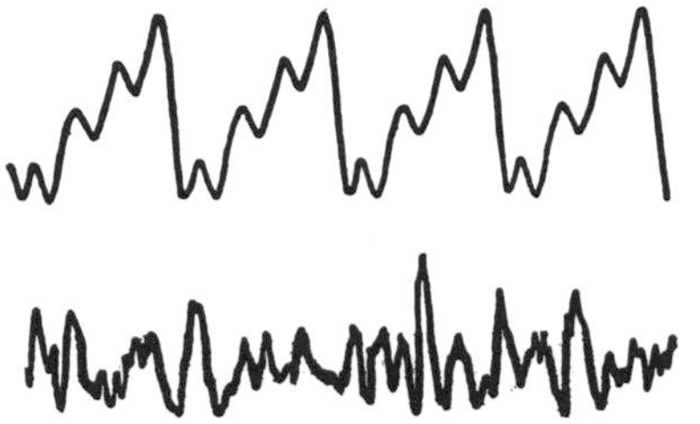

Fig. 32. A periodical vibration, a musical tone (*above*) and an unperiodical vibration, noise from a street (*below*)

The sudden change of the regular formant structure typical of the vocoid type is a distinctive characteristic of the extreme opposite class of sounds, the contoid. It may be effected either through a complete stop in the steady-state spectral structure, or by means of its replacement by an irregular, non-periodic noise spectrum. The so-called stop on the one hand, the steady-state vowel on the other are the two extremes as far as acoustic and articulatory distinction is concerned. The open vocal tract in combination with a laryngeal tone creates a vocalic timbre due to a formant structure. The completely or partly closed vocal tract implies an interruption or a disturbance of this timbre, thus creating variation and repetition, two necessary conditions for the sound-wave being used as a means of communication. The same idea has been expressed, in articulatory terms, as a distinction between opening and closing movements ("Öffnungsbewegung" and "Schließungsbewegung" respectively), e.g. at a very early date by E. A. Meyer, and later by P. Menzerath ("Öffnung — Schließung" = vocoid, and "Schließung — Öffnung" = contoid). On the physical level, however, no clear-cut division is possible between the phonetic types, the definite categorisation into discrete units being the result of an application on the physical continuum of a pattern (a quantization;

cp. p. 28). Vocoids and contoids represent two extremes with, in between, all possible gradations.

Contoid distinctions are in a way more complex than vocoid distinctions. There is less correspondence between physical phenomena and linguistic units within the consonantal type than there is among vocoids. This is particularly the case on the acoustic level. Synthetic experiments have proved that consonant distinctions very often may be manifested either by means of friction or explosion noise or through modifications

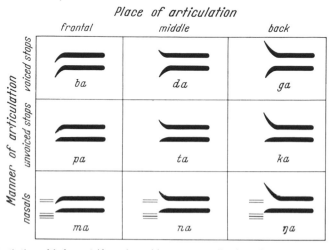

Fig. 33. Synthetic models for contoid-vowel transitions, corresponding (according to examination by auditory tests) to distinctions of place and of manner of articulation of contoids, to the distinction between voiceless and voiced ($p \sim d$, etc.), and between nasal and oral ($b \sim m$, etc.). According to the results obtained at the Haskins Laboratories

of the vocalic spectra (transitions; see Fig. 33—34). Recent discoveries have even proved the existence of transition phenomena in the fricative noise of contoids due to the influence of neighbouring contoids, which may be identified only through these transitions.

The undifferentiated friction noise is spoken of in acoustics as "white noise". Its acoustic structure is predictable, since there is the same probability for any frequency to be present in such a sound complex. All frequencies have the same intensity throughout the audible area. This sound thus has no "colour" (therefore its name). All friction noises utilized in human speech are spectral modifications of the white noise. [s], [ʃ], [f], [θ], etc. are distinguished by means of the relative intensity of the different parts of their spectrum alone: highest for [s], lower for [ʃ], still lower and also weaker for [f] and [θ] (two contoids which, on account of their low audibility, are often confused in languages which use them, particularly in children's speech, in vulgar or dialectal

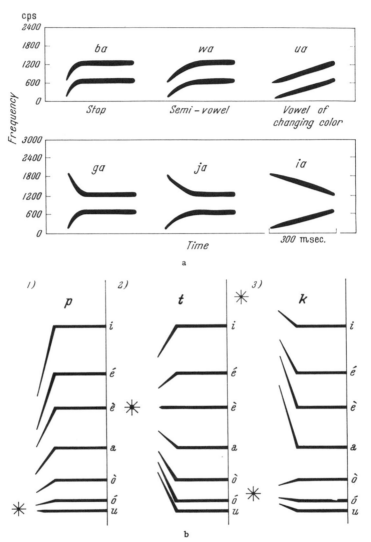

Fig. 34a. and b. Two specimens of synthetic patterns for contoid-vocoid transitions. In (a) above, No. (1) represents a stop contoid + a vocoid; No. (2) a continuant (frictionless) contoid + a vowel; and No. (3) diphthongs (gradual passage from one formant structure to another). The auditive tests made with these patterns have proved the potential distinctive character of the *rate of transitions*. In (b), No. (1) represents transitions characteristic of [p] + different vocoids; No. (2) is [t] + the same vocoids; and No. (3) represents [k]. For [p] and [t] the transitions — which in live speech is the effect of the changing resonance of the vocal tract during the passage from contoid to vocoid position — all aim at a given point on the frequency scale (marked *). This is the so-called *locus* of the contoid (the common denominator for different transitions). The locus is low for [p], higher for [t], which is in complete accordance with the way in which they are produced. As for [k] there seem to be two loci, one (low) for the dark vocoids, another (higher) for the clear types. This also is in perfect conformity with articulatory facts, since we know that the occlusion point of the [k] and [g] types varies with the surrounding vocoids (palatal occlusion before [i], velar before [u], etc.). It also confirms the structural interpretation of [k] as a neutral (non differentiated) contoid as opposed to [p] and [t], just as [a] is within vocoids. From MARGUERITE DURAND. Cp. hereto also Chap. IV, Fig. 48 and 51

speech, etc.; this is the case for instance in English and in Spanish[1]). Such contoids are **voiceless**. The **voiced** type of fricative implies the addition of a periodic wave movement and of a certain formant structure to the noise (types $[z]$, $[ʒ]$, $[v]$, $[ð]$, etc.). The distinctive factor traditionally spoken of as voice also seems to be manifested by other physical variables (intensity of the noise, abruptness of the for- mant transitions, etc.; see Fig. 34). See also Chap. IV. The least differentiated, or the most neutral of the frica- tive types is the so called $[h]$ contoid (in Engl. *he, hat,* Germ. *Hut,* etc.). The friction noise is generated in the glottis and the colouring is brought about by the supra- glottal cavities which nor-

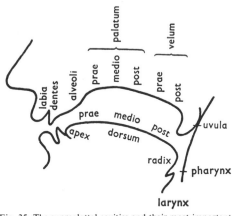

Fig. 35. The supraglottal cavities and their most important parts (with Latin denominations)

mally take the position of the following vocoid. This was the reason why certain traditional phoneticians talked about the different $[h]$-types as "voiceless vowels". If $[h]$ is called neutral it is because it has no

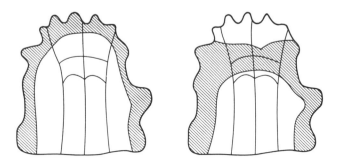

Fig. 36. An example of palatographic investigation of articulations. Stop phase of a dental (postdental) occlusive consonant (*left*) and of an alveolar stop (*right*). Cp. Fig. 35. The shaded area indicates the contact surface between tongue and palate

resonance properties — no supra-laryngal characteristics — of its own. It therefore often appears as a product of neutralization or confusion of consonant distinctions (in evolutionary phonetics as well as in defec- tive speech; see Chap. XI). The glottal stop $[ʔ]$ occupies the same position within the system of occlusive contoids.

---

[1] See also Chap. XI.

Traditional phonetics distinguishes between stops (occlusives), i.e. momentary contoids, such as [p], [t], [k], and prolongable contoids, such as [m], [l], [r], [s], or [v], the first type implying a complete closure of the vocal tract, with as a consequence an interruption of the sound and a silent phase, the second characterized by some kind of constriction or partial closure, or intermittent opening and closing, i.e. fricatives ([f], [v], [s], [ʃ], etc.), constriction, nasals [m], [n], [ŋ]), with an open nasal passage and a closed oral one, laterals

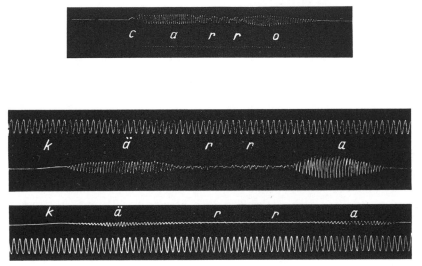

Fig. 37. Kymograms of different r-types: Spanish double -rr- (*top*), Swedish rolled -rr- (*middle*), and South-Swedish uvular, fricative -rr- (in the same word; *bottom*)

([l]), with an oral air passage which is closed in the middle of the mouth and open on both sides, and affricates ([t͡ʃ], [d͡ʒ], [p͡f]), a kind of combination between the first (stop) and the second (fricative) type. Distinctions may be made according to the presence or absence of voice (glottal vibrations), e.g. [f] ~ [v], [s] ~ [z], and according to the place of articulation ([p] labial ~ [t] apico-alveolar, [ɲ] palatal ~ [ŋ] velar, etc.). The Fig. 35 gives an approximate idea of the principal articulatory regions in the mouth (together with Latin denominations from which most phonetic terms are derived).

Other contoid types are possible and exist in certain languages. The clicks do not suppose any expiration but are brought about through a double closure and a rarefaction of the air contained in the chamber thus formed. When the front closure is released, the air rushes into the cavity. The same effect may be obtained by means of an oral closure and the lowering of the larynx with the glottis closed (implosives). The opposite type, i.e. an increase of the air pressure in the cavity is obtained if, under otherwise analogous conditions, the larynx is thrust upwards (ejectives). Cp. p. 37.

Numerous other distinctions may be obtained and are utilized in different languages, such as glottalization and aspiration. We do not need to enumerate them all here. What has been said is enough to give a general idea of the distinctive possibilities put at the disposal of man. Compared with this abundance of potential sound differences, the number of linguistic distinctions actually utilized in any given phoneme system is extremely reduced.

Finally, the sound source itself is subject to variations which condition a number of so-called voice quality differences. The traditional distinction made e.g. in song technique between chest register and falsetto is based on two different kinds of functioning of the vocal cords,

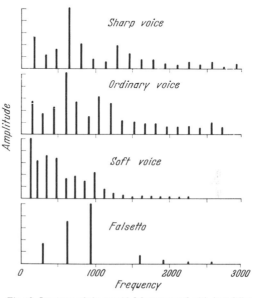

Fig. 38. Spectrum of the vocoid [a] pronounced with four different types of voices (from CHIBA and KAJIYAMA). Frequencies on the *x*-axis, intensities on the *y*-axis

with, as a consequence, a corresponding difference in the acoustic structure of the laryngeal tone, and in the harmonic structure of the sound emanating from the speech apparatus. The picture in Fig. 38 shows the spectrum of the vocoid [a] pronounced in a chest register and with an ordinary (not particularly sharp or soft) voice and of the same vowel pronounced in a falsetto register (according to CHIBA—KAJIYAMA).

Other factors which influence the voice quality are for instance the duration of the closure phase and the completeness of the closure, both of which have importance both on the intensity of the voice and on its aesthetic qualities. The problem of intensity will be treated below. For evident reasons, there are no clear-cut limits between the types thus distinguished; intermediate possibilities are therefore theoretically innumerable. Voice quality distinctions are rarely used for linguistic purposes. They are essentially responsible for the indi-

vidual characteristics of a person's voice and, in that respect,
carriers of information. Though they have no strictly linguistic importance, they may, however, give a listener information about the speaker
(symptom function; cp. Chap. IX) or be used as a stylistic tool, and have
either an intended or an unintended influence on the listener (as signal),
etc. The different functions of such variations were mentioned even by
the early German phoneticians (MERKEL, SIEVERS) and have been
studied recently by FELIX TROJAN. This aspect of the problem will be
treated in Chap. IX. The Danish stød accent, which has a distinctive
linguistic value, may to a certain extent be called a voice quality distinction, as its physiological manifestation is some kind of sudden,
intense innervation of the respiratory muscles and a corresponding
disturbance of the vocal cord vibrations, which become slow and irregular. Register differences may also, to some extent, be determined
by tradition and convention, and, in such a case, are not exclusively
due to a speaker's anatomic and physiological dispositions. Several
linguists have pointed to the high falsetto-like voice of the Lapps.
It is equally a matter of fact that certain rural regions in Sweden are
characterized by a high voice register (particularly in men's voices).
TOMÁS NAVARRO and other Hispanists have established essential differences in the average pitch between different Spanish speaking
areas (lower in Castilian, higher in Andalusia and in Latin America
where for instance Santo Domingo and Colombia are said to have a
relatively lower register, Mexico, Havanna, and Buenos Aires a higher
one), etc.

The source of the sound is, essentially, responsible for two other
important distinctive possibilities. The periodical opening and closing
of the glottis may be effected at more than one speed. The rates of
vibration speed which may be achieved in the larynx run from about
80 (even exceptionally as low as about 60—70 in the lowest male voices)
to about 12—1300 c/s (high soprano voices; in exceptional cases even
higher). In normal speech they range from about 100 c/s to about
500 c/s. The range for one individual is, in a normal conversation,
rarely more than one octave (cp. below), often much less, though in
special cases, e.g. under strong emphasis or emotion, it may be considerably more. The frequency of the glottal vibration is the physical
counterpart of the auditory and functional concepts of pitch and
melody. Our ear has long been supposed to react to variations in fundamental frequency according to a logarithmic scale. A doubling of the
frequency is always heard as the same interval, i.e. the octave in
music. The Fig. 39 shows a gradually changing frequency (of two Swedish words) plotted against a logarithmic scale. The frequency variation has been measured by means of E. A. MEYER's so-called "Tonhöhen-

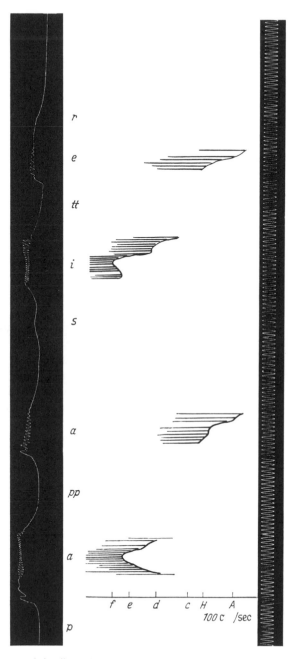

Fig. 39. Frequency variation (intonation) in a Swedish sentence (*pappa sitter*) measured by means of E. A. MEYER's "Tonhöhenschreiber". *Left*, kymographic recording of the sentence; in *the middle*, intonation curve (logarithmic scale); *right*, time curve (100 c/s)

schreiber". The curves shown in Fig. 40 are characteristic of the two Swedish word accents (acc. 1 and 2).

The linguistic utilization of pitch differences will be discussed in Chap. IV. In normal speech, the fundamental frequency is never absolutely constant. It varies, though often only slightly, from period to period. The difference between constant — or quasi-constant — and varying pitch is that between **musical tones** and **speech**. In music, the intervals between the notes correspond to conventionally fixed intervals, **semi-tones, tones, minor thirds, major thirds, fourths, fifths, minor sixths, major sixths, octaves,** etc. In speech, there are constant glides and less regular intervals. The

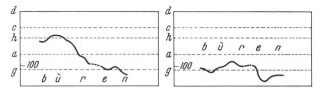

Fig. 40. Frequency variation plotted against a logarithmic scale (the word melody of two Swedish words *búren* 'the cage', with acc. 1, to the left, and *bùren* 'carried', with acc. 2, to the right)

number of distinctive and conventional intervals is also much smaller than in music, whose structure is more rigid. More about these questions in connection with word and sentence pitch (Chap. IV)[1].

In recent years the current musical (logarithmic) scale as a reflex of man's reaction to frequency variations has been questioned and a new scale proposed which is based on judgement tests concerning people's perception of a doubled pitch. This so called **mel scale** is more favourable to frequency differences than the logarithmic scale in the lower register and less favourable in the higher part of the frequency domain, which accords well with our actual reaction to pitch variations.

It is important to stress in this context that measured in mels the smallest perceivable difference experimentally established between two pitches is almost constant ($^1/_{20}$ mel). This is not so if the traditional musical scale is used. Other factors of importance are that the bandwidth of frequencies within which amplitudes are not superimposed because of the masking effect (cp. below) is one mel, and that frequency domains of equal importance for the audibility of speech are also about one mel.

Finally it should be noticed that some acousticians, for speech frequency curves, use a scale which is linear up to 1000 c/s, and thereafter logarithmic. The scale as such is of course indifferent from

---

[1] At different times, different pitches have been adopted for the musical scales. In scientific contexts, the standard frequency for *a'* is 426.7 c/s (for *c'* 256 and for *c''* 512, etc.). The standard now valid in music is *a'* = 440).

the point of view of the acoustical parameters on which speech is based. But an appropriate scale favours the parallelism between the visual and the corresponding auditory pattern and thus makes the scientific analysis of the latter easier.

The amplitude of the glottal vibrations, i.e. of the fundamental of the laryngeal tone, is one of the physical facts underlying the so-called intensity of the sound produced, though the amplitudes of the harmonics are of importance too.

A few remarks may be necessary in order to clear up the concepts of intensity and loudness and related phenomena. The propagation of an acoustic wave is accompanied by the trans-mission of energy through the medium in question (air etc.). When a sound-wave emanates from a point source, the energy spreads uniformly from the source in all directions, if the medium is uniform and unless reflection or refraction interfere. If in the following figure (Fig. 41), where S is the source, I is the amount of energy per unit area of the medium in one second, the area being perpendicular to the direction of propagation, and r_1 the radius of the sphere through which the energy passes,

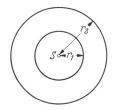

Fig. 41. The propagation of a sound-wave from a source (S); r = radius of the sphere

the total amount of energy passing through this sphere will be $4\pi r_1^2 \times I_1$. In the same way, if the radius of the sphere is r_2 (twice as large as r_1 in our figure), the total energy will accordingly be $4\pi r_2^2 \times I_2$. If the total amount of energy is assumed to be constant, we get the equation

$$4\pi r_1^2 \times I_1 = 4\pi r_2^2 \times I_2$$

whence

$$\frac{I_1}{I_2} = \frac{r_2^2}{r_1^2} .$$

The intensity of a sound produced by a given source is consequently inversely proportional to the square of the distance from the source.

To avoid confusion, the intensity as defined below is also called physical intensity. It is physically measurable and is a function of the amplitude and the frequency of the vibrating body. It is pro-portional to the square of both. A doubling of either consequently implies a four times higher intensity, since this doubling in either case implies that a twice larger path has to be covered by the vibrating body in the same amount of time, thus consuming a four times higher amount of energy.

Intensity (I) in a plane progressive wave is more exactly given by the formula $I = p^2/\rho\, V$, where p is the root mean[1] square value of the

[1] The mean value because generally intensity is due not to one but to several sources of sound.

sound pressure, ρ is the density of the medium and V the velocity
of the sound-wave in the medium. It is thus defined as a rate of flow
of energy. The ear, however, reacts logarithmically to variations of the
physical intensity. This means that the change in sensation is not
proportional to the absolute increment of intensity but to the fractional. It is therefore convenient to use a scale for heard intensity
differences, in which steps correspond to equal fractional increments.
The scale generally used is the decibel (db) scale, based on logarithms.
On such a scale, a difference between two intensities, I_0 and I_1, is said
to be x decibels if

$$x = 10 \log_{10}\left(\frac{I_1}{I_0}\right) \, .$$

This is a ratio of intensities and consequently supposes an absolute
reference value, a level from which the ratio can be measured (as is
the 0 level on a thermometer). The value chosen for this threshold
of audibility is mostly 10^{-16} W per square centimeter at 1000 cycles/
sec. Under such conditions, a two-fold increase in intensity corresponds
to 3 db, a ten-fold to 10 db, etc. The whole range of audible intensities
from 10^{-16} W/cm^2 to 10^{-3} W/cm^2 is covered in 130 db steps. Instruments
used for intensity measurements are calibrated so as to read directly
the intensity levels above a chosen zero. It will be clear from this that
the reaction of the ear is complicated by its different sensibility in
different domains of frequency[1]. The place of the minimum sensibility
level of the human ear on the frequency scale may be seen from Fig. 42,
which also shows the so-called pain level where the sound pressure
ceases to be acceptable to a human being. Accordingly, the variations
of sound pressure and of intensity, in order to be used in communication,
have to remain inside the area shown in this figure. Our possibility of
discriminating between intensity stimuli, as between all other sensations
registered by our perception organs, is consequently regulated by the
famous law of Webner-Fechner, according to which the objective
increase in stimulation must be higher, the stronger the stimulus, in
order to be perceived as identical[2]. Hence the need for special perception
measures (just as octaves, semi-tones, and the other musical intervals,
as well as the mel, are perception measures on the frequency level).
A decibel is sometimes, though inaccurately, defined in more popular
contexts as the least difference of intensity between two acoustic
stimuli which our ear can perceive. A more strictly perceptional measure

---

[1] See Fig. 42, from which it is to be seen that the 1000 c/s frequency level
chosen for the reference point of the db scale is within the optimum frequency
range of the human ear.

[2] In strict formulation: The increase of stimulus necessary to produce a just
perceptible increase of sensation is proportional to the pre-existing stimulus.

of intensity, is the phon based on tests of perceived equality in intensity. In Fig. 42 (lower part), any line corresponds to a certain intensity level independently of its actual place on the frequency and

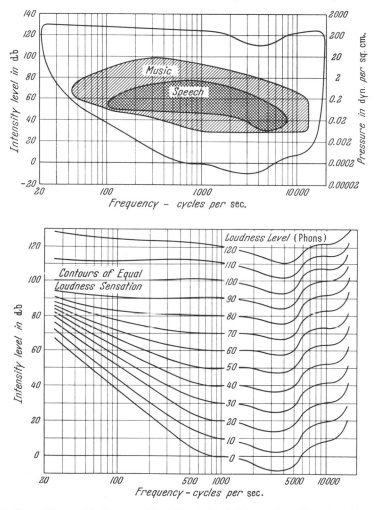

Fig. 42. The audible area of the human ear (*above*). The relationship between physical intensity and frequency on the one hand, and the ear's perception of *loudness* and *pitch* on the other (*below*). Any point along one of the curves is perceived as having the same loudness as any other on the same curve, indepedently of intensity and frequency

db scales. Any point on such a line has the same level of audibility. This level in phons for any tone is equal to the intensity of a 1000 c/s tone with the same intensity, expressed in db above the reference level. In the same way as for frequency, a direct measure — the sone — has

been introduced to in order to measure the perceived intensity differences. Thus a tone of two sones is by definition twice as strong as a
tone of one sone. In order to double the heard intensity the hearing
level in phons has to be increased by 9 db (for stronger sounds).

What has been said so far is valid for simple tones. The intensity
of complex tones depends on the amplitude and the frequency of each
of the components. It is, however, not equal to the sum of them but
represents a certain reduction which takes place in a rather complicated way, which we shall not consider in any detail here.

A few points are, however, worthy of some attention. If two vibrations are presented simultaneously to a human ear, the impression of
intensity is equal to the sum of both, always provided that they are
not too close to each other on the frequency scale. For in that case
the weaker is masked by the stronger. Within a certain bandwidth
the intensities are not superimposed on each other. This bandwidth is,
as was said above, equal to a mel.

If two vibrations of the same frequency stimulate our ear simultaneously, we also have to consider their phase, which is due to the
direction of the movement of the vibrating bodies. If this direction is the
same, as has been illustrated in our Fig. 43 on the following page (p. 65),
the effect is a two-fold amplitude $(B+C=A)$ and consequently an
increase of the intensity. This is the resonatory reinforcing effect (see
hereto also p. 48 ss). If they are in opposite phase, as is shown in Fig. 44,
the effect becomes the difference between the amplitudes $(B-C=A)$.
If the relation is more complicated, the resulting effect also becomes
more complicated (phase distortion). The ear is often said to be indifferent to phase, but recent discoveries seem to indicate that at least
some qualitative differences are due to a difference in phase. In any
case, phase does not seem to be linguistically relevant.

The subjective, or perceptual, sound intensity (often termed
loudness) is one of the correlates of the linguistic distinctions known
as intensity (or dynamic) accents, sometimes also called stress
accents. Recent discoveries have, however, proved that what we call
stress, as a linguistic phenomenon, is very often based on other physical
correlates (intonation, length, vowel colour, etc.). This problem will be
discussed in Chap. V.

To sum up, the acoustico-phonetic analysis of the speech-wave gives
us a fairly exact physical description of the kind of stimuli which reach
our hearing mechanism. Even the most complex speech-wave may be
exhaustively described in terms of frequency, amplitude, and time.
But such a description does not tell us anything about how these
stimuli are transformed into auditory reactions, nor — and still less —

into perceived speech patterns. In a corresponding way, the physiological analysis of the speech mechanism may give a picture of the procedures used by man in order to produce the sounds in accordance
with the social norm, though these data only partly cover the intentional
acts of will executed in order to realize the linguistic model. Further-
more, there is no one to one correspondence between acoustic pheno-

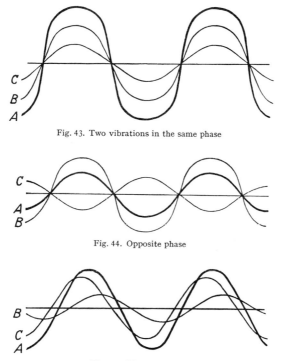

Fig. 43. Two vibrations in the same phase

Fig. 44. Opposite phase

Fig. 45. Phase distortion

mena and articulatory procedures. A sound is an acoustic phenomenon
and cannot be described in terms of tongue positions and lip rounding
but must be described in terms of acoustic variables (cp. above). This
is the principle. But on the other hand, the shape of our speaking
mechanism reduces considerably our possibilities to vary the production
of sounds. At any rate, one way of pronouncing the sound type prescribed by the norm is probably easier and more natural than another,
theoretically possible pronunciation. And as the differences between
people's speaking apparatuses are relatively very small, it is a fact
that, within one and the same speech community, articulatory variation
is slight and that the sounds used in a language are produced in a way
which is fairly constant from one individual to another. This implies that

the articulatory description of speech sounds given by traditional phonetics is much less inconvenient in practice than it may seem from a theoretical point of view.

We shall examine in detail in the two following chapters not only the way in which these potential distinctions are actually made use of for communication purposes and in phonemic systems but also the role played by the purely physical — acoustic and articulatory — analysis in the structural description of the linguistic expression.

Chapter IV

Segmentation. Forms of Expression. Oppositions and Distinctions. Paradigmatic Structures

It has already been pointed out that the sound-wave emanating from the mouth of a speaker is physically a continuum. Both the wave form as such — in the form in which it appears when registered for instance on an oscillograph film (Fig. 14) — and the picture given by a sound spectrograph (Fig. 47) on the basis of a formant analysis, show no more than an incessant variation of the different parameters mentioned in Chap. III. Even in cases where typical segments of an apparently steady-state nature may be seen, there is hardly any possibility of indicating an indisputable point where one segment starts and the preceding one ends. The classical distinction established for instance by the phoneticians of last century between typical sound positions and transitional sounds ("glides", "Gleitlaute", "Übergangslaute", etc.; ELLIS, MERKEL, SIEVERS) does not hold. Everything is transition. And even if one factor, e.g. voice, or nasality, may be said to cease at a given point (in the original complex curve, or on the spectrogram), this factor only rarely coincides with the other factors which together characterize a given segmental unit (e.g. a vocoid or a contoid). Even the early kymograms revealed the existence of transitional phases without any independent linguistic or communicative function. See e.g. Fig. 46, where the three phonetic features of voice, nasality, and degree of opening overlap in different directions. The apparent steady-state character of the vocalic portion on the kymogram is due to the defective registration of the vocal periodicity by the kymograph which normally only registers the fundamental. The same portion of speech is rendered in Fig. 47 by a sound spectrograph.

The concept of continuum also implies either complete identity throughout — e.g. a straight line or an unchanged simple tone —, or a series of ever-changing events where the same configuration never comes back again. Neither of these is capable of conveying information,

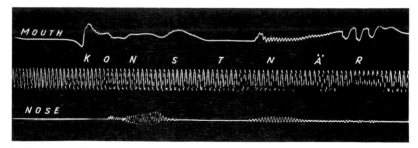

Fig. 46. Kymographic recording of the Swedish word *konstnär* 'artist', phonetically [*'konst,nɛ:r*]. *Above,* the mouth curve (air stream through the mouth with vocalic vibrations); *below,* the nose curve (air stream through the nose, so-called nasality). *In the middle,* time curve (100 c/s)

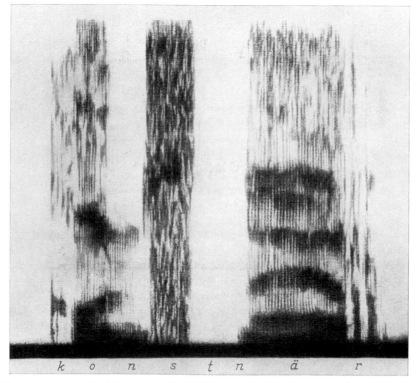

Fig. 47. Sonagram of Swed. *konstnär* (cp. Fig. 43). Filter: 300 c/s. Scale linear, 2000 cycles per inch. The transitions from consonant to vowel and from vowel to consonant are particularly distinct in the [ɛ]. The final [r] has three thrills. Notice the presence of vowel formants in the rolled [r]

and would be useless in human communication. GEORGE MILLER puts this as follows:

"If an object did not appear similar to itself, if recurrences of an event did not seem the same, if members of a class bore no ressemblances to one another, if relations could never be seen as alike, in short, if every event was new and unfamiliar, the commonplace stability of the perceptual universe could never be constructed out of the raw material of our experience and the world would necessarily remain a blooming, buzzing confusion. The first step toward discovering order and meaning is to recognize that something we have experienced before is now occurring again."

In another fairly recent paper MARTIN JOOS has made a series of statements about language and about linguistics as a "discrete mathematics", opposed to the continuous one (infinitesimal calculus etc.). "All continuity, all possibilities of infinitesimal gradation, are shoved outside of linguistics in one direction or other."

Before we go further into the problem of linguistic form let us start our analysis from the opposite end, the linguistic message, and find out what the relationship is between the continuous physical reality as reflected by the acoustic and physiological analysis of the speech event, and the structured linguistic reality, which comes out of a linguistic, structural analysis of the same event, as it is executed by the receiver. In order to do this, it necessary to start from a text[1], i.e. from an utterance. If we take the utterance (text) *the boys are playing in the street*, we know (from Chap. I) that it is built up by a content (signified) and an expression (signifier), thus:

content   *'the boys are playing in the street'*

expression   [ðə ˈbɔiz ə ˈpleiiŋ in ðə ˈstriːt]

where the content, here symbolized by the text written in ordinary letters, stands above the line, the expression, symbolized by a phonetic transcription, below. We obviously have to do with a chain of signs (cf. Chap. I), each of which has its content and its expression. The content is easily analysed into smaller elements. We can distinguish the following semantic units: 'boy', 'play', 'street', and the following grammatical (in traditional terminology morphological and syntactical) units: two articles (*the*), a plural ending (*-s*), a verb ending (*-ing*) together with the auxiliary verb form *are* making up a progressive form, a preposition (*in*) marking the relationship between the verb and the noun 'street', and finally a straight word order (*the boys are ...* as opposed to *are the boys ...*). Any of these elements is, at least to a certain extent, independent of any other, in the sense that none of them are automatically conditioned by the context, though congruency

---

[1] It sometimes seems convenient to use *text*, in accordance with glossematic terminology, about any kind of linguistic utterance or message, long or short, spoken or written.

limits e.g. the choice of verbform (*is* — *are*) versus substantive (*boy* — *boys*). The articles may be replaced by other units, e.g. *the boys* by *two boys, some boys, my boys,* or by zero (*Boys are ...*), *the street* by *a street, our street,* etc. The *-s* may be replaced by zero (*the boy*, with a necessary change of *are* into *is*), *are* by *were, have been, will be,* etc., *are playing* by *play, in* by *near, opposite,* etc. Finally the semantic elements may be replaced by almost any others: *boys* by *girls* or *children, play* by *sing, shout,* etc., *street* by *garden, wood, house, kitchen,* etc. By this analysis, which has been made here only as an example, and which may be carried still further, the content utterance has been cut down into a series of discrete content elements (cp. Chap. II and X).

All the replacements made during this analysis have, however, brought about a corresponding change on the expression level, i.e. a change in the set of expression units. This procedure is called a c o m - m u t a t i o n.

In a corresponding way, a c o m m u t a t i o n t e s t may be carried out on the expression level, i.e. a given segment be supposed to be replaced by another in order to examine whether such a replacement would imply a change of the content or not. In such a case, we have to start from the assumption that some kind of preliminary s e g m e n - t a t i o n has been tried, either on a purely auditory basis[1], or by imposing some pattern — the correct one or any other — on the physical conti- nuum. We can e.g. divide the content into three m e a s u r e s by count- ing the "accents": [ðə ˈbɔiz ə] — [ˈpleiiŋ in ðə] — [ˈstriːt]. Every measure may be replaced by another, say the first by [ðə ˈɡɔːlz wə] or [ə ˈkæt iz]. But these measures are all built up of s y l l a b l e s, e.g. three in the first, four in the second, etc. Any syllable may be replaced by another English syllable, e.g. [plei-] by [ʃaut-], [striːt] by [wud], etc. Any of the changes proposed so far would produce a different content, whereby it should be noticed that also a nonsense content, or lack of content, is a different one. If [ˈbɔiz] is replaced by [kraːts], this means only that the potential sign *crarts* has not been utilized in the English system, though it is in perfect conformity with its structural rules. Syllables, however, are composed of still smaller elements. This statement can easily be proved by a continued commutation test. The initial segment of [bɔiz] is inde- pendent of the following vocalic one. It is possible, and gives another good English word, to say [tɔiz]. The vocalic element may be replaced by [ai], [ou] (i.e. in our example [taiz], [baiz], [bouz], [touz]) or by monophthongs, such as [baːz], [biːz]. Finally, the third element [z] may

---

[1] We have already stressed the fact that the result of an auditory segmentation always depends to a great extent on the previous experiences — i.e. mostly the phonemic background — of the listener. These play an important part and are, in the case of so-called naive listeners, decisive.

be replaced by zero ([*bɔi*], [*tɔi*], [*ba:*], [*tu:*], etc.) or by other elements: [*bɔil*], [*tɔil*], [*toun*], etc. Of course, the first element may also be replaced by zero: [*aiz*], [*ɔil*], [*oun*], etc. If the text had been long enough, we could have tested all possible replacements by making commutation with all units encountered in our corpus. A native informant, or a dictionary, can confirm the existence, or non-existence, of signs resulting from such commutations. In principle, the native speaker will also be able to tell us if a given combination is a potential sign or not. The phonemic analysis should, however, be based, in the first instance, exclusively on conventionally existing signs. Only when the distributional rules have been determined, based on a statistically adequate material, will it be possible to classify a non-existent combination as a potential sign (as an "English not-word").

A series of commutation tests will very soon result in the discovery that certain elements occur only in **marginal** positions. In our example, it would not be possible to replace [*ɔi*], or any other vocoid, by zero, [*bz*] being an impossible English syllable, and a corresponding sign consequently an impossible English word or not-word. The marginal units must not occur alone. Most of the English ones are possible initially and finally ([*nɔt*], [*tɔm*], [*sʌm*] etc.), [*h*] only initially ([*hæt*]), [*ŋ*] only finally ([*kiŋ*]). Groups like [*pr*], [*br*], [*str*] are possible only initially, whereas such groups as [*lz*], [*ps*], [*ts*] are possible finally, and only there. Units like [*ai*], [*a:*], [*εə*], on the contrary, are acceptable English words. They do not suppose the presence of any member(s) of the other (marginal) category. Thus it proves convenient to set up, for English (and for a very large number of other languages), **two sets of minimal expression units: conditioning and conditioned** or **central and marginal**, i.e. in traditional terminology, **vowels and consonants**.

The procedure briefly described here gives an example of a purely **functional**, or **structural**, definition of expression units. A description of this kind gives us the **form** of the linguistic expression, form of syllables, of groups (measures), and of possible larger units. It is made on an entirely different basis from the traditional phonetic description of the expression **substance**. (The question of a corresponding form : substance dichotomy on the content level will be discussed in Chap. VIII.) A similar, purely formal description of an expression system was carried out by SAUSSURE in his famous reconstruction of the vowel system of primitive Indo-European (Chap. I, p. 12).

A further analysis of vowel-consonant distribution in English results in a further splitting up of the vowel category into two sub-classes according to their possible function as final or not final. If we take units like [*si:k*], [*fɔ:k*], [*sɔ:s*], [*ba:k*], [*tu:l*], the final consonant may

be replaced by zero: [si:], [fɔ:], [sɔ:], [ba:], [tu:], etc., all of which
are well-known English words. But if we choose another series of vowels,
commutable with those already given, i.e. [i], [u], [ɔ], [ʌ] in [sit],
[fut], [kʌt], the final consonant is no longer commutable with zero.
Syllables like *[si], *[tu], *[nʌ], if final and stressed, would not be
English[1]. We consequently get one series of vowels which can be stressed
and final, another which cannot. The latter category (in the position
mentioned), supposes a following consonant. This grouping of vowels
into "possible" and "impossible" in final stressed position corresponds
to the traditional phonetic distinction between l o n g and s h o r t vowels.
It gives us another example of a functional or structural classification[2].

When giving the above examples of expression segmentation and
expression analysis we started from a kind of phonetic transcription
of the text which was intended to give a rough idea of the sound-wave
as it is interpreted preliminarily by a native ear, accustomed to phonetic
analysis, i.e. the kind of transcription currently used in elementary
schoolbooks of English. We must, however, notice that this pronunciation is not the only possible one, and that, in fact, we can undertake
changes on the expression level which do not involve any content change.
Let us take the syllable [ə] in our example, which is the expression of
a sign written are, the content of which is 'are'. Consequently, according
to SAUSSURE, the sign in question may be symbolized as follows:

$$\frac{\text{'are'}}{[ə]}$$

with its content and its expression. But this expression may be replaced
by another element [a:] without any change on the content level. A
pronunciation [a:] is a slow, emphatic, or pedantic realization of the
form are, and the variation between [a:] and [ə] is a stylistic one (though
the [ə] pronunciation is not found finally). It m a y have an informative
value but on another level than the one taken into account so far (cp.
Chap. IX)[3]. In the same way, the form [ðə] in certain contexts is automatically replaced by [ði] ([ðə 'bɔiz] but [ði 'ʌðə 'bɔiz]). The choice
between [ðə] and [ði] is conditioned by the following phoneme or by
the degree of stress. [ðə] and [ə] are said to be w e a k or i m p l i c i t f o r m s
of the f u l l, or e x p l i c i t f o r m s [ði:] and [a:]. A setting up of the
phoneme inventory of a language must be made on the basis of full
forms (of words, or morphemes) as well as on the maximal distinctive

---

[1] They appear in polysyllabic groups: ['betə], ['ʌtə], ['hɔtə], etc.

[2] Another question is if, and under what conditions, this classification is the
definitive one from a structural point of view. This problem will be discussed later.

[3] A third (contextual or regional) variant is of course [a:r], or with weakened
/r/-forms. We do not take into account here the possible phonemic interpretation
of Engl. are as /a:r/.

capacity of the language ("the fullest, optimal code at the command of the given speakers"; JAKOBSON-FANT-HALLE). Consequently, our text was not long enough to give examples of the possible word (morpheme) variations and to establish the full forms.

The commutation test supposes two procedures, which both likewise are of equal importance in the language mechanism itself: identification and opposition (or distinction). If the two units — both represented in our example above — [b] and [t] are classified as functionally different on account of the difference in meaning between, say, [bɔi] and [tɔi], this implies that we consider the rest of the two chains as identical. In series like *pot, not, hot, lot, what, shot,* or *sat, sad, sack sag, sap,* only one unit is varied. The rest remains the same. Metrical procedures such as rhyme and alliteration imply identity as well as opposition. Their metrical effect depends on both.

The commutation test permits an exhaustive functional (linguistic) segmentation of the sound-wave, i.e. it gives us the smallest possible independent linguistic units on the expression level. Any commutable segment which cannot be split up by a new commutation into still smaller elements is a minimum unit. And every minimum unit must either be identified with, or opposed to any other minimum unit in the text examined. All units thus identified with each other belong to, or, in linguistic terms, are allophones[1] of one and the same phoneme.

It is important to realize that linguistic function is the principal basis for such an identification, not physical similarity. And it is particularly important to point to the profound difference between the two kinds of classification, a difference reflecting the one which, in general terms, also may be said to characterize psychological methods as opposed to physical. GEORGE M. MILLER has pointed out that similarity between objects, events etc. may be defined either by means of a psychological method, or by means of a physical. To the psychologist, two phenomena are identical if a group of test persons — properly chosen — find them identical. To the physicist they are identical if measurements of them show little difference. The analysis undertaken by phoneticians of the interrelationship between the physical input — the sound-wave — and the perception of this input as a phoneme sequence must consequently be made as a matching of these two series of events — the physical and the psychological — against each other. The results obtained from the analysis of one level do not necessarily tell us anything about those to be expected on the other. The more analytic-synthetic experiments that are carried out on phoneme

---

[1] This term is used here with reference to positional as well as to free variants.

perception and phoneme identification, the higher will be the predictability of one set of events from our knowledge of the other. But it is
essential to realize that this correspondence between physical and
perceptual facts is never more than a question of probability.

Three conditions must be fulfilled if two units are to be regarded as
allophones of the same phoneme: 1. they must be functionally identical,
i.e. be substitutable in identical environment, or have complementary distribution; 2. they must belong to the same structurally defined class, and 3. they must have certain distinctive features
(cp. also Chap. VI) in common. Consequently, two units are members
of two different phonemes 1. if they are commutable in the same
environment, or 2. if they belong to different structurally defined classes,
or 3. if they have no distinctive features in common. This means that
the grouping of minimal expression units into phonemes may be made
according to their distribution, e.g. as marginal and central units
(cp. above) into vowels and consonants. Consequently, any vowel is
supposed to be opposed to any consonant only on account of their
belonging to different distributional classes[1]. And any consonant may
be regarded as opposed structurally to any other consonant with which
it does not share any consonantal distinctive features. Thus the famous
problem of the [h]- and [ŋ]-sounds in English and in other Germanic
languages may be solved through a reference to this third rule. They
have complementary distribution — [h] appears only at the beginning
of a morpheme, [ŋ] only at the end of one or between vowels — but
have no other distinctive feature in common than that of being consonants.

It is evident that another kind of segmentation of the sound-wave
and other classifications of the expression elements than the functional,
or structural one proposed above are possible and for certain purposes
appropriate. We could for instance distinguish between such elements
as can be heard as different by a human ear and such as are auditorily
identified (in suitably arranged identification tests). A classification
based on this criterion would, however, have the disadvantage of being
determined to a large extent by the discrimination possibilities of an

---

[1] In many languages, there are examples of a free variation between vowel
and consonant, particularly between /i/ and /j/, /u/ and /w/. This is the case in
French where /j/ in *bien*, /w/ in *moi* have often been interpreted as non-syllabic
variants of the /i/- and /u/-phonemes, on account of the free variation in words
like *lier*, *louer*, phonetically [lie] or [lje], [lue] or [lwe]. It seems preferable, however,
to look upon such examples as so called word-variants, with variation in the
phonemic make up of the morpheme (just as there is variation between ['aiðə]
and ['i:ðə], sc. *either*, in certain kinds of English). The definition of the "semi-
vowels" in question as structural vowels leads to serious difficulties which cannot
be discussed here. We find exactly the same problem e.g. in Spanish.

individual whose discriminative capacity depends on his phonemic
background and his phonemic experience (cp. above), on his training
to listen to sounds, and particularly to speech-sounds, and on individual
auditory characteristics. It is not possible to distinguish, in a general
way, between sounds which can be discriminated and those which
cannot. Any sound difference can be recognized as different from another
by a human ear after sufficient training if the distance between the
stimuli lies within the physiological possibilities of our auditory mechanism (see Chap. III, Fig. 42). As all sound differences actually used in
linguistic communication, for evident reasons, are to be found considerably above the lower threshold of auditory discrimination, it goes without
saying that our capacity to hear linguistically distinctive sound differences is essentially determined by factors other than physiological ones
(assuming of course, that our hearing capacity is physiologically normal).
For even a very limited experience of foreign languages, of language
teaching, or of bilingualism tells us that everyone does not hear all of
the distinctions used in linguistic communication. In fact, the so-called
naive speaker hears only the differences used as distinctive in his own
language.

On the other hand, it is a matter of fact that many of the units set
up as allophones on the basis of commutation are often so different
phonetically that the phonetician has no difficulty at all in classifying
them, on a physiological or acoustic basis, as definitely different types.
It is, however, important to remember that, when doing so, the phonetician undertakes a classification which is based on substance, not
on function, and that such a classification is subject to criticism for
being arbitrary[1]. On the other hand, however arbitrary such a grouping
of speech-sounds into types may be, it is useful for practical, pedagogical
and other purposes. It is, for instance, the principle behind the so-called
phonetic alphabets[2], theoretically impossible but practically neces-

---

[1] It is arbitrary because the point of departure chosen lies outside the object
of analysis which in this case is a communication system, not a physical event.

[2] The principle of any phonetic alphabet — of which that of the "International
Phonetic Association" (dating from 1886) is the best known and the most widespread — is "one symbol for one sound". A symbol supposes a class — not just
an individual —, and as the classification of the speech events in the sound-wave
into classes is necessarily arbitrary, as long as the substance structure is the only
criterion, the choice of a given symbol for a given sound must always remain
controversial. In reality, phonetic transcription has always been, and always
must be, at least partly phonemic. When opposing two sounds by choosing different
symbols and when identifying them by using the same symbol phonetic transcription has always to a certain extent taken into account linguistic function and
phonemic points of view. Distinctions which are commonly used in the best known
languages have got their symbolic counterparts in the international alphabet,
but not rare distinctions.

sary and pedagogically indispensable. It should further be noticed here that many of the sound types classified as allophones by means of the commutation test may be looked upon as functional, distinctive units on other levels of linguistic communication than the one taken into account here (Chap. IX). When we talk about "sounds" in the present context, we consequently understand phonetic types independent of their linguistic function and distinguished roughly by certain phonetic differences (of articulation and of acoustic structure), differences which fall within the range of possibilities set up in our preliminary survey in Chap. III.

We are going to consider a few examples of expression structures and of phonemic systems, vocalic, consonantal, and prosodic. But before doing so, we have to consider two basic concepts: distinctiveness and distribution.

The first two steps in the structural analysis of the linguistic expression, the preliminary segmentation and the classification of the minimal units into phonemes, must be followed by a third step which implies a structural analysis of the oppositions, with a view to establishing, as a final result, the paradigmatic structure of the language. The relationship between the units distinguished must be determined on the basis of distinctive features, a concept which will be treated in more detail in Chap. V. The author of these lines is convinced of the necessity of taking into account for this kind of structural analysis even criteria which belong to the domain of the sound substance of the expression. Distinctions suppose differences. It is the task of instrumental and experimental phonetics to determine the physical facts behind the differences perceived and, consequently, behind the distinctions utilized for communication.

Though this survey is not intended to give any complete orientation about the methods used in modern phonetics, it may be useful to mention — without going into any detail — some facts of importance for the understanding of the results achieved in this field. A few further questions of method remain to be dealt with in another context later (Chap. V).

Instrumental phonetics may be said to work along two parallel lines. One is the physiological analysis of speech production, i.e. of the way in which our organs of speech produce the necessary sounds. The other is the acoustic analysis of the sound-wave. Both imply a description of physical facts and may in principle be carried out without consideration of any possible communicative function of the events analysed. The technical devices used are taken over from acoustics and from physiology. But, in fact, no really phonetic research is undertaken, or has been undertaken, independently of linguistic categories and linguistic or communicative functions. The acoustic or physiological events which actually take place in speech processes are innumerable. The phonetician, when planning an instrumental analysis, must make a choice, thereby concentrating his interest upon certain phenomena and disregarding the rest. If his background and interests are linguistic, the phonetician evidently chooses those phenomena which play a part in communication and those events through which linguistically relevant differences and qualities are manifested. Any phonetic research worthy of this name has its starting-point in linguistically, i.e. functionally, defined categories, and proceeds from those to the physical phenomena through which they are manifested in speech. Instrumental phonetics can answer the question of how linguistic distinctions and linguistic functions are realized physically but can never give any answer to the reverse question of which, or how many, linguistic categories have to be accounted for in the linguistic description.

As a rule, phonetic analysis reveals a whole series of physical differences between the units examined. The question then arises which of these differences is the one which, in the interpretation process, is to be regarded as the essential "cue" to the distinction under examination. Only one method of solution is feasible for a question of this kind, namely a synthetic experiment. Thanks to different technical devices, which cannot be described here, it is possible to produce synthetic speech by combining artificially the different parameters, or variables, of which the speech-wave is composed, and to vary one factor at a time, leaving the rest intact — a procedure which is only possible with synthetic speech. The result of the variation is checked by auditory tests. Thanks to this speech synthesis, it has become possible to check, at least to a certain extent, not only the results obtained from the structural analysis of the distinctive features, but also the instrumental data (cp. also Chap. III and V).

Instrumental analyses of articulations and of speech-waves have revealed that no two pieces of speech are physically identical. Identification, as well as opposition, consequently supposes that certain characteristics are taken into account, and others disregarded[1]. If the two [t]:s in *street* [*stri:t*] are identified as one, though they are clearly phonetically different, this identification is made on the basis of certain

---

[1] This is the principle for any kind of classification. It will be discussed further in connection with content analysis. We know from the physiology of perception that the same is true for any kind of conscious, intelligent perception, which by definition supposes classification, i.e. identification (and opposition). See hereto also Chap. I, the example quoted p. 14.

qualities which they have in common and which oppose them to all other expression units of the language capable of taking their place in the chain[1].

Let us start with the English consonant system — or part of the consonant system — to illustrate problems and methods. And let us suppose that, after the necessary commutation tests, we have set up among others the following preliminary minimal units: $/p/$, $/t/$, $/k/$, $/b/$, $/d/$, $/g/$. An analysis of their combinations in English syllables permits us certain conclusions as to their distribution in the language. Both occur in initial as well as in final position in the syllable: examples $/pa:/$, $/\Lambda p/$, $/tu:/$, $/ɔ:t/$, $/ki:/$, $/da:k/$, $/ba:/$, $/kæb/$, $/do:/$, $/bə:d/$, $/gou/$, $/dɔg/$. They are marginal units. Initially, they enter into combinations with "liquids": $/prei/$, $/tri:/$, $/braun/$, $/drai/$, $/grou/$, $/plei/$, $/blou/$, $/glaid/$, except t with l (tl- being an impossible English initial), the "dentals" and "palato-velars" also with $/w/$, in $/twin/$, $/dwel/$, $/kwi:n/$ etc. Finally, they admit several combinations, among which we mention those with l ($/kætl/$, $/teibl/$, $/str\Lambda gl/$), with nasal ($/oupn/$, $/'ga:dn/$), and with $/s/$ ($/outs/$, $/pə'hæps/$), most of which are morphemic compounds (for the concept of 'morpheme', see Chap. VIII). A systematic study of the possible combinations of these phonemes and of their frequency, in the vocabulary and in a text, will reveal some of the syntagmatic laws of the system (cp. below). It allows us to state that some marginal elements admit one order in syllable-initial, both orders, or only the ·reverse one, in syllable-final position (e.g. $/sp/$, $/st/$ initially and finally, $/ps/$ or $/ts/$ only finally; $/fl/$ initially, $/lf/$ finally). Some marginal units manifest a clearcut tendency to appear in close contact with the central element (the vowel) and may be classed as vowel-adherent (those are in fact the most "vocalic" ones, such as liquids or nasals), others prefer extremely marginal positions. Stops are normally less vowel-adherent than fricatives, nasals or liquids (e.g. $/-ft/$ but not $/-tf/$ finally, $/tw-/$ but not $/wt-/$ initially). Thus, the marginal units may be grouped according to their rank order and categories set up with the possible distribution as the only criterion. More about the concept of rank order and consonant distribution will be said in Chap. VII.

Let us choose the least vowel-adherent type of marginal units (contoids) and compare them with the rest of the contoids. It is easy to see that they have certain physical qualities in common which distinguish them as a group from all others. They imply on the articulatory level a complete momentaneous interruption of the air-stream followed by

---

[1] Distribution alone is not sufficient to identify them, because other phonemes (e.g. $/p/$ and $/k/$) would be possible in the same position. Function alone does not permit to decide if initial $/t/$ is to be identified with final $/t/$ or with final $/p/$, etc.

a sudden opening. This corresponds, on the acoustic level, to a silent or semi-silent, phase (the occlusion) and to a sudden change in the sound-wave, brought about by the opening or closure of the vocal tract. It consequently seems possible to look upon the sudden spectral change and the relatively silent phase involved as a distinctive feature which opposes these contoids to all others on the acoustic level, and on the complete closure of the air passage as the corresponding physiological charac-teristic. Thus /p/ is opposed to /f/, /b/ to /v/, /d/ to /ð/ and so forth by means of the relevant difference in English between 'stops' and 'fricatives'[1].

Even a superficial phonetic inspection of the six phonemes under discussion results in a classification into two series with three in each: /p/, /t/, /k/ versus /b/, /d/, /g/. A commutation test easily proves the func-tional value of the distinctions /p/—/b/ etc.: /pai/∼/bai/, /tai/∼/dai/, /koul/∼/goul/, or in final position /kæp/∼/kæb/, /hæt/∼/hæd/, and so forth. Phonetic analysis reveals several more or less easily defined physical differences between the two series, among others a difference as to glottal vibrations (/p/ is voiceless, /b/ voiced, etc.), a difference of aspiration (/p/ is aspirated, /b/ non-aspirated), of intensity (/p/ is supposed to be a "fortis", /b/ a "lenis", etc.), and of formant transition (cp. Fig. 33—34). It seems to be a fact that at least the differences of voice, of intensity and of formant transition are all capable of functioning alone as cues to the distinction perceived. This is a result which has been arrived at in repeated synthetic experiments and which linguistic evidence indicates as probable.

In the same way we have to define phonetically the differences between the pairs /p/∼/b/, /t/∼/d/, and /k/∼/g/ respectively. The arti-culatory distinctive factor is here the so-called "place of articulation" and the distinctions are traditionally described as labial versus dental (alveolar) versus (palato-)velar. The acoustic counterpart is on the one hand a difference in the formant structure of the explosion noise (lowest for the labials, higher for /t/—/d/; concerning /k/—/g/, see Fig. 34), on the other a difference in the transition from vocoid to contoid (contoid to vocoid).

If our distributional analysis had been exhaustive, we should have made an interesting discovery regarding the combinatory possibilities of the contoids, and particularly of the stops. After /s/ in the same syllable only one member of each of the three pairs is possible, i.e. in

---

[1] Though it would for certain purposes be very useful to generalize a termino-logy referring to acoustic characteristics when talking about speech sounds, and a corresponding terminology with reference to physiological events when talking about articulations and articulatory possibilities and types, we prefer to use, for the sake of convenience, the current terms, though it will be clear from what has been said here that they are not very appropriate.

traditional transcription /p/, /t/, and /k/ (/spai/, /stei/, /skai/). A combination /sb/ etc. is not English and an opposition /sp/ ∼/sb/ consequently impossible. This means that the /p/, /t/, /k/ in words like *spoon*, *street*, *sky* do not stand in opposition to /b/, /d/, /g/. The voice distinction is no longer linguistically valid. A stop after /s/ in the same syllable is consequently one out of three possibilities, not one out of six, as it is in other positions. Its amount of information is smaller and its predictability greater. Its qualities of voice, of force, its lack of aspiration, etc. are redundant.

A new problem of interpretation arises, however, in a case like this. How is it possible to identify the /p/ in /spai/ with the one in /pai/, an identification which is obviously the cause of the phonetic transcription traditionally used in this case (and evidently of traditional spelling)? A phonetic analysis reveals a difference between the two /p/:s, in so far as the first is aspirated ([p^h] in narrow transcription). /p/ in /spai/ is non-aspirated like /b/, voiceless (and probably a fortis) like /p/. In structural terms we have neutralization or syncretism after /s/ in the same syllable. Structurally the /p/ in /spai/ is neither a /p/ nor a /b/ but rather the common denominator of both, a unit which is undifferentiated with regard to the distinction voiced ∼voiceless (fortis ∼lenis). In the terminology of the Prague school, we have to do with the archiphoneme /P/. The basis for this concept of archiphoneme is the assumption that one of the two opposed series is to be regarded as marked, i.e. characterized by a quality lacking in the other series, which is unmarked. /b/ would thus be /p/+ voice, /d/ in the same way /t/+ voice, etc. The unmarked type is the one which is realized phonetically in positions of syncretism. Consequently there may be said to exist structural evidence for the interpretation of /p/ as unmarked and /b/ as marked and consequently an objective reason for identifying the /p/ in /spai/ with the one in /pai/. But the whole argumentation is based on the assumption that voice is the distinctive feature of the /b/- /d/- /g/ series as opposed to the /p/ series. If aspiration is chosen as the distinctive feature, our argumentation does not hold, and the unaspirated contoid in /spai/ should be written phonetically */sbai/. It is the task of instrumental phonetics to answer the question of what is distinctive and what is not, among the physical differences which actually exist between the linguistic units set up on the basis of commutation and distribution. This is the point where instrumental analysis, synthetic experiments, and auditory tests come in as an unavoidable part of the structural analysis. We leave out of the discussion here the question of the correctness of the interpretation given above of the English system of stops. We regard it as a working hypothesis. It is interesting to make a comparison with Danish which, at least initially, has the same system as English

with two series and the same combinations with /s/. But in Danish, the
/b/—/d/—/g/ series is definitely voiceless and the /p/—/t/—/k/ series
strongly aspirated. In Danish, it is consequently convenient to look
upon aspiration as the distinctive feature and to identify the unaspirated
contoid in the /s/-combination with /b/ and to transcribe it as /sb/ (in
accordance with current usage in Danish phonetics, but in contradistinction to official orthography which has sp- as in English). It should
be stressed that the groups in question (in English spy and in Danish
spille etc.) are phonetically more or less the same. Even in a so-called
phonetic transcription, structural points of view are, and must be,
taken into account.

Let us now start from the assumption that voice is the distinctive
feature in the English stop series. We shall revert to problems of this
kind a little later (Chap. V). And let us for the moment use the traditional
articulatory terms for the localization feature. We thus get the following
system of English stops:

	voiceless	voiced
labial	/p/	/b/
dental(-alveolar)	/t/	/d/
palato-velar	/k/	/g/

with neutralization of the voiceless ∼ voiced distinction in position after
s-, i.e. /P/, archiphoneme phonetically identified with /p/ ([p] as opposed
to the [pʰ] of other stressed syllable-initial positions).

It should be noticed that the aspiration feature consequently is
redundant in the English system. As such it contributes to a correct
identification of the message and supports efficiently the important
distinction between voiced and voiceless stops. It is certainly not due
to chance that this redundant feature is lacking in the position where
the voiceless series cannot be opposed to a voiced one, i.e. after /s-/,
where /b/ etc. are impossible and the possibility of confusion is therefore
excluded.

Thus, the grouping of /p/, /t/, /k/ and /b/, /d/, /g/ into two parallel
series is based on commutation and, therefore, on linguistic function.
From this point of view, /p/ is defined as simply being opposed to /b/,
to /t/, to /m/, etc. The purely formal description is exhaustive, when all
/p/'s relationships with all other expression units of the paradigm(s)
to which it belongs are sufficiently defined. The formal discription
states oppositions and sets up paradigms. The distinctive feature which
underlies the opposition and through which the distinctions are manifested in speech, on the other hand, has to be stated in terms referring
to the sound substance. In the author's opinion, the purely formal structural description and the substance analysis of the distinctive features

are different levels of abstraction with which we shall have to deal later.

It seems convenient, in the author's opinion, to introduce a terminological and conceptual distinction between opposition, which is a formally described linguistic function, and distinction, which is a linguistically relevant phonetic difference. According to this terminology there is opposition between /p/ and /b/ in English — but not e.g. in Finnish —, because the commutation test results in two different words if one, in given contexts, is replaced by the other (/pai/ ∼/bai/). In English, the difference between voiceless and voiced stops is a distinction because it is used to manifest a phonemic opposition. Consequently opposition belongs to the form domain, distinction to the substance domain, but even so to a substance which is linguistically formed, whereas difference refers to physical facts and events (of physiology or of acoustics) independent of any linguistic function. This terminology consequently reflects the three levels of expression analysis as it is mostly carried out in modern phonemics: 1. the formal setting up of phonemes (oppositions) (the strictly functional analysis), 2. the definition of the distinctions and distinctive features which manifest the oppositions, and 3. the purely physical description of allophones and of all other phenomena involved, directly or indirectly, in the speech process. It will be pointed out later (Chap. V) that particularly stage No. 2 in this analytic procedure may have different degrees of abstraction and, according to that, be of more or less general validity.

The preceeding analysis thus resulted in a paradigm based on two series of oppositions, one realized as a distinction between voiceless and voiced, the other as a distinction of explosion frequency (or of locus-frequency; see Fig. 34) on the acoustic level, or as a distinction of localisation on the articulatory level. These distinctions are the same within the two series voiced and voiceless, /p/ ∼/b/ being a difference parallel with the one between /t/ and /d/, /k/, and /g/. This implies that four distinctions give six expression units (phonemes). The introduction of only one additional distinction, say one between dental and alveolar (high and slightly lowered explosion frequency), gives two new phonemes: /t̬/ and /d̬/ and the following paradigm:

$$p \quad b$$
$$t \quad d$$
$$t̬ \quad d̬$$
$$k \quad g$$

a system used in certain languages (among which could be mentioned the Mapuche language of Southern South America, and also Swedish if, for special, purely structural reasons, the alveolar units were not to be analysed more conveniently as clusters of /r/+ dental).

On the other hand, many languages have poorer systems. One without any distinction of voice is very common, in fact much more widespread among the world's languages than the one given above (which is found in English, German, French, Swedish, Italian, Spanish, etc.). Finnish has e. g. no distinction of voice nor have most non-Indo-European languages.

The interruption type of contoid (stop) may be opposed to a nasal type, based acoustically on the addition of a "nasal formant", that is on a special low resonance, in articulatory terms a distinction between open and closed nasal air passage. Hence the following (English) paradigm:

$$
\begin{array}{ccc}
p & - b & - m \\
| & | & | \\
t & - d & - n \\
| & | & | \\
k & - g & - \eta
\end{array}
$$

which is, however, subject to a severe restriction of distribution as far as the nasal $/\eta/$ is concerned. A language which has a distinction between $/t̪/$ and $/t/$ etc. will probably also have one between $/n̪/$ and $/n/$.

Consonant paradigms are always, however, more complicated than this. They normally have at least some sort of distinction between **interrupted** and **continued**, i.e. in acoustic terms between a sudden change in a vocalic spectrum as opposed to a more gradual one and, as a consequence thereof, a continued noise, on the articulatory level between an occlusion and a narrow air passage, say $/d/ \sim /ð/$ (in English $/dei/ \sim /ðei/$, $/{}^{l}læðə/ \sim /l{}^{l}æðə/$). In the same way $/v/$ (in ${}^{l}veri/$) may be opposed to $/b/$ (in ${}^{l}beri/$) etc. The distinctions are parallel, in English, to those between $/t/$ and $/θ/$ ($/tin/ \sim /θin/$), $/p/$ and $/f/$ ($/pain/ \sim /fain/$), with the following extension of our paradigm:

$$
\begin{array}{lccccc}
\text{Labials} & p & - b & - m & - v & - f \\
& | & | & | & | & | \\
\text{Dentals(-alveolars)} & t & - d & - n & - ð & - θ \\
& | & | & | & & \\
\text{Palato-velars} & k & - g & - \eta & &
\end{array}
$$

Two aspects of this system should be noted. Firstly, two potential distinctions in the velar series are not utilized, since English lacks the velar fricatives $/\gamma/$ and $/x/$. For the opposition $/ð/ \sim /θ/$, it is difficult to find minimal pairs (e. g. *thigh — thy*), but both are admitted in the same context. Secondly, the nasal series does not know any distinction of voice. Voice in combination with nasality is consequently a redundant feature which may be lacking in certain cases of assimilation in combination with voiceless consonants.

This grouping of the phonemes into series or bundles in which one distinctive feature is kept constant and another is varied is an expression of the principle of economy. The same difference distinguishes /p/ from /b/, /t/ from /d/, and /k/ from /g/. And one factor only (localisation) is different in the pairs /p/ ∼/t/, or /d/ ∼/g/, equally one in /p/ ∼/f/ and /t/ ∼/θ/ (the labio-dental articulation of /f/ is redundant, and so is the interdental place of articulation of /θ/). English is said to have a correlation of voice, a correlation of nasality, etc. Several parallel series of correlation (e.g. the English stop and nasal series) are sometimes said to be a bundle of correlations (TRUBETZKOY's "Korrelationsbündel", French "faisceau de corrélation"). The principle of economy consists in the use of the same difference to distinguish between several phoneme pairs. An "economic" system is consequently easier to master than one which supposes the manoeuvering of as many distinctions as the number of functional units. The tendency towards greater economy is probably an important factor in evolutive phonetics. An economic system demands less effort, on the auditory as well as on the articulatory level. Discrimination between many units becomes easier if our ear can listen to, and recognize the same differences in varying combinations than if it constantly has to react to completely unrelated stimuli. Conversely, the fewer the articulatory movements and positions to be combined in realizing a given system, the easier will be the task of maintaining the necessary distinctions and the wider will be the permitted margin of error. It goes without saying that on all levels (auditory, articulatory, linguistic) the mastering of a system like the English stop paradigm we have just discussed is less complicated, and consequently functions with more accuracy (less loss along the communication chain), than if for example we had to distinguish /p/ and /b/ by means of voice, /t/ and /d/ by means of aspiration and /k/ and /g/ by means of, say, glottalization (see Chap. III, p. 57).

One of the first tasks of a phonemicist who has to undertake the description of a language is the establishment of its set of phonemes. Phonemisation implies the reduction of an unlimited number of variants to a limited number of invariants. If the aim is a practical one — e.g. the invention of a convenient writing system for a scriptless language, or the adoption of an adequate transcription system for language teaching — or a more theoretical one, the main concern of the phonemicist is to arrive at a sufficiently small number of minimal units (phonemes). The first phonemicist, in fact, was the man who invented the alphabetic script. The smaller the number, the simpler the description. And it is undeniable that, in any science, a description which needs a smaller amount of data is superior to one which supposes a larger number, supposed that the description is equally exhaustive. Phonemisation is only one aspect of the universal scientific search for generalities. The final scope of scientific analysis is to make general statements about a material. A description which characterizes a linguistic system by means of 40 phonemes is consequently, in principle, superior to one which uses 100 or 150 "sounds".

But how far is this statement valid? It would at first sight seem to be a satisfactory solution to stop when you have found the single phonemes (i.e. when you have reduced the variants into invariants and the complexes into single units). We have seen, however, that the phonemes are the result of our interpretation, and that only the distinctions are undisputably ascertainable. There is nothing in structural theory that prevents us from interpreting a French nasal vowel as a structural complex consisting of a vowel + a nasal phoneme, nothing either that prevents us from classifying it as a single phoneme. One interpretation may have certain advantages, the other may have others. The undisputable fact is the distinction between /a/ and /ã/, etc., and only that.

As was pointed out above, the analysis of spectrograms as well as the study of articulatory movements (e.g. on radiographic films) have persuaded phoneticians of the non-existence of stable phases corresponding to the successive phonemes of the structurally interpreted chain. No physical analysis can tell us if a given configuration has to be interpreted as one or two or more phonemes. On the one hand, single phonemes often present several rather easily delimited phases (a stop e.g. an occlusion + an explosion + an aspiration, etc.). On the other hand clusters often show a high degree of co-articulation which implies that what is perceived as a sequence of phonemes (pl-, -tl, etc.) is in fact a complex of simultaneous articulatory events. There may be more evidence in a spectrogram for a splitting up of an English /p/ into several units than for the interpretation of /pl/ or /kl/ as clusters. Consequently, segmentation must be based on structural evidence, not on physical.

Many languages outside Europe have series of so-called nasalized stops as single phonemes: /mb/, /nd/, /ŋg/. Such a transcription, in traditional phonetic script as well as in current European orthography, is of course due to Indo-European prejudice in phonemic interpretation. In many African and American languages, these phonemes are undoubtedly single phonemes. Several structural facts prove the correctness of such an interpretation. These languages have no consonant clusters. An interpretation of these three consonants as clusters would imply the introduction into the system of a distributional type unknown except for the examples created by the analysis itself. The frequent use of these phonemes in initial position, where a cluster consisting of nasal + stop would be particularly improbable in a language without other clusters, is a further argument. A syllabation of the type *si-mba*, *Ru-a-nda* is natural, and seems the only possible to the native speakers of these languages. And finally, the systems do not know any voiced stops (*b, d, g*) outside the particular position after homorganic nasals. In Guaraní (South America) the same units (*mb* etc.) are allophones of the nasal phonemes /*m*/ etc. in prevocalic initial position except before nasal vowels (which are independent phonemes in the language). A biphonematic interpretation of such units would consequently imply the setting up of a new series of phonemes known exclusively in the positions under discussion. It would be an extremely unsatisfactory phonemic solution. It would be identical with an interpretation of English or German unaspirated [*p*], [*t*], [*k*] (after *s* in the same syllable, in *spy* etc.) as separate phonemes.

A few further examples of the same kind of problem may be interesting. At first sight nothing would seem to prevent us, either, from analysing Amer. Engl. /ʃ/ as /s+j/ in the dialects which have no (phonetic) cluster /sj/, and from transcribing (with HARRIS) /sjai/, /sjrimp/, etc.[1] (for *shy, shrimp*), or from interpreting say Swed. /ʃ/ as /r+s/ in the dialects that pronounce the cluster *rs* as a single /ʃ/-like fricative (with ELERT)[2]. But there is a limit which the principle of simplification must not go beyond. If phonemic simplications of this kind lead to the introduction into the system of combinations otherwise unknown — just as in the African examples quoted —, thus imposing on the language consonant distributions for which there is no other evidence than the one obtained by the interpretation, this must definitely be characterized as wrong. English does not have an explosive cluster /sjr/. Nor does Swedish have any initial cluster /r/ + fricative (or /r/ + consonant). The functioning of the language mechanism consequently does not give any evidence for the splitting up of English /ʃ/ into /s+j/ or of Swedish /ʃ/ into /r+s/ (except, however, for syllable final or intervocalic position where there is, or may be, syncretism between /ʃ/ and /rs/).

When certain phonemicists, for the sake of simplification, have gone as far as in the examples just mentioned, they seem to have overlooked that they have taken a step beyond the phonemic level of language analysis, and proceeded to the splitting up of the phonemes into distinctive features, as visualized by JAKOBSON-FANT-HALLE the final step in an analysis which implies a successive reduction of the linguistic

---

[1] HARRIS uses /sy/ for /sj/.

[2] In most parts of Sweden the (postvocalic) cluster *rs* is pronounced as one single fricative sound, a kind of /ʃ/, and as the /ʃ/-phoneme (in many people's speech identical phonetically with *rs*) is only initial, except for loan-words and onomatopoetica, ELERT has proposed to interpret any /ʃ/ as a cluster /rs/ in any position and consequently transcribes *sjö* [ʃøː] as /rsøː/, etc.

expression down to its simplest, most general and least numerous elements. If we interpret /ʃ/ as /s+j/ in a language which does not give any structural or distributional evidence for it, we simply split it up into /s/ + compactness (see below), i.e. we isolate one of its distinctive features, thus confusing the phoneme with one of its minimal elements. The same could of course be said regarding the interpretation of French /ã/ etc., as /a/ + nasal etc., though there seem to be much better evidence for, and less difficulties with, this solution than with the others mentioned. TRUBETZKOY's remark to the phoneme definition that the phonemes are the smallest units following each other ("in noch kürzere aufeinanderfolgende Einheiten") is important. Linearity implies a boundary between two levels of description. A Swedish alveolar [ʈ] in *kort* is phonemically a sequence of /r/+/t/, not of /t/+/r/, whereas /y/ may be characterised indifferently as /i/ + labiality or as labiality + /i/. Consequently labiality is a distinctive feature of /y/; alveolarity is not a distinctive feature of [ʈ] but a manifestation of the /r/-phoneme.

A further reduction of the minimal units may sometimes be undertaken for practical reasons. This is e.g. the case when a language uses complex letter-groups when faced with a lack of adequate symbols for certain phonemes (Germ. *sch*, Engl. *sh*, French *ch* for /ʃ/). The written language may in such cases represent a more advanced analysis of the expression than is possible in its corresponding spoken form. When taking over an alphabet from another language — as has been the case for all European languages, where a variety of the Latin or of the Greek alphabet is used —, there is, if the borrowing system is the richer of the two, a choice between introducing additional symbols (by means of diacritic signs or otherwise) and accepting inadequate figures, resulting in phonemic confusion (e.g. Italian *e* and *o*, each representing two phonemes), or the use of different letter-groups. If the borrowing system is poorer, the application of an inadequate alphabet on this system may result in an unmotivated splitting up of single units into two graphic ones. This happens when certain modern languages use *c* or *z* (in loanwords) together with *s* for the unique /s/-phoneme (e.g. in Swedish), or when English uses *ch* in Greek loan-words (originally with an aspirate stop phoneme) without any correspondence in the phonemic system of the language. It may seem to be a certain advantage not to learn, and to teach, too many different signs. In fact an over-restricted set of symbols offers the evident advantage of being a simpler paradigm than a richer one. But, on the other hand, what is gained in the way of paradigm simplicity is lost in the syntagms which become the more complicated, the poorer the paradigm is ("paradigm" in this case = the set of graphic units). The Germans are spared the necessity of learning a special sign for their /ʃ/-phoneme but have to pay for this by writing the three letters *sch* every time the phoneme occurs[1].

The "phonological" concepts of relevancy and irrelevancy implied the assumption that certain physical characteristics of the expression unit — defined in acoustic or in physiological terms — were decisive for the identity of the unit, others not. The problem consequently often arose which of several actual sound differences was to be classed as the relevant one (a question to which we shall revert in Chap. V). Let us just mention here that the JAKOBSON-FANT-HALLE system of distinctive features is based on the same assumption and that, consequently, an analysis along these lines must precede the setting up of all the schemes which are widely used to illustrate the form, or the structure, of an expression system.

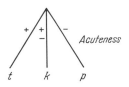

A convenient method of illustrating graphically the distinctions used by a given phonemic system and the hierarchy according to which the system is built up has been proposed by GUNNAR FANT and MORRIS HALLE. We are going to apply this procedure to consonant systems of varying complexity starting with the simplest possible system of stops which we regard as basic in all

Fig. 48. The minimal system of basic consonantal oppositions. The distinctive feature here is only acuteness. It should be noticed that the existence of fricative phonemes supposes that of stops, but not inversely. All languages have stops, some lack fricatives (JAKOBSON)

linguistic structures and corresponding to the minimal vocalic paradigm set up already in Chap. III, and then analysing the complete French system, remarkably rich and characterized by some peculiar and very uncommon distinctions (p. 88).

If we go over to vowels, it may be convenient to start with the system characterized above (Chap. III) as basic, i.e. a system of three members of maximal acoustic distinctions which is a paradigm with a first distinction between a compact and a non-compact (diffuse) spectrum (cp. above), /a/ versus /i/ or /u/, and a second distinction between the diffuse type of spectrum between an acute and a grave one, i.e. /i/ versus /u/. The compact phoneme /a/ is neutral as far as acuteness is concerned. This system is known from, among others, certain American languages (Quichua, etc.). It is schematized in Fig. 50 and 51.

---

[1] This is only a particular instance of a general phonemic law which implies a reversed proportion between the number of phonemes and the length of syntagms. A language with a small number of phonemes, in order to obtain the same number of signs as a richer language, has to make its syntagms longer (the length measured in number of phonemes). It is only natural that it should be valid also for the graphemic level.

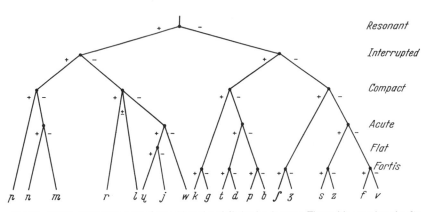

Fig. 49. French consonants grouped as a hierarchy of distinctive features. The positive member of a distinction is marked +, the negative −. In the cases where there are three members, the intermediale (neutral) one is marked ±. To the right, the distinctive features. Thus the first basic distinction is the one between resonant and non-resonants (i.e. presence or absence of formant structure). The second division is based on the distinction between interrupted (stops, nasals) and non-interrupted (liquids, fricatives), the third, fourth and fifth on the place of the dominating frequency regions of the noise or of the resonant spectrum (cp. above, Chap. III) on the frequency scale, the sixth on the so-called intensity of the noise (valid only within the non-resonant group)

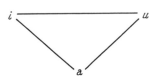

Fig. 50. Minimal vocalic system

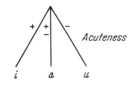

Fig. 51. Minimal vocalic system (Fant's scheme)

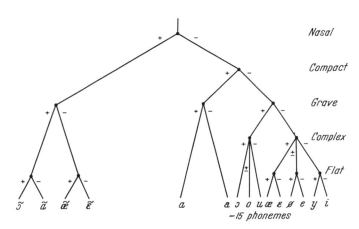

Fig. 52. Scheme of the French vocalic system (the so-called [ə] muet is left out)

If we apply the above graphic form on French consonants we get the scheme of Fig. 49.

It may be instructive to compare this scheme with the one proposed for the /p, t, k/ system. For some examples of more elaborate systems, see also Chap. III. As a specimen of complex vocalic paradigms we also give here schemes of the French vowel system (see Fig. 52 above) and, of the Swedish system (according to FANT; for another graphic presentation, see Chap. III, p. 50):

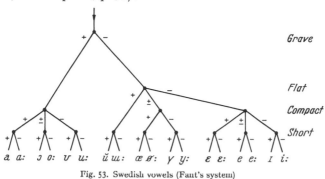

Fig. 53. Swedish vowels (Fant's system)

Although vowels are syllable nuclei and in a certain sense dominate the surrounding consonants[1], they may be subject to restrictions in their amount of information, conditioned by their being in a syllable

---

[1] Traditional phonetics taught that consonants are often articulated within a resonance room already formed for the following vowel, that e.g. the lips are rounded and protruded and the back of the tongue drawn backwards at the same time as, or even before, the tongue closes the air passage for [t] in [tu:], and that, in a corresponding way, the vocal tract remains in its vocalic position, as far as this is possible, when a postvocalic consonant is pronounced. We now have the necessary spectrographic evidence for these phenomena on the acoustic level. We know that vowel formants are to be seen in the consonant spectra, and we know that, in a certain sense, the syllable may be defined as an acoustically determined unit, dominated by the vowel and by its resonance, giving to the surrounding consonants the specific colour which indicates their participation in the acoustically determined syllabic unit. This particular vocalic colour of the consonants in a syllable is, of course, predictable from the vowel quality, and consequently non-distinctive. Such consonant colour may, however, in cases of reduced vowel length and/or intensity, be the essential, or sometimes the only manifestation of a vocalic, phonemic opposition. Thus, a palatalised [t'] with an i-colour in its explosion (and aspiration) phase, and distinct from an ordinary [t], may under certain structural conditions be regarded phonemically as a sequence /t/ + /i/. Consequently what is simultaneous on the substance level often has to be interpreted structurally as a linear sequence of two consecutive units in a determined order (cp. p. 84—86). If this interpretation is accepted, the difference between [t] and [t'] in the given system may be said to be distinctive but not phonemic (cp. p. 81), since the phonemic opposition is one between /i/ (or other vowel phonemes) and zero.

which may, in some way or other, be dependent on a preceding or following syllable. The following cases of syncretism or of reduction of the
distinctive possibilities of vowel phonemes are well-known examples.

In many languages there is so-called vowel harmony, complete
or more often partial. This means that the vowel colour of one syllabic
nucleus is determined by that of another. In Turkish, the plural ending
is *-lar* or *-ler* according to the vowel of the word stem (*at* 'horse', plural
atlar, but *gül* 'rose', plural *güller*). In Finnish, the vowel of a postponed
morpheme is for instance *a* or *ä* (an open [ɛ]-sound) depending on the
colour (grave or acute) of the stressed vowel (always the first syllable)

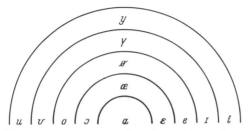

of the stem, e. g. the inessive
case *-ssa* or *-ssä* (*talossa* 'in
the house' but *metsässä* 'in
the wood'). This means that
the distinction /a/ ∼ /ɛ/,
which exists in other positions, is neutralized in a
case like the one just mentioned, and that the distinctive value of the opposition
/a/ ∼ /ɛ/ in Finnish is limited to certain positions. It

Fig. 54. An early attempt to schematize vocoids according to
distinctiveness and hierarchic relations was made by WINTELER
(reproduced in SIEVER's "Grundzüge", 2nd ed.; his phonetic
symbols have been changed in the above reproduction)

goes without saying that a language which permits both $A + \ddot{A}$ and
$\ddot{A} + A$ (besides $A + A$ and $\ddot{A} + \ddot{A}$) in two consecutive syllables is
richer in communicative possibilities than one which must have either
$A + A$ or $\ddot{A} + \ddot{A}$.

French has traces of vowel harmony in the sense that the distinction
half-closed ∼ half-open — the functional role of which is, however,
extremely restricted — may be neutralized completely in unstressed
syllables where the degree of opening (compactness) is determined by
the vowel of the stressed syllable (e. g. *été, laisser* with [e] in the first
syllable but *était, laissait* with [ɛ] or the intermediate variant [ę];
heureux, jeudi with [ø], but *jeunesse* with [œ], etc.). Old Swedish had
systems of vowel harmony and of so-called vowel balance, which
still survive in certain dialects and imply an alternation determined
automatically by the quantity of the stressed syllable of the word.

Rules of vowel harmony may be still more complicated. ROMAN
JAKOBSON reports that in a Palaeo-Siberian language (Gold) a word
must contain either compact (*o, a, e*) or diffuse vowels (*u, ǝ, i*). In Ibo
(West-Africa), it is impossible to have two successive vowels distinguished
by only one degree of opening (compactness).

In English as well as in German, Swedish etc., unstressed syllables
admit a reduced number of vowel distinctions as compared to stressed

syllables (for vowel qualities as an indication of stress, see p. 110).
Vowel length is for instance neutralized in unstressed syllables in the
three languages mentioned. We have mentioned above (p. 71) that
English does not use vowel length as distinctive in final stressed open
syllables and that consequently the distinction between, say, /i:/ and /i/
(/si:n/ ∼ /sin/) is neutralized in e.g. /si:/ (here the only possibility).
In Swedish, labiality (flatness) is not distinctive in unstressed syllables.
The same is true of German. The Italian distinction between /e/ and
/ε/ is valid only in stressed syllables. Spanish manifests a tendency to
reduce its vocalic distinctions in unstressed syllables to the three basic
units /i/, /u/, and /a/. The South American language Guaraní (in Paraguay
etc.) has a distinctive nasality of vowels in initial syllables but extends
the nasality automatically to the rest of the word, where consequently
it is a redundant, non-distinctive feature, predictable from the first
nasal vowel of the word.

The distinctive features described and discussed so far have all been
examples of phenomena used to characterize units which are often called
segmental phonemes, i.e. the smallest functionally independent
segments in the chain (roughly speaking vowels and consonants). Thus
voice may be supposed to characterize /b/ as opposed to /p/ in French etc.
But there are other contrastive elements in language which serve to
oppose longer units (phoneme combinations such as syllables, groups,
and periods) to otherwise similar units of the same complexity. Those
are what certain linguists call suprasegmental phonemes and
others prefer to call prosodemes (or prosodies). We have talked
above (Chap. III) about variations of fundamental frequency (pitch,
melody, intonation). This variable is never used to oppose a segmental
phoneme to another. A vowel remains the same — under certain restrictions which depend on the definition of vowel colour — if it is
pronounced on a higher or lower fundamental frequency, if the fundamental is a monotone or if it is varied (the latter is of course the case in
normal speech), etc. But certain languages use variations of pitch in
order to oppose groups of phonemes to each other, thereby changing
the corresponding content. Chinese is the best known of the so-called
tone languages. As all words in Chinese are monosyllabic, we can
without any practical inconvenience talk about words, when syllables
would have been from our point of view the proper term[1].

In Peking Chinese four different tones (or word-tones) may be
combined with an otherwise identical phoneme sequence. They are
numbered from 1 to 4 and described in handbooks as being respectively
1 level —, 2 rising /, 3 "broken" √, and 4 falling \. It goes without

[1] The problem of the word as a possible phonetic unit will be treated p. 137.

saying that tones as well as segmental phonemes occur in the speech
chain in a considerable number of contextual variants, the melodic
characters of which may often be rather different from the type described as being the primary one. A few other examples will be given.
In the Vietnam language there is said to be six phonemic tones: 1 high
plain (neutral), 2 high melodic (as slight rising), 3 high glottal (the vowel
of the syllable is "split" by a glottal stop and the second of the two
halves has a higher pitch than the first), 4 low plain, 5 low melodic
(rising from No. 4), 6 low glottal (the same musical level as 5 interrupted
by a glottal stop). In a case like this, the physical manifestations of the
word tones are not all purely musical (i.e. variations of the fundamental
frequency) but may be manifested partly by means of other acoustic
qualities (in this example an interruption of the regular wave form of the
musical tone). In many languages which are classed as tone languages it
is a matter of fact that the oppositions in question are not strictly
speaking tonal, and that other criteria than tone levels or tone inflec-
tions contribute to their manifestation. An example of an original tone
distinction which has been supplanted by a voice quality distinction
(an interrupted versus a non-interrupted tone movement) is given by
the so-called Danish stød.

Other typical examples of tone systems are found in African languages. In Yoruba, any syllable may be pronounced on three different
tone levels: high, mid, and low. A word *bá* (high tone ⁻) means
'meet', *ba* (mid tone —) means 'hide', and *bà* (low tone _) means
'perch' (WARD). Consecutive syllables may consequently have independent tone levels. An example: *ó bá* (high∼high) 'he meets', *a bá* (mid∼
high) 'we meet', *ó ba* (high∼mid) 'he hides', *a ba* (mid∼mid) 'we hide',
etc. In the same way, the Ibo phoneme sequence *akwa* with two high
syllables (⁻ ⁻) means 'cry', with two low syllables (_ _) 'bridge',
with high + low (⁻ _) 'cloth', and with low + high (_ ⁻) 'egg'
(WARD). This is not the place to give a definite structural analysis of
such tone systems, an analysis which in very many cases is difficult
because of the incomplete or inaccurate descriptions given in traditional
handbooks. At least in many cases, the examples given of gliding and
other complicated movements are to be interpreted as contextual
manifestations of a small number of basic phonemic tones. IDA WARD
tells us that in Yoruba a falling tone may cover two vowel sounds,
the first high, the second mid or low, and that a rising tone may cover
a low followed by a higher tone (*bɛɛ ní* 'yes' being either ⁻ _ ⁻ or
\ —). It is quite evident that the latter (falling) type is one of several
possible manifestations of the phonemic distinction high∼low, in this
particular case a contraction of a short (implicit) form of the full (ex-
plicit) type ⁻ _. A close structural analysis of a tone system may be

supposed, in most cases, to result in a considerable reduction of the number of phonemes and in a simplification of the physical definition of the distinctions which realize them. Cp. hereto also p. 163.

The analyses given so far as examples of phonemic and prosodic paradigms and hierarchies have been based on the sound substance and on the grouping together of distinctions into parallel pairs or series made on the basis of physical resemblances and differences. This may in numerous cases be the only practicable way of undertaking a classi-fication of phonemes and other expression units (cp. below). It should, however, be borne in mind that such a classification, at least very often, runs the risk of being more or less arbitrary. The numerous cases of conflicting interpretation of the same material given by different phone-micists are proof enough. It is therefore important to underline that quite often — though by no means always — it is perfectly possible to give structural evidence for a classification, not only of allophones into phonemes (cp. above), but also of phonemes into pairs, series and paradigms. There is no doubt that a classification established that way has a higher degree of objectivity than one which supposes sub-stance criteria.

We have already mentioned German as an example of a language which neutralizes the distinction of voice in consonants in word-final position. If a verbal form like *ich habe* /'ha:be/ has a syncopated form *ich hab* /ha:p/ with an automatic change of /b/ into /p/, or if we find in the morphological paradigms alternation between /p/ and /b/ (e.g. in *grob* /gro:p/, *gröber* /'grø:bər/, *Tag* /ta:k/, *Tage* /'ta:gə/) this is structural evidence for setting up pairs like /p/—/b/, /t/—/d/ (not, for instance, /p/—/d/ or /t/—/b/). This case is simple, because the substance analysis also gives a fairly unambiguous interpretation. But there may be cases where this kind of evidence is much less transparent than in English or in German. TRUBETZKOY gives (in his "Grundzüge") an example from Mende (a West-African language, Sierra Leone), where there is a grammatical alternation not only between /p/ and /w/ (a voiceless ~ voiced opposition, where the plosive feature of the /p/ and the rounded and fricative features of the /w/ are redundant) but also between /t/ and /l/ under the same conditions. Consequently, the relation between /t/ and /l/ is exactly the same as that between /p/ and /w/. Thus /l/ has to be classified as the voiced counterpart of /t/, in that voice (or perhaps intensity) is the distinctive feature, while the lateral feature is redundant. Though the phonetic differences may be the same, a lateral dental consequently has to be treated very differently in a system which has a /d/ as the voiced counterpart of /t/ and a distinction between laterals (liquids) and stops (as is the case in English and in the other European languages: Eng. /dei/ ~/lei/ ~/ðei/), and in a language where an otherwise isolated /l/ can take the place as the otherwise non-existant voiced counterpart of /t/.

Thanks to analytic procedures of the kinds exemplified above, the linguistic expression can be segmented into discrete elements. For the linguist undertaking a preliminary expression analysis of an unknown language in order to establish the form of the pattern, and for the native listener, the task is the same in one sense: both have to quantize the continuum of the sound wave and, consequently, to carry out an appropriate segmentation. The difference between one and the other is that for the linguist the task is, through trial and error, to arrive at the form of the pattern, i.e. the number and interrelations of functional units by which to interpret the expression, whereas the native listener has to apply the right code, already known, to the continuum and identify the stimuli as allophones of the units which build up this code. In both cases, we have to do with a reinterpretation of something continuous as something discrete. In fact, language identification and speech production, and in a word human linguistic interpretation, imply an unceasing passage from one to the other of these two levels. The linguistic message is discrete, the medium is continuous. LEIGH LISKER calls it the "physically continuous versus the perceptionally discrete nature of speech".

Any linguistic unit has to be classed as discrete. There is no passage possible from one phoneme to the other. It is a case of either /i/ or /u/, /p/ or /b/, /s/ or /ʃ/. A word accent is either grave or acute (if there are two), either high, mid, or low (if there are three units), etc. This implies that any phonemic change must by definition be a substitution, not a gradual passage. The glide belongs to the substance, not to the form level of language. This is a basic principle in the language mechanism, and it is valid, in the author's opinion, to the same extent for prosodic as for so-called segmental units. The differences of interpretation proposed and undertaken by different writers are often due to a confusion of levels.

In a certain sense, however, there may be said to be a kind of continuity e.g. between two phonemic systems, one of which is richer than the other. Let us take as an example Italian vowels which form a triangle of seven phonemes

All these oppositions can easily be exemplified by means of minimal pairs. But all do not have the same degree of stability. The distinctiveness of the $/e/\sim/\varepsilon/$ and $/o/\sim/\mathfrak{o}/$ distinctions is not as indisputable as that between, say, $/i/\sim/e/$ or $/a/\sim/u/$. For many words there is hesitation in cultivated speech between the two degrees of opening, a hesitation which is due to the mixed character of standard Italian. Consequently we may easily imagine a gradual passage from the full system with seven phonemes to the reduced system with only five, with, as the last step before the complete generalization of the poorer system, a situation where just a few words are distinguished by means of the critical oppositions, or its distinctive value is utilized only in situations where the risk for confusion and misunderstanding is great. Parallel examples can be given from Swedish, where the $/e/\sim/\varepsilon/$-distinction in many regions is precarious, or from French, where in the nasal series, the labialized nasal phoneme $/\tilde{\oe}/$ tends to disappear. As far as only paradigmatic relations are concerned, a system remains unaltered independently of the modifications suffered by the statistical distribution of its members. But if we look upon distribution even in its widest sense as part of the structure, any change in the occurrence of a linguistic unit must be said to imply a modification of the structure of the language.

Other instances of pretended continuity have been quoted by DWIGHT L. BOLINGER, who mentions cases of sound symbolism, e.g. when the increasing closeness of a vowel is used as a symbol of increasing smallness, or the lengthening of a vowel (in *la-a-a-rge* etc.) becomes an expression of greatness. Even if, at least in some of the examples quoted by BOLINGER, this interpretation should be correct, it does not affect the general validity of the statement made about the discreteness of linguistic units. It is doubtful if sound symbolism may be said to belong to the sphere of linguistically structured messages, even if "linguistic message", in accordance with the points of view in Chap. IX, is taken here in its widest sense. I quote from BOLINGER: "A phoneme is by definition a meaningless sub-unit. Since it is meaningless, variations in its structure can be dismissed as accidental or as imposed by some higher layer and hence irrelevant to the phoneme itself. The moment we step across the threshold of symbolism, however — of phenomena in language that are coded to correspond to phenomena in larger areas of behaviour — we are in a different world. It should never have been assumed that the techniques that worked below the threshold will work just as well above it. With the phoneme, the all-or-one is everything. Above the phoneme, the all-or-none is adjustable." A way of defining language would be to say that it starts and ends with discreteness. Such a definition would account for instances of sound symbolism of the type referred to by BOLINGER, without affecting in any way the principle of the discrete character of human language. To some people this might seem a circular definition. To this it may be objected that there are other criteria which permit us to draw the border-line between language and other types of social behaviour and that these criteria give more or less the same delimitation of what we conventionally call language.

One of the most important discoveries of structural linguistics is the universality of the hierarchic structure of the linguistic expression. The discovery was made by ROMAN JAKOBSON, or at least first formulated by him in strictly scientific terms. It was due on the one hand to the comparative confrontation of different phonemic structures with each other — described in strictly structural terms —, on the other to the systematic study of defective (children's and aphasic) speech which was for the first time made possible thanks to a strict application of the phonemic principle. The panchronic laws for phonemic structure formulated by ROMAN JAKOBSON — summarized in the thesis of the primarity of extreme distinctions over more subtle ones (implying e.g. that no language has fricatives which does not have stops, and that labialized vowels suppose back vowels but not inversely) — express the fundamental principle underlying the form of human language as a means of communication. This principle seems to be the same in other communication systems invented or utilized by man.

Chapter V

Redundancy and Relevancy. Levels of Abstraction

The analytic procedure described in the preceding chapter was based on the supposition that one single feature may constitute the difference between pairs in opposition and pairs in contrast, following the type example that /p/ is identical (structurally) with /b/ except for one feature, the distinctive voice and that, consequently, /b/ can be regarded as /p/+ voice, etc. In a corresponding way, French or German /y/=/i/+ labiality, French /ɛ̃/=/ɛ/+nasality, etc. In other words, we suppose that in the sound wave (phase 7 of our scheme, Fig. 3) certain physical features are necessarily the carriers of information about certain discrete minimal units (phonemes, etc.). Within the Prague school, the establishment of relevant versus irrelevant sound features was one of the essential tasks of the phonemic analysis, as was pointed out in Chap. IV. The theoretical foundation of the concept of relevancy was laid by KARL BÜHLER ("Prinzip der abstrakten Relevanz"). Numerous are the discussions in phonological literature about interpretations of this kind, numerous the answers given by different phonemicists. In certain cases, such questions may be resolved with reference to structural facts (e.g. distribution). In other cases the answer may seem arbitrary, due to superficial analogies, to the speakers' subjective feeling, to orthography, etc.

A very important distinction has been established by W. S.-Y. WANG and CH. J. FILLMORE between extrinsic and intrinsic cues to phoneme identification. A redundant phenomenon is extrinsic if it reflects the speech habits of a particular community, intrinsic if it is due to the speech mechanism in general. Only extrinsic cues may play a part in communication (cp. particularly Chap. IX). This is why they alone may become important for the evolution of sound systems. Many mistakes have been made in evolutive phonetics because of ignorance of this basic distinction. The same distinction was already made by OTTO JESPERSEN in his analysis of linguistic quantity (duration) and was taken over in a somewhat modified form by the author of this book (distinction between "subjective" and "objective" quantity). According to the scholars quoted, vowel duration, an important cue to the opposition -dd- ~ -tt- in Amer. English (ladder ~ latter), has already taken over the responsibility for this distinction in question in some American dialects.

When I tried, many years ago, to analyse the French consonant system from a phonological point of view in an attempt to answer the question what was relevant in oppositions like /p/ ~ /b/, or /s/ ~ /z/, I arrived at the conclusion that intensity was relevant and voice a concomitant factor. My argument was that, in cases of assimilation, the fortis-type (/p/, /t/, /k/, /s/, /ʃ/, /f/) remains "strong" though it may become voiced by assimilation to a following consonant (coupe de champagne [kup̬ də —], sache bien [saʃb̬jɛ̃], etc.) and the lenis-type become voiceless without loosing its lenis-character (absolu [abs̥ɔly], rez-de-chaussee [red̥ʃose]). Consequently intensity was the only stable factor and should be looked upon as distinctive or relevant. There seems to be no doubt that, even if assimilation takes place, the distinctions remain valid, at least as a potentiality. /b/ is opposed to /p/ exclusively through intensity, not an account of voice. This argumentation, however, overlooks the fact that, even if intensity is the distinctive factor in these cases of assimilation — and must be, because there is no other —, this does not necessarily prove that the same stimulus is the cue to the identification of the units in question when the difference of voice is there. We have learnt from synthetic experiments that different cues may be used for the same distinction in different contexts. In the French system, consonant intensity is a potential distinction which serves as cue to the phonemic opposition of "voice" when intensity is the only remaining variable, but only there.

In fact, up till quite recently, structural linguistics often had no possibility of answering questions of "relevancy" and "distinctiveness". Structural analysis can inform us about oppositions, distinctions, contrasts, and distributional limitations (neutralization). Instrumental analysis can discover the physical facts corresponding to the linguistic realities. The more accurate and detailed this analysis becomes, the more numerous the physical data obtained and the more complicated their mutuous relationships. Only the recently discovered synthetic methods, however, can give a definite answer to questions of this type. By varying one feature at a time, it is possible to do what the human speaker cannot, isolate one sound feature from another and examine its role in communication processes.

Two examples, both taken among the prosodic features, will be given here just to illustrate the connection between structural and instrumental analysis and the role of synthesis in solving the problem of relevancy and redundancy. Our first example will be the syllable problem, our second a so-called word accent. In both cases, the phenomena as well as the tentative solutions of the problems they imply are mentioned as examples of a method for handling linguistic facts and for solving linguistic problems. The question of "right" or "wrong" is not taken into account at all.

Since the very beginning of scientific phonetics it has been regarded as axiomatic that phonemes are grouped into larger units, called syllables. The concept of syllable is e.g. implied in the distinction between vowels and consonants (central and marginal units; cp. Chap. IV). In many languages, the syllable is undoubtedly a structural unit, sometimes a very important one for the economy of the language. The number of syllables may for instance be linguistically relevant. It would be impossible to imagine the basic role played by the number of syllables in Romance metrics if this had not — at least in the past — been the case in the systems of these languages. In Modern Spanish there is a distinction between syllabic and non-syllabic phonemes which may be regarded as an opposition in the number of syllables, e.g. /lei/ ~ /le'i/, sc. ley 'law', lei 'I read', /r̄ei/ ~ /r̄e'i/, sc. rey 'king', rei 'I laughed'. These distinctions can thus easily be interpreted as oppositions between a smaller and a greater number of syllables, i.e. between different syllabic segmentations of a phoneme sequence. If this interpretation is accepted, the non-syllabic character of the [i̯] in ley, rey will be predictable — from the monosyllabicity of the group — and thus be regarded as redundant, just as the syllabic character of the [i] in lei, rei is predictable from the dissyllabic character of the respective groups.

But not only the number of syllables but also the syllabic boundary, or the syllable division, may be a linguistically relevant phenomenon, which means that an otherwise identical phoneme sequence may be the expression of two different contents, according to the place of a syllabic boundary within the sequence. A type $A|PA$ is another sign than $AP|A$. DANIEL JONES has given numerous English examples of distinctions of this kind. We quote the following:

1. /mai|'trein/   'my train'
   /mait|'rein/   'might rain'
2. /'nai|treit/   'nitrate'
   /'nait|reit/   'night-rate'
3. /ðæt|'siŋk/   'that sink'
   /ðæts|'iŋk/   'that's ink'
4. /ə|'neim/   'a name'
   /ən|'eim/.   'an aim'.

Within each of these four pairs of syntagms, there is at least one factor which is different and which manifests the distinction on which, in turn, the difference of content is based. According to DANIEL JONES, to whom we owe these and other examples of the same kind, as well as important studies on them, the two members of the pairs quoted are not identical (not "homophones"). Alternatively, at least, there exists a possibility of distinction which may be utilised if a speaker wants to secure an undisturbed arrival of the message. The linguist, on his first level of analysis, consequently simply discovers the existence of a difference in content and of a corresponding difference of expression. The first task of the phonetician is to define — in acoustical or articulatory terms, or both — the differences which he hears or which, if he is a native speaker, he believes he makes when pronouncing one or the other of the quasi-homonyms. JONES gives, for the examples quoted above, among others the following data:

1. in /mai|'trein/ ai is fully long, t strong, r voiceless;
   in /mait|'rein/ ai is shorter, t weak and r fully voiced.
2. = 1.
3. in /ðæt|'siŋk/ s is strong; in /ðæts|'iŋk/ s is weak.
4. in /ə|'neim/ n is strong; in /ən|'eim/ n is weak.

If this collection of data is correct, we consequently have to do with a number of consonantal differences ("strong" versus "weak", "fully voiced" versus "/partly/ voiceless") and also of a vocalic difference ("longer" versus "shorter"). Let us suppose, too, that our collection of data has been fairly exhaustive — which in our example is evidently not the case. We are thus faced with a series of differences which have to be examined auditively and instrumentally. These differences may consequently be supposed to be present in any sound wave which has to transmit the linguistic signs, or sign combinations, mentioned. Now the second question arises. Are all the physical differences that are actually found in the sound wave and the differences of articulation reflected in the curves obtained, also distinctive in the sense that they are indispensable for a correct identification of the message? Or are only one, or two, or three, of them distinctive and, if so, which of them? And finally, is it possible to find a common denominator which summarizes all the differences actually found, a distinction of which the differences present in the sound wave are the manifestation? In other words, are the differences mentioned (of length, of voice, of "strongness", etc.), and all others, predictable from this common denominator and consequently to be classified as combinatory, or redundant? This is a typical problem in structural expression analysis. It implies the need of reducing the great number of physical facts to a small number of functional distinctions. This step must then be followed by a third one, the establishment of a limited number of phonemic oppositions, i. e. of the phoneme inventory of the languge.

In our example, it seems a priori probable that the physical differences reflect some more general difference of which they are the consequences. If we suppose the existence of a syllabic boundary as a distinctive factor, we can look upon the differences mentioned above as manifestations of this syllabic boundary, and say, generally speaking, that one of the main variations within consonants is one of force. A consonant is stronger at the beginning than at the end of a syllable. From this there follows other secondary differences: the shorter vowel in the closed syllable, the voiceless *r* after the strong *t* (whose assimilatory force is stronger than that of the weak one), etc. But this is a hypothesis, and it has to be checked. Traditional instrumental phonetics had no possibility of going further into such problems. Continued analysis and continued collecting of more material may make one solution more probable than another but will never give the definite answer. Here is the point where synthesis comes in.

The syllabic boundary has been explained by traditional phoneticians in different ways. On the articulatory level, attention had been drawn to the tension of different articulatory muscles (larynx muscles, respiratory muscles, etc.), to the periodicity of the expiration movements (STETSON's "puff of air from the chest", etc.) and to the opening and closing movements of the upper speech organs, of the jaw, etc. On the acoustic level, the decrease and the following increase of the intensity curve had been taken as the manifestation of syllable division. On the other hand, some phoneticians had simply denied the possibility of finding physical correlates to the syllabic unit which was explained as being exclusively a "phonological" unit, i.e. determined only by rules valid within a given system and consequently its definition a matter of distribution (cf. Chap. VI). This hypothesis, interesting and adequate though it may seem in certain cases (examples below), does not work when we have to deal with languages like English, German, or Swedish, where it seems to be a fact that the syllabic boundary alone is, or may be, distinctive, and that there is, consequently, a distinction between $/A|PA/$ and $/AP|A/$. Distribution alone does not cover this case.

The phonetician, on this level of research, is faced with a number of differences whose distinctiveness he has to test: the intensity of the consonant at the boundary, the vowel length in open and closed syllables, the force of assimilation of consonants in implosive and explosive position, etc. Let us pick out one factor, the degree of influence of the respective consonants (explosive and implosive) on the surrounding sounds, or the degree of fusion between sounds belonging to the same syllable as compared to those belonging to different syllables (examples above: $/-t|rei-/$ versus $/-|trei-/$ with a voiceless r in the latter case, a shorter $/ai/$ versus a longer one according to the place of the following consonant). And let us suppose, as a pure hypothesis, that this difference is reflected in a difference in the degree of influence on the spectrum of adjacent vowels, so that the formant transitions (cp. Chap. III) are more typical and more regular when the consonant belongs to the same syllable, less typical or lacking when the consonant belongs to another syllable and that, consequently, the syllable is in a way a kind of acoustic unit.

This was the assumption I started from when I made my syllabic experiments at the Haskins Laboratories in New York in 1955. I painted artificial spectrograms of the type vowel-consonant-vowel. The vowel had three formants, the consonant was intended to be a stop (rendered by just a silent phase and the formant transitions characteristic for the combination; Fig. 33). Two kinds of variations were made: the place of the transition (only on the first vowel and only on the second), and the duration of the occlusion phase (i.e. the silence). The question to be answered by the listeners was: you are going to hear a sequence of a vowel plus a consonant plus a vowel; do you think that the consonant belongs to the first or to the second syllable? (forced choice of one alternative). The result may be seen in Figs. 55, 56, and 57. It confirmed the hypothesis in the sense that the difference in transitions was heard as a difference of syllable division under the condition that the distance between the vowels (i.e. the duration of the occlusion) was not too short. If it was less than 50 msec the "consonant" was always judged to be explosive, the most common type and accordingly that which one is inclined to hear when there are no strong cues to a different interpretation.

This result is far from being a definite answer to our question. It has, however, given us information about one physical factor which, at least under favourable conditions, is capable of producing the impression of a linguistic syllabic boundary. It remains to be examined if other physical phenomena (e.g. the intensity of the consonant alone, certain assimilatory phenomena alone, vowel length alone, etc.) can produce an identical auditory effect. In this way, it will be possible one day to list which phenomena have this capacity, and which not. There

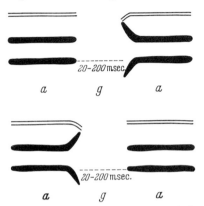

seems to be no doubt that, at least in this particular case, there are several cues to the distinction. On the other hand, it also seems evident that some of the differences actually present in normal speech are just combinatory phenomena which alone do not provoke the impression intended.

Fig. 55. Synthetic pattern for the two syllabic types *V/CV* and *VC/V* used to auditory tests concerning syllable boundaries (the "Pattern Playback" of the Haskins Laboratories). The distance between the two vocalic patterns was varied in 10 steps

Our second example is a little more complicated. Swedish has a phonemic word accent which may be described structurally in the following way (only essentials have been taken into account). Words of more than one syllable and stressed on any other syllable than the last one are characterized by an accentuation which is indispensible for a complete and exhaustive phonemic description of the sequence and which opposes units which are otherwise phonemically identical. This is true in principle even if the accent, in very many cases, is predictable from a knowledge of the morphemic structure of the syntagm, and even if its importance in the economy of the language is restricted to a rather limited number of minimal pairs. Examples such as *ánden* 'the duck' ∼ *ànden* 'the ghost', *búren* 'the cage' ∼ *bùren* 'carried' (past participle), *tánken* 'the tank' ∼ *tànken* 'the thought', *kómma* 'comma' ∼ *kòmma* 'come', *knúten* 'the node' ∼ *knùten* 'tied' (past participle) may be sufficient to prove its phonemic character, at last in dissyllabic words. If the last syllable is stressed, there is no accent distinction. If the word, in the sentence, ceases to carry the stress, the accent opposition is neutralized.

For a native speaker without any linguistic training the words mentioned are just "different". He normally hears the difference but is in most cases unable to give any meaningful description of what he hears or believes he does when he pronounces the words. That the phonetic description of this accent distinction has been no easier for native than for foreign linguists and phoneticians is easily illustrated by a survey of literature on the subject. Auditory phonetic analysis has not succeeded in going very much beyond the primitive impressionistic descriptions given by untrained native speakers. In some cases, an impossible theoretical starting-point has excluded any possibility of success, even where instrumental methods have been used.

The second step to take, after the structural analysis, is to proceed to measure all imaginable facts which *a priori* seem possible as basis for the distinction. The first, and for evident reasons most probable assumption is that the difference is one of intonation. Measured curves of the variations of the fundamental frequency in fact show, and have always shown, a strikingly good correlation

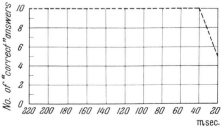

Fig. 56. Result of auditory tests concerning syllabic segmentation. On the *x*-axis the variations of duration of the silent phase ("occlusion"); on the *y*-axis the number of "correct" answers (correct here = in accordance with the hypothesis)

with the word accent, accent 1 showing one type, accent 2 another. My own measurements were carried out in various stages and with several years' interval (in 1938, in 1949, and in 1955). Particularly the second series gave a rich, homogeneous material from the south of Sweden and admitted a fairly detailed description of the differences of intonation which

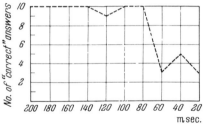

Fig. 57. For explanations, see Fig. 56. The number of "correct" answers is lower in this experiment but enough to be considered as a positive result

accompany, with a striking regularity, the two word accent types. It was limited to dissyllabic words. Nothing could, however, at this stage prevent a critic from asserting that the relevant factor in the accent distinction was nevertheless something else (intensity, duration?).

In 1955, when working at the Haskins Laboratories in New York, I took up the problem again, starting with a thorough instrumental analysis of a restricted and still more homogeneous material than the one examined in 1949. I examined all the factors which in the earlier discussion had been proposed as possible physical counterparts to the phonemic accent distinction (see Fig. 58). The form of the tone curve in the first (stressed) syllable — the analysis had for the sake of convenience been restricted also here to two-syllabic words — was the factor which showed the greatest regularity by far and the strictest correlation with the two groups of quasi-homonyms examined (see particularly Fig. 59, the overlapping of the intensity distribution and the absence of any overlapping for intonation). That duration could not be of any importance was immediately clear.

Words	Duration (msec)		Pitch		Intensity		Distance (in db) between max. of 1st and 2nd syllable
	1st vowel	2nd vowel	Max. pitch interval within 1st vowel (in cps)	Place of peak (in msec) from beginning of vowel	Max. range within stressed syllable (in db)	Place of max. (in msec) from beginning of vowel	
Accent 1							
vaken . . .	220[1]	100	65	30	25	60	12
biten . . .	200[1]	140	70	0	22	20	10
tuten . . .	200[1]	150	75	20	30	20	8
lipen . . .	200[1]	120	50	50	20	20	15
komma . .	120[2]	150	40	20	23	20	20
tanken . .	130[2]	60	70	30	30	20	12
buren . . .	150[1]	120	48	30	25	20	10
värken . .	150[2]	80	55	30	35	70	8
maten . . .	200[1]	100	50	40	30	40	5
bruken . .	150[1]	70	50	20	25	100	10
mean: long / short	189 / 133	109	57.3	27	26.5	39	11
Accent 2							
vaken . . .	220[1]	170	60	120	26	100	12
biten . . .	200[1]	130	35	70	27	40	10
tuten . . .	200[1]	70	50	80	25	50	7
lipen . . .	200[1]	80	80	80	22	50	8
komma . .	170[2]	180	60	90	20	40	6
tanken . .	180[2]	80	45	100	30	120	+10[3]
buren . . .	200[1]	130	65	90	20	50	10
verken . .	150[2]	60	60	100	22	60	5
maten . . .	220[1]	80	45	100	13	70	3
bruken . .	220[1]	80	35	80	20	110	10
mean: long / short	209 / 167	106	53.5	91	22.5	69	7.9 (of 9 cases)

[1] Phonemically long vowel.
[2] Phonemically short vowel.
[3] The second syllable had 10 db higher intensity than the first one.

Fig. 58. Presentation of possible physical counterparts to the opposition of accent in Swedish. The examples are quasi-homonyms

And still the answer obtained was not a definite one. It had been made probable that intonation must be a strong cue to the word accent. But how important is intensity variation? Are both necessary, or is one of them enough when the other is lacking? The analytic result had to be checked by means of a synthetic experiment.

The recorded sentences were passed through a Vocoder and the original varying pitch replaced by a monotone pitch of about 100 cycles per second. To my ear, any accent difference between the words under examination had disappeared. When I listened to the words in isolation, I was no longer able to hear which accent they had. This result would

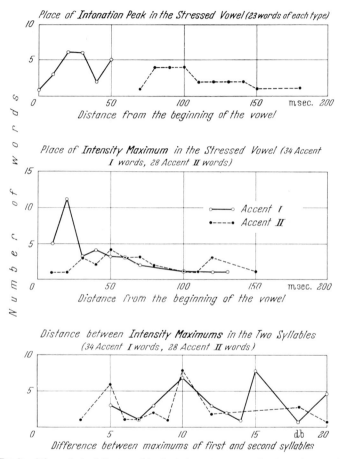

Fig. 59. Results of the analysis of three possible physical counterparts to the phonemic accent distinction in Swedish dissyllabic words. Only the intonation peak (*above*) shows any relevant correlation to accents

seem to be sufficient proof that pitch variations are indispensable for the accent difference. It remained, however, to be determined whether or not pitch phenomena alone were sufficient to give a satisfactory impression of accent 1 and accent 2.

For that purpose the recorded words were combined with different artificial pitch patterns (chosen essentially according to my earlier results). The pitch patterns were first varied as to the place of the pitch maximum (the peak) within the stressed syllable. If the peak was just at the beginning of the vowel, the impression of accent 1 was always absolutely clear. If the peak was placed at 100 msec from the beginning, the impression of accent 2 was just as definite. Even a peak at any later place within the stressed vowel gave a good impression of accent 2. If the peak was placed midway between the two ideal points (0 and 100 msec), the impression was confusing; I hesitated between accent 1 and accent 2. In some words, I felt inclined to interpret the intonation as accent 2 (e.g., in *buren*), in others as accent 1 (e.g., in *tanken*). In no case was the impression really acceptable as either of the two accents.

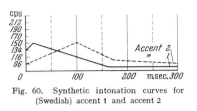

Fig. 60. Synthetic intonation curves for (Swedish) accent 1 and accent 2

As long as the peak remained within the first 50 msec from the beginning of the vowel, the impression of accent 1 was satisfactory, but as soon as the place of the peak was at 75 msec or later in the vowel, I had the impression of accent 2. These results can be seen in Fig. 60.

The pitch patterns were then varied as to the pitch range, i.e., the interval between the lowest point of the tone curve and the highest point reached (the peak), and also as to other details in the form of the intonation curve. These variations did not seem to have much influence on the accent type heard unless the deviations from the type patterns were considerable. An interval of only 30 cycles gave as definite an impression of the accent in question as one of 100 cycles (an octave), with the reservation that the very high peaks sounded less natural than the less extreme ones. Nor did it seem that the slope of the falling part of the curve was of any great importance for the accent type. The two curves indicated below as 2 and 3 gave equally good impressions of accent 1, whereas the curves 1 and 4 were hardly acceptable (Fig. 61).

In order to go one step further in trying to isolate the distinctive factor in question, I recorded a series of nonsense words (*bibbi, babba, bubbu; diddi, dadda, duddu; giggi, gagga, guggu; mimmi, mamma, mummu; ninni, nanna, nunnu; lilli, lalla, lullu*) pronounced with the accentuation which seemed most natural to me (i.e., accent 2). Spectrograms were made of the recordings and they were examined in the same way as the sentences. The length of the stressed syllables in these words, which had all been pronounced as short, showed an average value of about 160 msec with variations between 140 and 200. The peak was in all cases approximately 100 msec from the beginning of the vowel with the average at 100 (about one half of the cases) and with a variation between 80 and 120. The pitch pattern of these nonsense accent 2 words did not show any deviation from that which had been found for the "real" words.

When the natural, spoken pitch of these nonsense words was replaced by artificial pitch patterns, it was evident that if the peak was placed at 0 or 10 msec from the beginning of the vowel, the impression was clearly that of accent 1; if placed at 100, accent 2 was just as unmistakable. The intermediate position gave the same confusing impression as for the "real" words, though with a somewhat greater breadth of the indefinite domain. Thus peaks at 25 and 75 did not give quite satisfactory impressions of accents 1 and 2, respectively.

The first four groups of the nonsense words listed above were reconstructed artificially by means of painted spectrograms. The sound was recorded and passed through the Vocoder, where different pitch patterns were combined with the synthetic sound. Although there was no case in which the groups

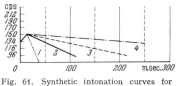

Fig. 61. Synthetic intonation curves for (Swedish) accent 1. Nos. 2 and 3 were the best, 1 and 4 hardly acceptable

in question sounded "natural" to my ear, I could easily recognize a combination of the pitch type ∧ with such synthetic groups as *babba*, *dadda*, *diddi*, etc. as accent 1, and the corresponding combinations with the pitch type ⌒ as accent 2.

As regards the place of the peak within the stressed syllable, I noticed that extreme types were necessary, i.e., the peak at 0 and 100 msec from the beginning respectively, in order to provoke a really satisfactory impression of the accent type.

Since it may seem, subjectively, that a certain difference in length is combined with the word accent distinction (and some phoneticians have maintained that this difference is rather important), I thought it could be of interest to find out whether or not differences in duration were capable, alone, of yielding any impression of an accent difference. I painted 5 different spectrograms of the group /papa/, where the relative length of the vowels were respectively: 300—100, 100—300, 200 — 200, 250—150, and 150—250 msec, and listened to the sound from the playback (with a monotone pitch of 120 cps). None of these were capable of giving any impression of a word accent distinction. The type 200 — 200 was heard as a spondee word (a type which is not unknown in Swedish), the types 300—100 and 250—150 as if they were stressed on the first syllable (but without any word accent qualities), and the type 100—300 as if it was stressed on the second syllable. As for the type 150—250, I hesitated whether to class it as stressed on the second syllable, or as a spondee word.

In order to examine the linguistic role of the intensity differences between accents 1 and 2 (cp. below, Fig. 62), I listened to the words as originally recorded (in context and in isolation), except that intensity variations had been removed by the Vocoder and associated equipment. The absence of intensity variation did not seem to have any influence on the word accent perceived; the identification of the accent, even with isolated words, was just as easy without intensity variations.

I then tried to impose different intensity patterns upon the words in question. Accent 2 words were combined with a falling intensity curve within the stressed syllable, with a peak at the beginning of the vowel (a fall of about 15—18 db). Accent 1 words were combined with a rising intensity accent with the maximum at about 100 msec from the beginning of the vowel (rise of about 15—18 db). In no case did this artificial intensity pattern serve to change an accent 1 word into an accent 2 word, or vice versa.

In the same way, I applied to the different words a difference in intensity between the two consecutive syllables. The reason for this was that the intensity of the unstressed syllable has sometimes been supposed to be an essential feature of the word accent. Linguistically untrained people often speak of a different stress on the second syllable of the word when they are asked to characterize the difference they make between two words differing in accent. The second syllable of accent 2 words is said to be more stressed than the corresponding syllable of accent 1 words. I listened to accent 1 words with an even (artificially imposed) intensity on both syllables, that of the unstressed one being about 5 db lower, and to accent 2 words with a corresponding difference of about 15 db. In no case did these variations have any effect on the word accent perceived, which remained the original one. When the different intensity patterns were listened to in combination with a monotone pitch, they did not give any word accent impression at all. Consequently, it is evident that intensity variations alone are not capable of yielding a word accent distinction. In all cases mentioned above, the words were listened to in isolation.

Spectrograms of whispered words (4 words of each kind) were analysed for intensity variations; they gave approximately the same intensity patterns as the words spoken with voice. The average value for the place of the maximum was 45 msec for accent 1 (values from 10 to 80), and 88 msec for accent 2 (values from 10 to 160). When I listened to the whispered words in isolation, I was quite unable to hear which word accent they had, although, when pronouncing them, I believed that I heard a clear difference. This result gives a further confirmation to my conclusion that the intensity difference, even if there is one in most cases, is not sufficient to function alone as the basis for word accent distinctions.

It seems that the existence of an intonation peak somewhere in the vowel of the stressed syllable is an absolute condition for the accent distinction under examination. A monotone pitch does not give any accent impression at all. I am inclined to regard the place of the peak

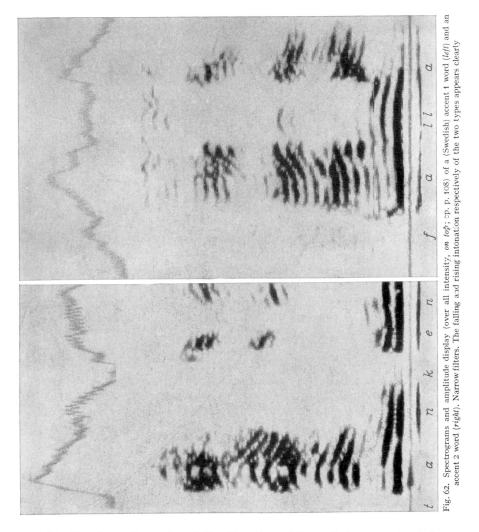

Fig. 62. Spectrograms and amplitude display (over all intensity, *on top*; *cp.* p. 108) of a (Swedish) accent 1 word (*left*) and an accent 2 word (*right*). Narrow filters. The falling and rising intonation respectively of the two types appears clearly

within the stressed vowel and the direction of the melody curve (mainly falling or rising) which follows from this difference, as the distinctive feature for word accent opposition. It can be concluded from the experiments made with nonsense syllables, artificial pitch, and synthetic sound groups that the pitch difference alone is sufficient to provoke a satisfactory impression of the two accents; the pitch difference should consequently be considered as distinctive, or phonemic.

From the studies involving intensity, it was evident that the intensity pattern could not alone provoke the impression of a word accent distinction. The intensity differences which undoubtedly exist in many of the cases examined are far less regular than the differences in intonation (no overlapping; Fig. 59). The relation, in average intensity, between the stressed and the following unstressed syllable of the word has evidently no importance for the accent distinction. Hence, intensity cannot be regarded as distinctive for word accent in Swedish. Rather, intensity differences are merely phenomena which normally (but not regularly) accompany the intonation pattern. They are redundant in the proper sense of this term.

Analogous experiments have been carried out on stress in English by D. B. FRY. His results (also produced at the Haskins Laboratories) were somewhat different from mine. He found for instance that intensity and duration were both sufficient cues for stress. Other experiments have given partly analogous, partly different results. Pitch also seems to be a possible cue for stress in English. It seems *a priori* possible that vowel colour may be one too. In such cases, the physical analysis cannot give any definite answer to the question of relevancy. The poorer a system is in distinctive possibilities, the greater the probability that one and the same opposition may be manifested through several physical differences. The richer the system the stronger the necessity to economize the resources, and the smaller the redundancy.

We have seen above (p. 92) that in certain tone languages some phonemic tones have other characteristics than differences of frequency and of frequency variations alone. The term "tone" may be looked upon as adequate if the elements in question occupy a given place within a system of oppositions which are essentially tonal. Under abnormal conditions tone distinctions may be replaced by other qualitative differences, such as vowel colour (formant structure, etc.). This seems to a certain extent to be the case in whispered Chinese where the tone oppositions are said to be conserved.

As far as prosodies are concerned it seems that even linguists with a definitely structural orientation have often overlooked the possibility — and necessity — of reducing a complicated physical cue to a simpler and more general phenomenon (a curve to a tone level, etc.). This is due to the refusal of some linguists to accept the articulated character of prosodies. In the author's opinion, a phenomenon such as intonation is structured in the same sense as the sequence of segmental phonemes and should consequently be looked upon as composed of smaller units. When, as in the result of the investigation quoted above (on Swedish word accent), we find a distinction between two curve forms — a falling and a rising — it seems to me that this can hardly be the final step of the analysis. The melody difference measured and tested is a distinction (in our sense of the word). There is no longer any doubt about that. But the two curves obtained are probably only manifestations of an opposition which ought to be described in physically less complicated terms, for which in Swedish I venture to propose — without having made the final auditory and synthetic tests and only as a working hypothesis —, the terms "low" and "high". If — as seems likely — this description covers a geographically larger region of the Swedish-speaking area than the more complicated curve-forms, we have arrived at a stage of higher abstraction and at a result of more general validity[1]. From a structural — and, generally speaking, a scientific point of view — the latter is "better" than the former.

Consequently, the relevancy on this more general level may be said to be the (relative) position of a point on the tone scale and the complicated curve-form a redundant phenomenon.

A still higher level of abstraction is arrived at when linguistic criteria alone are taken into account for the analysis, as is the case in glossematics and probably in SAUSSURE's theory: cp. e.g. his non-substantial conception of the phoneme in "Mémoire" (cp. Chap. I). Accent 1 may be described simply as the neutral, non-characterized accent, the only one in monosyllables and oxytones. Accent 2 is the positively characterized (marked) member of the opposition. It has +, when the other has —. The Swedish word accent may be described simply as an opposition between "tone" and "absence of tone", or, more generally speaking, between, say, "marked" and "unmarked" syllable sequences, whereby the positive (physical) qualities of the "mark" are left out of consideration. Our description has become one step more abstract and general. In this particular case, it becomes valid not only for the "tone languages" Swedish and Norwegian, but also for Danish, whose stød is at least roughly identical with the Swedish tone accent functionally but very different from it on the point of view of its physical manifestation[2].

These questions will be discussed again in connection with the problems of perception and interpretation (Chap. X).

---

[1] The melody differences which manifest the accent distinction are very different — even sometimes more of less opposite — in different parts of the country, which usually does not prevent, or even complicate, communication. This proves that identification of the linguistically relevant unit does not necessarily suppose identification of the physical details and that identity of form may be sufficient (cp. p. 116).

[2] I simplify deliberately. The Danish stød accent behaves differently in certain respects.

Scheme   *Levels of abstraction*[1]
                          (Example: Swedish word accent)

1st level   intonation   intensity   duration   syllable boundary[2]
of abstraction: ⌐ ⌐   ⌐ ⌐   — - ~ — —   - c | - ~ - | c -
                 Method: analytic, physical.
                 Discription not exhaustive.
                 Validity: the group of speakers examined.

2nd level   intonation   intensity duration syllable boundary
of abstraction: ⌐ ⌐   redundant
                 distinctive: curve-forms.
                 Method: analytic-synthetic, and auditory (psychological).
                 Description exhaustive as far distinctiveness is concerned.
                 Validity: the group of dialects represented in the material.

3rd level   intonation
of abstraction: ___ (low)   ‾‾‾ (high)
                 distinctive: level; redundant: curve-form + other variables.
                 Method: synthetic, and psychological.
                 Description exhaustive as above.
                 Validity: all Scandinavian dialects with phonemic tones.

4th level
of abstraction: —   +
                 opposition: presence — absence of mark.
                 Method: structural.
                 Discription exhaustive.
                 Validity: all Scandinavian dialects with phonemic word prosody.

The passage from description level no. 2 to 3 is a typical instance of quantification (cp. p. 28). The passage from no. 3 to 4 implies disregard of any substance, a purely formal description (in the sense of SAUSSURE or HJELMSLEV).

In the traditional terminology of the Prague school all the phenomena which accompanied a relevant difference were classed as irrelevant. This term has caused numerous and unhappy misunderstandings. The irrelevant phenomena have been spoken of as less important, less interesting, and even been regarded as lying outside the linguist's main concern. "Phonological" description was accused by traditional phoneticians of being inaccurate, just a rough, superficial survey of a few characteristics chosen more or less arbitrarily, and to which was opposed the "detailed", "exhaustive", and "accurate" phonetic description of

---

[1] This concept must not be confused with that of levels of analysis such as sentences, words, morphemes, phonemes (e. g. HERDAN: levels of linguistic form; HERDAN, however, clearly points out the necessity of establishing different levels of abstraction).

[2] Another redundant feature which might theoretically be supposed to be a cue.

the old school. It need not be emphasized here that this was a complete misunderstanding, a grotesque misinterpretation of some misleading and unhappy formulations in the publications of the early Prague phonologists or their successors. It proved, besides, a lack of acquaintance with the principles of scientific thought and scientific method as they have been worked out in modern philosophy, psychology, and natural sciences, and it consequently contributed to the sceptical attitude to linguistics which has long been so widespread among representatives of other fields. In structural linguistics, as in all scientific work, everything, any detail, however insignificant it may seem, is interesting and important. It is registered, described, identified, and classified according to its proper place within the hierarchy of the linguistic systems and subsystems. Modern linguistics therefore prefers redundant to irrelevant and opposes redundancy to relevancy, or to distinctiveness.

Redundant, in linguistic contexts, does not mean "superfluous". Redundancy by no means implies that something can be neglected. On the contrary, in modern communication theory, redundancy is a very important concept and the redundant phenomena extremely relevant (i.e. relevant for the communication process[1]). We have seen that redundancy is a matter of statistics, and consequently of predictability.

Let us suppose that, in e.g. *nitrate* ∽ *night-rate*, consonant intensity has been proved to be the essential distinctive feature, and that vowel length (in /-ai|-/ versus /-ait|-/) and consonant assimilation (in /-t|r-/ versus /-|tr-/) are classified as redundant. This implies that the latter phenomena are predictable from the intensity of the consonant and that they convey no other information than the one already present in the consonant distinction. Predictable are in that case also the potential differences in formant transitions, the importance of which had been proved by our experiment. But all these phenomena may nevertheless be extremely important for the interpretation of the message. The syllabic boundary — and the difference of consonant intensity which, in our discussion, we have supposed to be its essential physical counterpart — is a subtle distinction. The difference between an explosive and an implosive consonant may be supposed to be not very much

---

[1] The reason why the so-called relevancy of the Prague school was so often misunderstood was that it was not always explicitly pointed out in what respect the "irrelevant" phenomena were irrelevant. They are irrelevant to the establishment of the phonemic system of oppositions of a language (on the symbolic level; cp. Chap. IX), but only for that. But as this establishment was at the beginning the main concern of "phonological" analysis — just as it should be — it is easy to understand how the mistake came up. It is more difficult to realize that so many qualified linguists never became aware of their confusion.

above the discriminatory threshold of our ear. Its physiological counterpart may be supposed to be weak too and to get completely lost in
current speech in the numerous cases where misunderstanding is excluded. The presence of redundant cues to the distinction consequently
guards the message against misinterpretation. Vowel length, consonant
intensity (in the *t*) and assimilation (voiceless *r*) work together to secure
the interpretation of the word as *nitrate* and not as *night-rate*. Which
of them, in a given situation, is the best cue for a listener, is of course
impossible to say. Different speakers may react differently to different
cues. Synthesis can answer the question of the potential distinctiveness
of the various cues. The result, in effective speech, may be due to all,
or only to some of them. The more subtle a distinction is, the more
important is the presence of redundant information, of secondary cues.

There is of course in a message other redundant information than
phonetic (the amount of which is predictable from the phonemic and
distributional laws of the system), namely other linguistic information
(implied in the grammatical structure and in "meaning"), and extra-
linguistic information (implied in the non-linguistic context, or situation,
which excludes numerous linguistically possible interpretations, etc.).
We have already talked about the "experience" of the receiver (Chap. II,
scheme and comments). We shall have to deal more with these questions
later (Chap. X).

We have seen above (Chap. III) that formant transitions as well as
explosion noise may be sufficient cues to consonant distinctions. A $/p/$
may be identified and opposed to $/t/$ or $/k/$ either through its relatively
low frequency noise, or through the direction (downwards) of the transitions of formants 1 and 2. Which of these features is to be looked
upon as relevant (distinctive) and which as redundant is under such
conditions simply a matter of statistics. That feature is distinctive
which in listener tests gains the highest percentage of identifications in
synthetic experiments of the kind mentioned above. We also have to
take into account the fact that one cue may be the essential one in one
context, another in another context, and that, consequently, the seeking
for just one distinctive feature may be illusory. There seems to be
no doubt that in French, voice is the normal cue to the distinction
$/p/ \sim /b/$ etc. in initial position and between vowels but that, in certain
assimilated groups $/pd/$, $/td/$, $/kb/$ etc. (where one phoneme, here the first,
is assimilated in respect of voice and becomes voiced without being
confused with its voiced phonemic counterpart), the fortis $\sim$ lenis-
distinction becomes the operative one. Another difference, the duration
of the closure phase, seems to play a major role in the voiced-voiceless
distinction in certain contexts in Amer. English, a shorter duration being
heard as "voiced", a longer as "voiceless" (LISKER). It should be added

that the factor which according to perception experiments seems to be the principal cue (according to our definition), may be replaced as the operative factor by another, if the listeners constitute an abnormal group, e.g. in auditory capacity (the hard of hearing, etc.). So formant transitions are the principal cue to consonant distinctions for persons whose capacity to hear, or to discriminate, high tones is reduced or lacking. My synthetic experiments with Swedish word accents seem to have proved that neither intensity nor length variations alone, though undoubtedly present as redundant features, in that particular case were able to function as cues to the prosodic distinction examined.

It seems convenient, starting from this definition of redundancy, to establish a distinction between statistically predictable phenomena, of the kind mentioned here, on the one hand, and other characteristics in the sound-wave which may, or may not, be present in it — phenomena which, seen from the point of view of the symbolic function of language, may seem to present a random distribution in contradistinction to the redundant phenomena. Let us mention as examples such features as voice quality, the presence of intensity of higher vocalic formants, certain "unpatterned" intonation contours, nasality. Such phenomena, though present in the sound-wave, do not contribute to the identification of the linguistic units. They are neither distinctive (in the sense in which this concept has been taken so far), nor redundant. For those we propose the term irrelevant, but still it is extremely important to stress that irrelevancy here is viewed linguistically and does not imply irrelevancy in any other respect. We shall see in a later chapter that such phenomena may become relevant and distinctive and play an important communicative role on other levels of communication (Chap. IX). Cp. hereto also FILLMORE's and WANG's distinction (p. 97).

It will appear from other chapters but will be stressed here too, that distinctiveness and relevancy are not in principle a question of absolute values (of frequency, of intensity, of colour, of duration) but of relative values, and that identification supposes comparison. A tone language which uses pitch levels (high ∼low, etc.) as distinctive, is not forced to use any absolute levels. High and low are determined in relation to each other and to the average pitch level of the speech. A high tone in a man's voice may be lower, in cycles per second, than a low tone in a woman's. In the same way, stressed and unstressed syllables etc. are relative to each other and to the context as a whole. That a vowel is "long" does not mean that it is longer than any "short" vowel, only that it, in the given context, is longer than an otherwise identical "short" vowel would be in the same position.

The same is valid, though it has not always been observed, for purely qualitative distinctions. The Danish vowel system has a distinction of compactness — diffuseness of four degrees (i: — e: — $ε$: — a: /mi:$lə$/ ∼ /me:$lə$/ ∼ /$mε$:$lə$/ ∼ /ma:$lə$/). Phonetically, the third degree /$ε$/ is exceptionally closed ([$ẹ$]) and the fourth remarquably palatal [$æ$], or even [$ε$]. Foreigners identify Danish /a/ in *tale* etc. with [$ε$], not with [a]. It is, however, the most compact (open) of the Danish front vowel phonemes. All these vowels have allophones in combination with r which are definitely more compact (open) than the common allophone, with the result that /a/ becomes phonetically [a] or even [$ɑ$], that /$ε$/ becomes a very open [$æ$], and that /e/ sounds more like [$ε$] and [i] like [e]. Consequently, the "same sound" [$æ$] is in certain positions an allophone of /a/, in others of /$ε$/. The /$ε$/-phoneme in combination with r is often more open than the /a/-phoneme in other positions. A Dane does not hesitate to identify the vowel in /$rεt$/ (phonetically [$Ræt$]) with the one in /$hεst$/, and the vowel in /'ra:$sə$/ (phonetically ['Ra:$sə$]) with the one in /'ta:$lə$/ (phonetically ['$tε$:$lə$]). He is not confused by the overlapping between the phonemes /$ε$/ and /a/. In a given position the identification is sure. [$æ$] in [$Ræt$] is identified as an allophone of /$ε$/ because, in the given position (after r-), the system also offers a more open possibility. And [$ε$:] in *tale* is identified as an allophone of /a/ (with [a] in *rase*) because in the position in question it is the extreme possibility. Consequently the distinctiveness of a given vowel is not to be found in any particular formant structure or in any given tongue position, but in the relation to the other possibilities offered. The distinctive feature of Danish /a/ is that of being the most compact vowel admitted by the language in a given position. This is a phenomenon which plays an enormous part in the identification of a message — particularly in communication between people speaking partly different dialects.

A still more striking example of the relative character of relevancy and of distinctive features is given by LADEFOGED and BROADBENT who have found out that the identification of the vowel of a synthetic word (as /i/, /e/ or /$æ$/) was dependent on the vowel values of the introductory phrase used ('please say what this word is'. /bit/, etc.). These values consequently functioned as reference points for the identification. This is a fact which is evidently responsible for the way in which we interpret the phonemes of other people in spite of undeniable differences. As soon as we have got a few specimens of the other person's phoneme values, we have the reference to which we can correlate the auditive stimuli without being disturbed by their being different from the values we use ourselves. This is equally true for prosodic features and probably explains why in different dialects of tone languages people understand each other — and are not even struck by the discrepancies — although there may be considerable differences and overlapping in the musical manifestations of the respective units (so in Swedish for instance, where accent 1 in one dialect may be identical with accent 2 in another, musically speaking, and yet not present any serious obstacles to identification). That linguistic pitch levels as used in sentence prosody are relative, varying as to their place in the tone scale with the variations of the average laryngeal frequency — e.g. differences between men, women, and children — is a well-known fact.

The concept of relevancy has of course played an important part subconsciously in the traditional classifications drawn up by pre-structural phoneticians. It is closely connected with the concept of distinctive feature as this has been worked out, on the basis of TRUBETZKOY's phonological theory, by ROMAN JAKOBSON. The distinctive feature concept and the binary theory will be further discussed in Chap. VI.

Chapter VI

The Distinctive Feature Concept.
The Binary Choice

The concept of distinctive feature is just as basic in structural linguistics as are the phoneme and the sign. This concept is in fact a necessary consequence of the phonemic principle, and more particularly of phonemic classification and of phonemic codes, in so far as these are based on physical criteria[1]. It thus follows automatically from what was said above (in Chap. II) about the communication process and about encoding and decoding of a message. If the linguistic mechanism is a game with oppositions and identities, we have to face the problem: what is the minimal difference between the terms of an opposition? The answer must be that the slightest difference admitted between two phonemes is a distinctive feature. A phoneme thus becomes a bundle of distinctive features. Those are the ultimate distinctive units in language, the atoms of linguistic structure.

A consequence of this definition of the phoneme as a bundle of distinctive features is, as was pointed out already in Chap. IV, that any phoneme in a linguistic system can be described in terms of yes-or-no-answers to questions about distinctiveness (see the JAKOBSON-FANT-HALLE system, Fig. 63, p. 118). The English phoneme /p/ can be exhaustively described by means of the following distinctive features: consonantal — non-consonantal, interrupted — not interrupted, tense — not tense, grave — not grave, nasal — not nasal, or, more accurately, by an enumeration of which of these the phoneme has, or has not. Thus /p/ is

---

[1] In glossematics, where substance is not taken into account, the definition of the phoneme consequently becomes different and, as a consequence of this, the word phoneme itself replaced by the substantially neutral ceneme.

	#	h	d	ð	z	t	θ	s	n	b	v	p	f	m	g	ǵ	ž	k	č	š	ŋ	l	i	ə	u	e	a	o
1. Vocalic/Non-vocalic	−	−	−	−	−	−	−	−	−	−	−	−	−	−	−	−	−	−	−	−	−	+	+	+	+	+	+	+
2. Consonantal/Non-consonantal	−	−	+	+	+	+	+	+	+	+	+	+	+	+	+	+	+	+	+	+	+	+	−	−	−	−	−	−
3. Compact/Diffuse			−	−	−	−	−	−	−	−	−	−	−	−	+	+	+	+	+	+	+		−	−	−	+	+	+
4. Grave/Acute			−	−	−	−	−	−	−	+	+	+	+	+									−	+	+	−	+	+
5. Flat/Plain																							−	−	+		−	+
6. Nasal/Oral			−	−	−	−	−	−	+	−	−	−	−	+	−	−	−	−	−	−	+							
7. Tense/Lax			−	−	−	+	+	+		−	−	+	+		−	−	−	+	+	+								
8. Continuant/Interrupted	−	+	−	+	+	−	+	+		−	+	−	+		−	−	+	−	−	+								
9. Strident/Mellow			−	−	+	−	−	+							−	+	+	−	+	+								

Fig. 63. JAKOBSON-FANT-HALLE's analytic transcription of the phonemes of English (Received Pronunciation). "The phonemes may be broken down into the inherent distinctive features which are the ultimate signals" (Preliminaries)

exhaustively described by the following properties: consonantal +, interrupted +, tense +, grave +, nasal −. Any change in the pluses and minuses implies another phoneme, or a hole in the system (cp. the examples above).

The question of whether, or to what extent the speaking individual is conscious of the independency of phonemic units has already been touched on (Chap. IV). Some evidence was given for the assumption that this is so (p. 72). The same question may be asked of the distinctive features — are speakers aware of them as independent units? It seems, to the author at least, that the speaking individual has no conscious feeling for the complexity of the minimal expression units in the same way as he has for the bundles of distinctive features, i.e. the phonemes. A naive speaker will hardly be able to tell us if there is more kinship between /p/ and /b/ than between /p/ and /v/, and would probably not understand the point if it was explained to him that just one feature distinguishes the first two but two features the members of the second pair. It would probably be very difficult to teach people to use an alphabet based on distinctive features, in spite of the restricted number of letters that would be needed for such a script, whereas experience has taught us that the mastery of a phonemic script is easily acquired.

But, on the other hand, we have some evidence for the opposite opinion. The way in which a person behaves when confronted with the phonemes of a foreign language is instructive in this respect. This is a question we shall have to face in a later chapter (X) in analysing the perception process in more detail. It may, however, be considered briefly here. When we hear a sound sequence in an unknown language, we try to segment it on the basis of the model we have in our own language. We refer the acoustic stimuli to the different phonemes of our own language, basing our identification on sound ressemblance and on distribution. An Italian "hears" a French /y/ as an /i/, etc. But it sometimes happens that a foreigner hears an unknown phoneme as two phonemes. I once heard a Russian woman pronouncing the Finnish word *yksi* 'one' as /juksi/. A Swede or a German "hears" the French or Italian /ɲ/ (Fr. *baigner*, It. *bagno*) as /n+j/. The examples can be multiplied. Such an interpretation implies that the listener decomposes the unit heard into its distinctive features, i.e. the /y/ into palatality (acuteness) + labiality (flatting). And as in Russian labiality supposes velarity, a Russian's only way of pronouncing both features is to make a combination of the two units /j/+/u/. In the same way, a German or a Swede cannot combine the two features of nasality and palatality (compactness) in a single phoneme. Finnish does not have any /f/ and originally substituted a group *hv* ([xv]) in loan-words (from Swedish or other languages), e.g. in *kahvi* 'coffee', earlier *rohvessori* 'professor' for the modern *professori* (with the initial cluster as well as *f* later adopted by the system).

A parallel analysis into distinctive features is made, as was pointed out in Chap. II, when the number of signs in an alphabet are not numerous enough to symbolize all the phonemes of a language. Swedish *sj* for /ʃ/ may be looked upon as an interpretation of /ʃ/ as /s/ + palatality (compactness). It can be objected, of course, that in this case the spelling is explained by historical facts[1] and that the other Swedish diagraphs do not admit any interpretation of the same kind. But we find similar phenomena in cases where a foreign phoneme has been introduced by loan-words and has to be written, in some way or other.

In native words, the [b], [d], [g] of Modern Greek are free variants of [mb], [nd] and [ŋg] and can be analysed convincingly as a nasal phoneme plus /p/, /t/, /k/. The nasal has disappeared in many dialects as an independent segment and is represented solely by the voice feature of the stop. This is also the case where the loss of an initial unstressed vowel brings a nasal + stop cluster into initial position (μπαίνω ['beno] <

---

[1] The Swedish /ʃ/-phoneme is recent and due to a fusion of *s* and a (primary or secondary) palatal. The spelling still reflects these historical facts (cp. the following words: *sjuk* 'sick', *skina* 'shine', *skjuta* 'shoot', *stjärna* 'star', all with initial /ʃ/, and etymologically related to English and German words, where partly the same phenomena have taken place, e.g. Engl. *ship, fish*, Germ. *Schiff, Fisch* with original *sk*, where the velar stop has been palatalized; in the latter case, Swedish has retained *-sk: fisk*).

ἐμβαίνω, 'I enter'). The large number of loan-words in Modern Greek containing [b], [d], [g] and unfamiliar clusters such as [mp] and [nt], mean that [b], [d], [g] must be recognized as separate phonemes. Greeks naturally write /b/ in loan-words as μπ and /d/ as ντ (μπιρα 'beer'). This implies an analysis into voice + (voiceless) stop (N+p, N+t) and the Greek has an unshakable conviction that he is actually saying [mp] and [nt].

In many cases of controversial phonemic interpretation the analysis of a given type of sound may result either in a bi-phonemic or in a mono-phonemic interpretation with a following analysis of the phoneme into distinctive features. Some phoneticians have e.g. analysed the Swedish so-called supradentals (an alveolar series of stops, a nasal, a lateral, and a fricative) as single phonemes with the alveolar localisation as the distinctive feature, responsible for the opposition to dentals; others have, on the basis of distribution and possible free variation, particularly at morpheme boundaries, classified them as clusters of /r/ + dental (an interpretation reflected in the spelling: *rt, rd, rn,* and *rs*). Cp. hereto HARRIS' interpretation of Engl. /ʃ/ (Chap.IV, p. 85).

Even if most of the spellings of this type have nothing directly to do with any — conscious or subconscious — analysis of the phonemes concerned, it is certainly a fact that spellings like Swedish *sj*, German *sch* or English *sh* are accepted less reluctantly and have probably survived more easily than if the phoneme /ʃ/ had been symbolized by means of completely hasardous letter groups (say *fl* or *kr*). If we find *sj* more "natural" it may be at least partly because we have a feeling of "kinship" between /s/ and /ʃ/. In languages which have chosen dia-critic signs to symbolize phonemes without correspondences in the Latin alphabet, the situation may have been similar (š for /ʃ/ or č for /t͡ʃ/ in several languages). When the Germanic umlaut-vowels were first written — i.e. felt to be phonemically distinct from the original ones — they were often symbolized by means of a combination of the symbol for the unaltered vowel + the one which had caused the change. Swe-dish and German *ö, ä* are typical examples of this (*o, a* + the sign of a palatal on top). Swedish *å* is in the same way *a+o* (on top), i.e. an *a* with a feature typical for *o* (labialisation). The invention of such graphemes supposes necessarily some kind of analysis into distinctive features (i.e. /ø/ is split up into /o/ + palatality, etc.), in just the same way as the Russian woman mentioned above analysed Finnish /y/ into /u/ + palatality.

Though sufficiently explained historically — as are most of these spellings —, the French diagraphs *an, on* etc., for nasal vowels can also be looked upon as symbolizing a distinctive feature analysis (/ã/ = /a/ + nasality).

Let us add to this that the concepts of "marked" and "unmarked" and the idea of "archiphonemes" connected with them discussed in Chap. IV (p. 79) ought to be taken into account here too. For if in a given language, say German, /b/ is to be interpretated as /p/ + voice (as can be seen from the neutralisation in final position, where [p] is the only admissible type), then we have another instance of distinctive feature analysis, voice being felt as one of the independent features which build up the "bundle" /b/.

The basic idea behind the distinctive feature concept such as it has been worked out by JAKOBSON-FANT-HALLE is that the receiver of the message, when listening to the sound-wave, is confronted with a two-choice situation and consequently has to choose either between two polar qualities of the same category (grave ∼ acute, compact ∼ diffuse), or between the presence or absence of a given quality (voiced ∼ unvoiced, nasalized ∼ non-nasalized). All identification of phonemic units thus supposes a binary choice. The phonemic code would consequently be a binary code. This idea is in accordance with one of the principles of information theory and is held by communication theorists as well as by neurologists as a necessary hypothesis for describing the transfer process (according to Chap. II). The binary code represents an extreme simplification and, therefore, the highest degree of efficiency. The message is reduced to a series of yes-no responses, as is the case in the Teletype code (see Chap. III, Fig. 10).

We have mentioned above that the transfer of the structured message from the brain to the peripheric organs which have to execute the articulatory movements anyhow implies an encoding into a binary code of the Morse alphabet type. The neural impulses are discrete. The responses of the neurons are yes-no responses. It still remains, however, to be proved that this is an argument strong enough also to make the binary principle the only possible basis for describing the decoding of the acoustic continuum of the sound-wave, i. e. for assuming that identification of expression units (phonemes) is always the result of a binary choice, never of a choice between several possibilities. Cp. e. g. the Swedish vowel system as it was illustrated in Chap. III (with three degrees of labialisation). We shall mention here just a few of the arguments which have been put forward against the binary principle.[1]

---

[1] TRUBETZKOY defended the binary principle e. g. when he held that no language had more than two degrees of phonemic length and that instances of three degrees given in the description of certain languages (Estonian) were due to misunderstanding and misinterpretation. It was formulated already in the phonological program presented by JAKOBSON, KARCEVSKIJ, and TRUBETZKOY to the First International Congress of Linguists in 1928.

D. B. FRY finds the idea of distinctive features attractive because of its simplicity and generality, and the theory of primary recognition as a result of a series of binary choices convenient from the point of view of information theory, but he does not look upon it in any sense as a *sine qua non*. One of the weaknesses of the binary theory is, according to FRY, that it never states quite clearly on which side of the border-line between psychology and physics it operates. This remark of FRY's is, in fact, a very important one. If the distinctive feature is a physical quality, this presupposes a one-to-one correspondence between physical facts and psychological (perceptual) phenomena which is contradicted by experimental evidence (synthetic tests, etc.). It should be added that if we pass over from the more general psychological to the strictly linguistic level, this one-to-one correspondence becomes still more dubious. FRY further stresses the fact — referred to in Chap. II — that the physical dimensions of the stimulus must be transformed into psychological dimensions in the listener and that, consequently, the first question to be resolved is what psychological dimensions are likely to be involved in the perceptual process which forms the basis of primary recognition. He regards four dimensions as fundamental: q u a l i t y, p i t c h, l o u d n e s s, and l e n g t h, as was already mentioned in Chap. II. They are basic in the sense that they are independent variables. Sounds c a n be produced (by a speech apparatus) which differ with respect to o n e of these dimensions but are similar in all the others.

It is important that the four perceptual dimensions set up by FRY on the psychological level have their approximate counterparts on the physical level in respectively f r e q u e n c y   c o m p l e x e s (and relations), (f u n d a m e n t a l)   f r e q u e n c y,   i n t e n s i t y, and   d u r a t i o n, all of which are physically measurable phenomena. It should, however, be added that all are not equally simple. We have pointed out in Chap. III that intensity is a function of amplitude and frequency. The frequency complex which underlies the perceptual concept of quality (colour) is already by definition a result of cooperation between different absolute and relative factors, particularly of frequency and intensity (see for further details Chap. III). Length may be due to a combination of duration, intonation, quality, and vowel-consonant relation (contact), or even be manifested by any one of them. Intensity may be manifested as duration, as we have already seen in Chap. V, etc.

According to FRY, the transformation of the physical speech input may be supposed to give rise, in the brain of the receiver, to patterns defined in a four-dimensional psychological space and recognized as given phonemes. This first act of primary recognition is succeeded by a second when one of the parameters is changed and the pattern modified. Some kind of hierarchy seems to govern this segmentation, since in most languages quality is the dominating factor. "Any part of the speech sequence in which the four-dimensional pattern remains the same, forms a segment for the listener and as soon as a change of quality of sufficient magnitude occurs, the recognition mechanism proceeds to another act of primary recognition."

Another critic, ANDRÉ MARTINET, accuses the JAKOBSON-FANT-HALLE system of being aprioristic, a pre-established system for which the authors have postulated general validity. MARTINET admits the necessity of defining the oppositions in terms of sound substance. These terms as such are indifferent, but any effort to make them descriptive (grave — diffuse, strident — mellow) will necessarily be arbitrary. What seems important to MARTINET is the proportionality of the relations between units, and this proportionality is revealed by the parallelism in the variations. And it can hardly be denied that at least some of the terms which JAKOBSON et al. have chosen to symbolize their fundamental entities — the distinctive features — seem arbitrary, even directly misleading. The idea of the universality of the basic features may seem fascinating but needs further evidence. MARTINET cannot accept the general validity of the binary choice. In fact, it seems as if several writers are inclined to look upon it as the simplest principle of interpretation, though by no means the only possible one. Compare e.g. J.C.R. LICKLIDER: "It is not yet entirely settled what the acoustic counterparts of some of the phonatory distinctions are, but it is nevertheless of interest to picture speech as the product of an encoding process that is governed by a set of decisions between paired alternatives". P. L. GARVIN regards prosodic features as "phonemic situations in which binary contrasts do not readily appear".

MOL and UHLENBECK have disputed not the concept as such but the correctness of the traditional description of the distinctive features in terms of two or three formants. No conclusive evidence exists to show that the ear is capable of executing a Fourier-analysis. Though the authors have put forward a different hypothesis for interpreting the hearing mechanism and phoneme perception they do not by any means consider the problem as solved.

In an article on the logistic foundations of binary phoneme classification UNGEHEUER makes an important statement about the increasing tendency to apply the concepts of formal logic within the domain of linguistics. It is, according to UNGEHEUER, essential to remember that the logistic calculus is only the adequate exterior presentation of data and that no symmetry or coherence may be forced on these data, a danger which is said to be particularly great in linguistics. The only aim of the symmetrical presentation is to make a logical presentation of the obtained data and of their interrelations. The collection of data cannot be replaced by logistic.

The basic idea of the Jakobsonian system is to be found, probably for the first time, already in an article by Viggo Brøndal. He broke with the orthodox theory that articulation was the necessary basis of phonetic description and moved towards an abstract conception of phonemes as types with variable manifestation and without any one-to-one connection with articulatory data ("types phoniques abstraits, réalisables phonétiquement de façon toujours variable et jusqu'à un certain point arbitraire, et qui, par conséquent, ne sont jamais liés à une articulation particulière et unique"). This was a conception dia-metrically opposed to that of classical phonetics with its doctrine that "each new position of the tongue produces a new vowel". Brøndal postulated a hierarchy of phonemes, where traditional phonetics had seen just differences and where any idea of differences in the complexity of phonemes was *a priori* excluded (/y/ was a "simple" as /i/, etc., a standpoint which can be maintained only from a purely physical point of view, not functionally). Ungeheuer, in drawing his readers' attention to Brøndal's important article, stresses the fact that the hierarchy Brøndal is talking about here is just the kind of theoretical logistic presentation of phonemic systems for which Jakobson's system is intended to be a general base and for which Ungeheuer has tried with considerable success to outline the fundamental logistic principles.

It is interesting to compare Jakobson's basic system with Winte-ler's scheme reproduced in Chap. IV (Fig. 54), where it may be seen how the front and the back series are represented as extreme contrasts in one dimension, the closed $\sim$ open distinction ($i \sim a$, $u \sim a$) in the other. The triangular form of the basic vowel system is clearly illustrated (it was in fact known already in the 18th century; Hellwag). More interesting, however, is the fact that the intermediate character of the "flatted" (labialized) series is correctly interpreted in spite of the author's articulatory starting point. The introduction of the vertical line in the scheme consequently implies the introduction of a more subtle distinction (intermediate between "grave" and "acute").

What is basic and general in the structure of the expression in human communication is firstly the minimal system of oppositions, based as it is on maximal distinctions, and secondly the rank order according to which this basic system is extended into more complicated ones (more in Chap. XI; cp. also Chap. IV). The distinctive feature is, just like the phoneme, a linguistic unit, which, as such, cannot be described either in perceptual, or, and even less, in physical terms but which has to be correlated in some way or other to pheno-mena on both these other levels. This is a critical point where linguistic theory has not so far found a definitive solution and where the efforts of linguists and phoneticians have to be concentrated. It is evident that the linguistic terms in which this linguistic concept has to be defined must be closely related to at least perceptual concepts, since linguistic identification is a kind of perception, though a perception determined by a very particular set of structured prejudices which may counteract the purely psycho-physiological process of auditory perception. FRY points out that whereas an Englishman identifies the *t* in *top* with the one in *stop*, the difference is easily perceptible to native speakers of many languages of India; and yet to these same people the vowels in *red* and *raid* — very different to English ears — seem almost identical.

If we use the concept of distinctive feature in the sense which seems to have become traditional — as a set of basic perceptual parameters to which correspond, though in an irregular way, certain physical parameters — this concept belongs to our level no. 2 in the scheme in Chap. V. On a higher level of abstraction, the same unit may also be manifested by means of some other distinctive features and still remain linguistically identical with itself, as long as its mutual relations to the other units, i.e. its place within a given system of oppositions (paradigm), remains unaltered. It is characteristic that the concept of distinctiveness has no place within glossematic theory. The level of abstraction on which this theory operates simply does not admit this concept. This of course does not prevent it from being extremely useful on lower levels.

H. J. ULDALL states this explicitly by saying as follows: "A 'phoneme' is generally understood to be a class of variants in the expression which are equivalent in respect of functions with the content, but there is not necessarily any connexion between such a class as a whole and any class of units of 'distinctive features', but each of the members of the class, the variants, is a terminal of a function the other terminal of which is a unit of 'distinctive features'. The 'distinctive features' form classes of their own, and the term 'phoneme' would be more reasonably employed on this level — in fact, in something like DANIEL JONES's sense of 'a family of sounds'."

Basic are 1. on the physical level the four parameters just mentioned; 2. on the perceptual level a corresponding set of psycho-linguistic dimensions, whose relations to the physical parameters are not yet thoroughly examined; 3. on the strictly linguistic level (structural, in a restricted sense), the fundamental oppositions common to all known languages of the world, the most resistant ones in aphasia, and first to appear in children's speech. That these basic oppositions are roughly identical, in speech communities and in individuals (even in their physical manifestation, though they have been defined so far only in functional terms), is a consequence of the fact that, notwithstanding minor genetic and individual variations, the human speech apparatus and the human perception mechanism are almost identical from individual to individual. As a consequence, the same machinery for realizing an expression system is at the disposal of all groups and individuals.

The general and basic factor in the most primitive type of linguistic opposition (checked $\sim$ unchecked, or consonantal $\sim$ vocalic) is at the same time a maximum opposition and an opposition of extreme simplicity. This is true also of the most primitive vowel system, the triadic scheme

$$i \quad u$$
$$a$$

If all languages which use just this primitive vowel system pronounce the vocoids (allophones) roughly as $[i]$, $[u]$, and $[a]$, the reason is to be found in what was said above. On the other hand, we know that such languages often admit a very free variation of allophones; the more variation we admit the greater the risk of phonemic confusion and over-lapping.

It seems evident to the author of this book that the reduction of the linguistic expression into a series of binary choices — of yes-no questions — is an extreme simplification and generalization which may be undertaken for, and justified by, special purposes, e.g. for economic transmission or for adequate script (specialised alphabets, etc.). The Teletype Code is such a case. Any of the three units in the triadic system above may be identified by at most two yes-no questions: either 1. compact $\sim$ diffuse, or 2. acute $\sim$ not acute, or 3. grave $\sim$ not grave. In all three cases, "yes" gives immediately the correct identification, whereas "no" must be followed by a second question, respectively 1. grave or acute, 2. diffuse or compact, 3. = 2.

It seems, however, that this is an oversimplification of a perceptual process which can just as well be regarded as e.g. a triadic choice. Psychological evidence seems to confirm the idea that man is capable of making such a choice and that, consequently, /i/ in the scheme above may be identified directly as being neither /u/ nor /a/, i.e. through its place in the triadic system.[1]

---

[1] "Aus der Zerlegbarkeit von Phonemen in binäre Simultankomponenten kann nicht geschlossen werden, daß die Phonemdistinktion innerhalb des Bereichs der Schallsignale tatsächlich nur auf zweiwertigen Urteilen beruht. ... sehr wohl denkbar, daß auch ternäre oder noch höherstufige Distinktionen eine Rolle spielen" (MEYER-EPPLER).

A further step towards a more solid basis for our evaluation of the supposed binary choice has been taken thanks to recent investigations of auditory perception and auditory similarity between phonemes and of the possibility of establishing a psychological (perceptual) space as a sort of transition stage between the phonetic and the phonemic analysis. We need a more objective measure of the perceived similarity of speech sounds than the purely impressionistic judgement of even an expert linguist. Such a technique is needed in order to test the validity of JAKOBSON's binary hypothesis. "If he is correct we should expect the sounds to form clusters in the psychological space such that each cluster marks the end of one of the dimensions" (LIBERMAN). Important contributions to this technique and to the solving of this great problem have been made by writers such as SOL SAPORTA, UNGEHEUER, and GÖTE HANSON. The results obtained so far do not seem to confirm entirely the hypothesis under discussion.

It consequently does not seem possible to answer the question of the binary choice and the binary code by a simple yes, or no. It is in itself not a "yes-or-no question". Any message can be broken down into a series of binary distinctions, as may be seen from the Morse alphabet (a two-symbol code like — ·). But neither the phonemic nor the graphemic code represent the final step of a possible analysis into minimal units (HERDAN). There does not need to be any discussion about the possibility of interpreting language as a code made up of binary distinctions. This seems on the contrary quite evident. The discussion concerns the question of whether, or to what extent, the human perceptual mechanism when at work in the process of communication actually fulfils such an analysis to the bitter end, and consequently if any expression paradigm set up in linguistic description of particular languages has to be based on the binary principle. This seems rather doubtful. On the other hand it may be that one day the investigation of "the possibilities [that] such a code (sc. a binary one) would afford us a common denominator of different languages" (HERDAN) will give a positive result.

The idea of the language mechanism as a manipulation of independent variables is supposed by LIBERMAN to be valid on the expression as well as on the content levels of language. I quote: "... we all know how morphemic elements are entered into various combinations to create a variety of words, each element having a particular identity or meaning which it retains regardless of the combination in which it occurs. Indeed, we may suppose that combining independently variable stimulus elements is a workable basis for perception in the language area and it is likely that this tells us something rather important about the human mind."

Chapter VII

Syntagmatic Structures. Distribution and Probability

Any one of the minimal units set up by means of the segmentation and the phonemic analysis described in the preceding chapters gets its linguistic value through its relations to the other units of the paradigm. Its amount of information is to a large extent determined thereby. The richer the system, the greater the amount of information of any of its units, and vice versa. But as a member of a given chain of expression units, i.e. in a syntagm, it necessarily also has given relations to any other units within the chain. These are the syntagmatic relations to which this chapter will be devoted. We shall soon see, by means of a few examples, that even the structure of the syntagm, and, more generally, of the complex expression units (syllables, groups, etc.) are of importance for the informative value of the phonemes. The laws of distribution valid for the building up of these larger units often strongly reduce the amount of information of each smaller unit. In no language is the combination of the phonemes, or more generally the putting together of smaller entities into larger elements, free. In most languages, it is subject to very strong limitations.

In our example in Chap. III (*the boys are playing* ...), we saw that the first segmentation into measures (according to the number of stresses) was followed by one into syllables. Like any other of the fundamental concepts in phonetics (vowel, consonant, etc.), the syllable may be defined in structural or in physical terms, in the latter case acoustic and physiological. The structural syllable (or the "phonological" syllable, as some phoneticians have called it) is a combination of phonemes into groups according to the rules valid for the language in question and consisting of one central unit — the syllabic nucleus — and one or more marginal units. There may — at least theoretically — be languages without this functional distinction between marginal and central units. They will consequently lack structural syllables, though they may of course have phonetic syllables, i.e. an organisation of the phonetic elements into acoustically and physiologically determined groups. The opposite situation, however, is theoretically inconceivable, as the linguistic function must necessarily correspond to some kind of physical manifestation. Otherwise the structural opposition would remain a never realized potentiality. The definition of the syllable as only a "phonological" unit is consequently unsatisfactory, though this by no means implies that its physical manifestation is always the same.[1]

---

[1] This is of course true of any linguistic element. Even if two systems have the same structural opposition between vowels and consonants, it is not *a priori* necessary — though statistically relatively probable — that this opposition in both cases is manifested through the same physical differences.

Let us as a starting-point for our discussion choose the system reconstructed, on the basis of comparative evidence, for Proto-Indo-European by CARL HJ. BORGSTRØM. He supposes that, at a certain stage of the linguistic evolution of this hypothetical language[1], the vocoids were just phonetic auxiliary elements without any linguistic function of their own except that of making the consonants audible. Those were the only distinctive units of words and forms, the only phonemes in the system. A phoneme was consequently manifested in the sound substance as a contoid + a vocoid. The importance of the contoid-vocoid transition for the identification of the consonant phonemes has been treated in Chap. III. The colour of this support vocoid, which was linguistically irrelevant, must have been dependent on the surrounding contoids. Let us symbolize it by [ə] and suppose a word containing the phonemes /p/, /t/, and /k/, phonemically /ptk/, phonetically [pətəkə]. Such a language would consequently lack syllables, or, more correctly, there would be identity between phonemes and syllables, and consequently no distinction between vowel and consonant (this distinction being defined as a function within the syllable). In our example above, [pə] is consequently a phonetic syllable, though phonemically it is the manifestation of a phoneme /p/, nothing more.

If we imagine, as a further step in a hypothetical evolution, that a distinction is created between three different vocoid colours and that the vocoid quality is no longer automatically determined by the context — no longer 100% predictable —, we get a linguistic system which knows an opposition between, say, /pi/, /pu/, and /pa/, and consequently phonemic syllables, analysable into /p/+/i/, /p/+/u/, or /p/+/a/. If then these /i/, /a/, or /u/ phonemes become capable of functioning alone as signs, whereas /p/, /t/ etc. have to be accompanied by one of those three, we get our functional distinction between conditioning and conditioned units, i.e. vowels and consonants. A syllable consisting of a consonant plus a vowel represents the most primitive, and without doubt historically the oldest, of all syllabic types, the only one which is general in all languages. We call it the open syllable. All languages have open syllables. Very many have only open syllables. No language has only closed syllables.

Let us assume from now on that all languages have syllables and consequently also an opposition between vowels and consonants. Our first concern will be the syllabic structure and a comparative survey of some structurally different syllabic types. It goes without saying, and follows automatically from what was said in Chap. III about the

---

[1] It is of no importance for our demonstration whether this language has existed or not. At some stage in the history of human language, however, such a system must have been a fact.

difference between vocoids and contoids, that the type exemplified
above (stop + vowel) constitutes the simplest possible syllable: extreme
closure + extreme opening — the articulatory manifestation of which
is, so to say, prepared in the infant's first babbling: *ababa — adadada*,
etc. (though such series have of course nothing to do with speech in our
sense of the word). The syllabic type /*pa-pa*/ is the first which appears
in children's speech.

The idea of the non-phonemic vocoid as an automatic, predictable
element in the chain of phonemes is an excellent starting point for a
study of syllables and syllabic structures. For such a development
perfectly explains the actual situation in the world's languages today,
i.e. preponderance of the open syllable. According to this view and
in full accordance with JAKOBSON's law (see Chap. IV and XI), it is also
natural — and confirmed by numerous data — that the open syllable
should be the first to appear in children's speech and the last to disappear in aphasia (more about this in Chap. XI).

The simple syllable *PA* is primitive in the sense that it gives a very
limited number of combinatory possibilities. Let us suppose a phoneme
system of a very simple type with eight consonants (say /*p*/, /*t*/, /*k*/,
the corresponding nasals, a liquid and a fricative) and the three basic
vowel /*i*/, /*u*/, and /*a*/. We get just 24 possible syllables. If the word
length were restricted to a single syllable, we should obtain just as many
words, an impossible set of communication possibilities for a human
being. All languages known today have developed their systems in one
direction or another. One possible method is repetition — *PAPA*,
PAPAPA, etc. /*PA*/ can be opposed to /*PAPA*/[1]. If, as a further
development of the distributional possibilities, /*A*/ in both may be replaced
by any of the other two vowels /*I*/ or /*U*/, we obtain 9 combinations
with /*P*/, and with the eight consonants as a whole 576 dissyllabic
"words", a considerable improvement. It can easily be proved that
already the introduction of syllable-initial clusters of two phonemes, stop
+ liquid, say /*PLAPLA*/ as opposed to /*PLAPA*/ or /*PAPLA*/ would
imply a multiplication by three (i.e. 1728 "words"), etc. And yet we
have not taken into account the monosyllable (/*PA*/, /*PLA*/, etc.). We
understand from these examples that we do not need to add very many
new possibilities (two series of stops, one single syllable-final consonant,
three-syllable "words", etc.), in order to obtain a very large number of
possible complexes, able to function as the expressions of signs.

---

[1] This is already a considerable increase of the linguistic possibilities and is
lacking in certain types of primitive structures. Small children neglect the distinction and say *papa* or *papapa*, *ma* or *mama* indifferently. Reduplication
puts this repetition to functional use. — The zero initial /*A*/ has been disregarded in
the above examples.

Japanese gives a good example of a primitive syllabic structure. The language has only open syllables, no consonant clusters and just five vowels. On the other hand, a word may contain several syllables. The Japanese so-called syllabic script with its 50 signs, one for each possible syllable in the language, is conditioned by this simple syllabic structure (see also Chap. II, p. 21, footnote). The more complicated the syllabic structure of a language, the less adequate a syllabic script system.

Even languages which admit implosive (= syllable-final) consonants and closed syllables as opposed to open ones, most often manifest traces of the primitive syllabic tendency towards the type $/PA/$. This tendency may be manifested in different ways. It may be that a language has initial but no final clusters, or that the number of phonemic oppositions is reduced at the end of syllables, or both. Even in languages where rather complex implosive groups are admitted there is often a striking tendency to assimilation or syncretism, of reduction in rapid speech, in children's speech, and as an individual characteristic in certain persons with a defective mastery of their phonemic system.

Instances of syncretism in implosive position are numerous. The German and Slavic unvoicing in final position belongs to this category. The Greek distributional law according to which any word must end in a vowel or in s, n or r with exclusion of all other consonants is another example of restriction of the same kind.

As typical examples of different syllabic (or to a certain degree morphemic) structures we can take on the one hand, Swedish as it has been analysed by BENGT SIGURD, and on the other Spanish as analysed by AMADO ALONSO and by the present author.

In the introduction to his analysis of the rank order of Swedish consonants SIGURD mentions two main ways of classifying phonemes: according to their distinctive phonetic features, or according to their ability to combine with the other phonemes in the speech chain. There is of course, at least theoretically, a third way: according to paradigmatic relations only (but it is, as was pointed out in Chap. IV, p. 75, doubtful whether this is practically possible). Already in 1952, ELI FISCHER-JØRGENSEN had expressed the opinion that the syllable was the natural unit for the study of phonemic distribution. It is in conformity with this principle that SIGURD analyses Swedish monosyllables. A monosyllabic word is of course a sign (or more exactly a semantic sign unit) the expression of which is monosyllabic. The concept "monosyllable" is consequently a shorter expression for this more detailed definition and may be used without too much inconvenience, after this reservation has been made. It is evident that among monosyllables are represented the most complicated syllabic structures existing in the language in question.

9*

Position

3	2	1	V	1	2	3

```
        3      2      1        V      1      2       3

   s + p ⎫                                  ⎧ s + {t
       b ⎪                                  ⎪     {k
   s + t ⎪                                  ⎪ ʃ
       d ⎬ + r                          r + ⎨ t + s
   s + k ⎪                                  ⎪ p
       g ⎪                                  ⎪ b
       f ⎪                                  ⎪ d
       v ⎭                                  ⎪ k
                                            ⎪ f + t
     s                                      ⎪ v
   s + p ⎫                                  ⎪ j
       b ⎬ + l                              ⎪ m
       k ⎪                                  ⎩ n
       g ⎪                                  ⎧ l
       f ⎭                                  ⎧ s + t
                                            ⎪ p
   s + p ⎫                                  ⎪ t
       b ⎪                                  ⎪ d
       f ⎬ + j                          l + ⎨ k
       m ⎪                                  ⎪ f + t
       n ⎭                                  ⎪ v
                                            ⎪ j + d
     s                                      ⎪ m
   s + k ⎫           } + V +                 ⎩ n
       t ⎬ + v                              ⎧ s
       d ⎭                                  ⎪ p
                                            ⎪ b
     s                                      ⎪ t
   s + k ⎫                              m + ⎨ d
       g ⎬ + n                              ⎪ f
       f ⎭                                  ⎪ n + d
                                            ⎩ j
   s   + p                                  ⎧ t
   s   + t                                  ⎪ d
   s   + k                              ŋ + ⎨ s + t
   s   + m                                  ⎪ k
       s                                    ⎩ n
       b                                    ⎧ s
       d                                    ⎪ t
       g                              j + ⎨ d
       ʃ                                    ⎪ k
       h                                    ⎩ f
       c                                    ⎧ s + t
                                            ⎪ t
                                       n + ⎨ d
                                            ⎪ ʃ
                                            ⎩ j
                                            ⎧ p
                                       s + ⎨ t
                                            ⎪ k
                                            ⎩ m
                                            ⎧ s
                                       t + ⎨ ʃ
                                            ⎩ m
                                       k + { s + t
                                            { t
                                       p + { s
                                            { t
                                       f + { s + t
                                            { t
                                       v + d
                                       g + d
                                       b +
                                       d +
                                       ʃ
```

Fig. 64. Structural formula for Swedish monosyllables. Only uninflected words are taken into account. According to SIGURD

SIGURD classes the Swedish consonants with regard to their relation to the syllabic nucleus V, and groups them according to their vowel adherence. In the following structural formula (Fig. 64) a plus sign to the left means that the preceding phoneme may be added to make an existing cluster, and a plus sign to the right means that the following phoneme may be added.

This formula does not imply that all the monosyllables which could be constructed within the limits of the structural pattern exist as words in the lexicon of the language. In fact, only a fraction of them actually do. As with any structural frame set up in linguistic description this formula gives us the possibilities of the language and, consequently, contributes to the determination of the informative value of each of the units listed. SIGURD establishes, on the basis of this formula, the following rules, where x and z represent any two consonants:

a) If there is the initial combination /xz-/, there is no initial combination /zx-/.

b) If there is the final combination /-xz/, there is no final combination /-zx/ (five exceptions).

c) If there is the initial combination /xz-/, a final combination of x and z, if it exists, either has only the form /-zx/ or both /-zx/ and /-xz/ (two exceptions).

SIGURD takes as an example the phonemes /k/ and /l/. They

combine initially in /kl-/ but not as */lk-/. Finally the distribution is reversed: /-lk/ but not */-kl/. The final combination is regarded as the inverted form of the initial /kl-/. Consequently /l/ always takes the position next to the vowel. It has a greater vowel adherence than /k/. If /k/ is combined with /r/ we find that we can have /kr-/ and /-rk/ and nothing else. /r/ is more adherent to the vowel than /k/. And if we finally combine /l/ and /r/, we find that only one combination is possible, sc. /-rl/ and that consequently r is more adherent than /l/. The rank order between the consonants under discussion is thus $r - l - k$. If $\dashv$ is chosen as the symbol of this adherence relation, we obtain the formula $r \dashv l$. Two Swedish consonants, viz. /h/ and /ç/, do not enter into clusters and do not belong to any adherence relation. It would bring us too far to develop here in more detail the distributional analysis undertaken by SIGURD and by a few other phoneticians who have taken up this sort of structural analysis, or to try and give a survey of the mathematical theory of relations presented together with SIGURD's paper by the mathematician LARS GÅRDING. We mention SIGURD's study just an example of possible, and necessary, syntagmatic descriptions.

Just as economy — i.e. the arrangement of the phonemes of a language into parallel series with a common distinctive factor (Chap. IV) — has been supposed to play a part in linguistic evolution, distribution may have similar evolutionary consequences in the sense that rare combinations tend to give place to more frequent ones. The phenomena traditionally called dissimilation, metathesis, and interversion are very often due to such a tendency.

Spanish gives us a great many examples of syncretism in syllable-final position. The phonemic system has three nasal phonemes: /m/, /n/, and /ɲ/, valid, however, only initially (and consequently between vowels, since any intervocalic consonant automatically becomes explosive). In final position, there is no opposition, the "place of articulation" of the nasal being automatically determined by the following consonant, if there is any; otherwise it is dental or velar indifferently (stylistic or regional variations); thus un beso [um'beso], un día [un'dia], un chico [uɲ'tʃiko], un gato [uŋ'gato], and jamón [xa'mon] or [xa'moŋ]. Phonemically we have to do with the archiphoneme /N/ in all these cases. The "place of articulation" consequently has no informative value. It is a typical example of redundancy. The quality of the following consonant is predictable from the nasal and consequently gives no further information.

If we go over to more dialectal or vulgar types of Spanish and look at the syllabic tendency as it is manifested in colloquial speech and in vulgarisms — to an astonishingly large extent the same all over the Spanish-speaking world — we find other striking instances of phonemic

confusion in syllable-final position. Many dialects tend to confuse *r*
and *l* and to pronounce either only one of them, or an intermediate
liquid known from many non-Indo-European languages.

Another distinction which is normally neutralized is that between
voiced and voiceless. A word like *doctor* may be pronounced with [*k*],
[*g*], [*ɣ*] or [*u̯*], or even without any implosive consonant at all, depending
on the degree of distinctness of the pronunciation used ([*dou̯'tor*] and

Swedish

/— m/ ======------[m] + all consonants (*omkring, omtala, omsluta,* etc.)
           ------[ɱ] + [f, v] (*om vi* — —; facultative variant)

           _—[m] + [p, b] (*en påse;* facultative variant)
/— n/ ≋≤≤≤------[n] + all consonants[1] (*en mås, ensam, en kung*)
           ---- [ɱ] + [f, v] (*en vas;* facultative variant)
           ˋ-[ŋ] + [k, g] (*en kung;* facultative variant)

/— ŋ/-----------[ŋ] + all consonants[2]

[1] Not before /k/ within the morpheme.
[2] Only at morpheme boundaries.

Spanish

        _[m] + [b, p, m]   *un beso*
       _[ɱ] + [f]   *un fósforo*
      _[n¹] + [þ]   *un ciego*
/— N/ ≋≤------[n²] + [t, d, n, l, r]   *un tonto*
      ˋ-[n³] + [ş]   *un señor*
       ˋ-[ɲ] + [tʃ, λ]   *un llano*
        ˋ[ŋ] + [k, g]   *un gato*

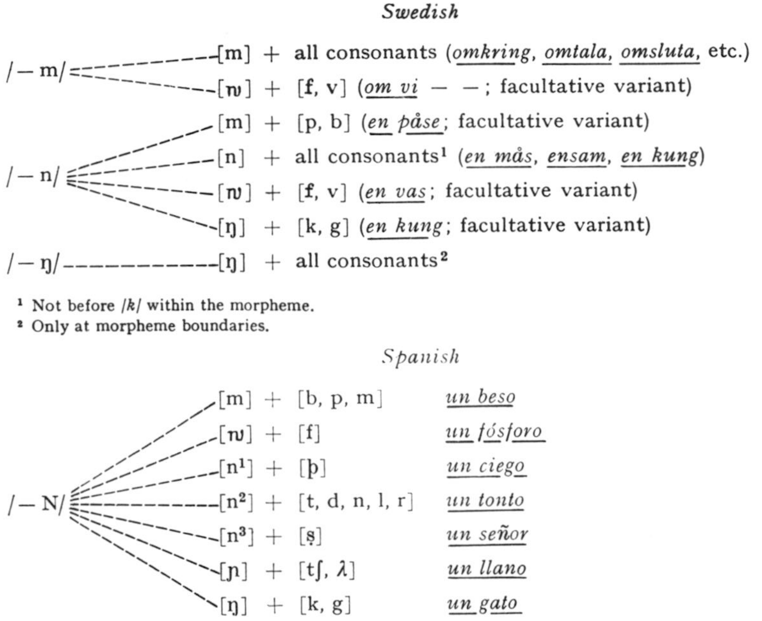

Fig. 65. A comparison between the behaviour and distinctive possibilities of nasals in syllable-final position
in Swedish (*above*), and in Spanish (*below*). Whereas Spanish has just one phonemic possibility — differently
manifested according to the following phoneme (here seven variants; the three types of [*n*] are respectively
interdental, postdental and alveolar) — Swedish has three (though with certain restrictions)

[*do'tor*] being definitely vulgar, [*doɣ'tor*] or [*doɣə'tor*] colloquial). This
implies that even the distinction between consonant and "semi-vowel"
is neutralized. Even other consonants tend, in vulgar speech, to be
reduced to semi-vowels, or to be dropped, at the end of syllables. Labials
and velars become [*u̯*] (*objeto* [*ou̯'xeto*], *capsula* ['*kau̯sula*]), dentals [*i̯*]
(*padre* ['*pai̯re*], *porque* ['*poi̯ke*], etc.). The Spanish system does not admit
palatals at the end of syllables (except [*i̯*]). If we add to this that zero
is another common colloquial manifestation of implosive consonant
phonemes, we arrive at the conclusion that the open syllable *PA* is
the ideal to which Spanish phonemic evolution tends. The famous
"aspiration" of implosive *-s* so far infects only the physical manifestation,
not the phonemic structure, but is on the other hand a stage towards

a non-differentiated consonant and, finally, zero (usually not arrived at yet in most of the Castilian dialects[1], but well-known e.g. from the phonetic history of French).

A comparison between Spanish and Swedish regarding implosive nasals is instructive (Fig. 65).

An example from an African language, Hottentot, will be given as an illustration of a still more marked tendency towards open syllables. The exceptions from the rule of the open syllable are twofold: implosive nasals (*m* and *n*), though with a restricted distribution and a phonemic status which is not quite clear, and implosive -*b*, -*s* and -*ts*, all three

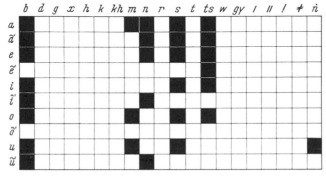

Fig. 66. Combinations of vowel + consonant in Hottentot. *Above* to the right, the four click consonants (cf. p. 56). According to Nienaber

with a grammatical function (-*b* a masculine ending, -*s* a feminine ending, and -*ts* a characteristic of the second person in pronouns and verbs), doubtlessly reductions of the original, full forms -*bi*, -*si*, and -*tsa*, consequently independent syllables. This example, quoted from G. S. Nienaber, also gives us an instructive instance of how a more complicated syllabic structure may arise as a secondary phonetic reduction of originally independent morphemes, each of which is in accordance with the primitive syllabic type. It is e.g. generally supposed that the numerous endings in Indo-European, Finno-Ugric, and other languages have originated as morphemes (words) which have given up their independence to become just indicators of a linguistic function[2].

---

[1] Even in the southern peninsular dialects where the -*s* is replaced by a lengthening of the preceding vowel or of a change of its quality (e.g. ['*gato*ʰ] > ['*gato:*] in Andalusian dialects) the -*s* may be said to be phonemically retained.

[2] Identical phenomena have sometimes taken place so recently that they may be followed in texts or in living dialects, e.g. the Scandinavian passive voice in -*s*, where the ending is a reflexive pronoun (*sik*, *sig*) added to the verbform, or the vulgar French interrogative particle -*ti* which is the pronoun *il* added, sometimes by means of an intrusive -*t*-, to the verb in so called double interrogative constructions (*mon père viendra-t-il?* 'will my father come?').

Modern Greek gives us another instance of "assimilation" and restricted distinctive possibilities at syllable boundaries. As in Spanish the "place of articulation" of an implosive nasal may be automatically conditioned by a following phoneme and there is consequently in this position only one nasal "archiphoneme" with indifferent localisation, e. g. the definite article τὸν τρόπο *ton* ¹*tropo* in contradistinction to τὸν πατέρα *tom* *pa*¹*tera*, or the particle σαν in σάν καὶ σένα *say* *kje*¹*sena*. But when in Spanish, as in French and other Romance languages, assimilation regularly affects the implosive element, Greek offers interesting examples of a double influence of the type $n+p>mb$, $n+t>nd$, $n+k>\eta g$, and even $n+ps>mbz$, etc. (e.g. στὸν Πειραιά *stom* *bire*¹*a*, τήν κόρη *tiŋ*¹*gori*).

Many of the juncture phenomena which in traditional phonetics were classified as instances of assimilation can be considered more adequately as cases of restricted distribution, namely all the cases where we have to do with the loss of a phonemic distinction within a syntagm. The paradigm remains unaltered but the number of combinations of the distinctive units becomes more limited than before (if the phenomenon is looked upon as a diachronic change, which it may, but need not necessarily, be); or than it would be without this restriction (if diachrony is left out of consideration, or no evidence about earlier stages is to be obtained). It seems in fact extremely important to make a clearcut distinction between phenomena of the type mentioned and real assimilations where the influence between phonemes concerns only their physical manifestation.

The so-called vowel harmony (already discussed in Chap. IV) implies that a vocalic (phonemic[1]) colour is totally or partly conditioned by the presence of another vowel phoneme in surrounding syllables or groups[2]. Two well known instances of this type of syntagmatic structure are Finnish and Turkish (examples, p. 90).

The same phenomena have already been mentioned under the heading syncretism in Chap. IV. We do not need to go into any further details here, nor do we need to make any calculations of the consequences for the number of distinctive resources of metaphony as compared with the absence of metaphony, or of syncretism versus non-syncretism. Let us just compare two artificial alternatives : a language having $PI - PU - PA$ in the first syllable and the same alternatives in the

[1] It is of course possible to talk about vowel harmony even when no phonemic restriction is implied (e.g. the slightly more open quality of the first [e] in French *était* as compared with the one in *été*).

[2] Vowel harmony may be caused by an initial syllable on the vowel of the following syllable(s), by a final syllable on the preceding one, by a stressed vowel on unstressed vowels or by unstressed on (preceding) stressed ones, etc. These are typical instances of differences of syntagmatic structure.

second (*PIPU*, *PAPI*, etc.), and another having automatically the same vowel in the second as in the first syllable (just *PIPI*, *PUPU*, etc.). The first language obtains through combinations of P + vowel 3×3 dissyllabic "words", the second only 3, and through addition of the monosyllabic type each another 3 (i. e. 12 versus 6 "words").

Syncretism means redundancy, and redundancy implies predictability of units, i.e. restriction of their information value. A syllable-final [*m*] in Spanish implies not only that a following explosive consonant must be labial but also that there must follow an explosive consonant, the condition for [*m*] to be implosive in Spanish[1]. But this redundancy also implies extra guidance to the identification of phonemic units. Consequently syntagmatic restrictions mean reduced possibilities of combination and therefore of opposition — with as a theoretical consequence the necessity of longer sequences to express the same amount of content — but at the same time more chance for correct identification of a phonemic sequence. A language where such restrictions are numerous is poor but easy to master. A richer system automatically becomes more difficult.

The way of grouping syllables into larger units as well as the delimitation of units are other effects of the peculiar syntagmatic structure of a language. We cannot any longer, on this level of analysis, avoid taking into account the sign function and, consequently, the content level of language. For even if segmentation is manifested strictly phonetically and, at least in principle, can be related to physical phenomena (formant transitions or chest pulses for syllables, etc.), and/or is reflected by conventional distributional rules (e. g. the presence of a stress on a syllable marking the beginning of a new segment in Finnish, and marking the end of one in French), it becomes almost impossible not to relate the segments obtained to corresponding segments on the content level (syllables or shorter syllabic groups to morphemes or words, breath groups to sentences, etc.).

The problem of the phonetic structure of the "word" and the "word as a phonetic unit" merits a few comments in this context. In our analysis carried out in Chap. IV we took into consideration the content level, when analysing expression, only for the commutation test, and vice versa. This is correct in principle. We cannot carry out a segmentation of the phoneme sequence starting from content units, and pretend e. g. that there is a boundary after a given consonant since this consonant is final in a word. In the French sequence *elle était une amie* /ε| le| tε| ty| na| mi/, which contains four words and six syllables, there is not one single instance of coincidence between a syllabic boundary and a word boundary.

---

[1] Since the labial nasal is never word-final.

Expression and content segments overlap. The word boundary falls within the syllables /le/, /tɛ/, /ty/, /na/. If, on the other hand, we take the German phrase *es war einmal ein Esel* /ɛs 'va:r ʔain'ma:l ʔain'ʔe: zəl/ we see that five of the six syllabic boundaries coincide with a morpheme boundary and that there is no word boundary that does not coincide with a syllabic boundary. The "linking" of a final prevocalic consonant is unknown in German[1], normal in French. This fact, together with a stress on any important word in the sentence, contributes to giving a certain phonetic independence to the German word as compared with French, and to making the German content units coincide with expression units to a much larger extent than is the case in French. It is a matter of fact that this way of expressing the difference of syntagmatic structure between the two languages is a simplification. More strictly speaking, German sequences may be cut down into phonetically characterised groups which in almost all cases may be correlated to corresponding content units (traditionally called words), without any overlapping between the two sets of parallel elements. As may be seen very easily the syntagmatic structure is completely different in our two examples given above.

The extent to which the "word" (used here with the reservation just made) remains phonetically unaltered in sign combinations expresses its degree of phonetic autonomy and consequently reflects the parallelism, or lack of parallelism, between content and expression structure, as far as segmentation is concerned. The examples mentioned above from Modern Greek illustrate another case of phonetic subordination of the word to the phonetic unity of the group. The famous Celtic alternation between initials is another instance of — or at least can be traced back to — a syntagmatic structure where even the initial of a unit (a "word") in spite of its "strong" character, is infected by combinatory laws[2].

When structural analyses of the kind mentioned above are extended to larger units (here for convenience called words of two, three, etc. syllables), sometimes interesting structural laws may be discovered. The

---

[1] Its absence is further marked through the existence, in Northern German, of a glottal stop at the beginning of the new unit.

[2] It should be noticed that in numerous instances of this kind the combinatory modification leaves the phonemic status of the unit intact, adapting its manifestation more or less to the surrounding phonemes. Consequently the distinctions are preserved. On the other hand such modifications very often result in a phonemic confusion or in some kind of automatic distribution, with a reduction of the distinctive possibilities as a necessary consequence. The "aspiration" of implosive -s in Spanish often results in initial alternation, e.g. *los vinos* [lo-ɸinoʰ], *las gatas* [la-'xataʰ] with, as a consequence (at least in the latter example), phonemic confusion (syncretism) between -s + voiced cons. and voiceless cons., i.e. /-sg-/ and /x/ (= the "jota" or *j*, *g* [*e, i*] of the orthography).

correlations between different characteristics often reflect qualities of extreme interest for judgements about the communicative efficiency of a linguistic system. For it seems to be a fact that languages differ considerably in efficiency from this point of view. It does not seem to be a general rule — as has been held by some writers — that poverty in one respect is automatically compensated by a rich development of expression possibilities in another, though this is of course often the case. An interesting example is quoted by FRANZ GIET from northern Chinese dialects with an extremely limited number of syllables (word elements), from 846 for the best equipped down

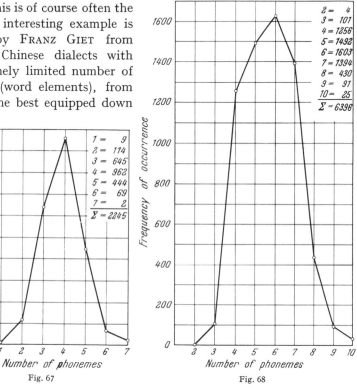

Fig. 67. Distribution of phoneme number in German monosyllables (x-axis = number of phonemes; y- axis = frequency); according to MENZERATH

Fig. 68. Phoneme frequency distribution in German dissyllables (cp. Fig.67; MENZERATH)

to 316 for the poorest, and having a number of distinctive tones which decreases with the number of syllables (and not conversely, as one would guess *a priori*).

German has like Swedish and the other Germanic languages a large number of possible consonantal combinations. The above graph (from MENZERATH) shows the distribution of monosyllables in German where the four-phoneme group is by far the most common (Fig. 67). The same graph for dissyllables has the aspect seen in Fig. 68.

As a contrast we also give MENZERATH's graph for words of seven syllables in German (Fig. 69). It is well known that there is negative correlation between word length and word frequency (ZIPF). MENZERATH has discovered (for German) another law of extreme interest and has summarized his results as follows: 1. the relative number of phonemes shows a decrease which is inversely proportional to the number of syllables; 2. the greater the number of syllables, the narrower the breadth of variation of the number of elements. (Fig. 70 below).

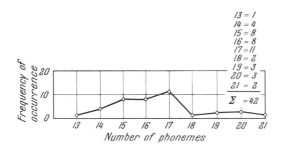

$13 = 1$
$14 = 4$
$15 = 8$
$16 = 8$
$17 = 11$
$18 = 2$
$19 = 3$
$20 = 3$
$21 = 2$
$\Sigma = 42$

Fig. 69. Frequency distribution of phonemes in German words of seven syllables (MENZERATH)

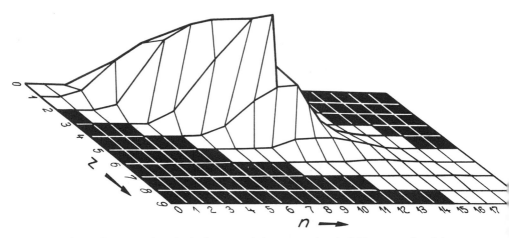

Fig. 70. Frequency polygon for the German vocabulary. z = number of syllables, n = number of phonemes. The summit is the most common word type ($n = 8$, $z = 3$, i.e. a three-syllabic word with eight phonemes)

If the restrictions on the number of phonemic combinations and phoneme sequences referred to above strongly diminish the chance factor in speech and consequently the information quantity of phonemic units, this is true also of the laws for phoneme frequency within the grammatical and semantic stock of units (signs) of a language. A phoneme may be predictable not only because it is the only one permissible in the given context, or one of only a few possibilities. But it may be more or less probable also because of its frequency rank in the language. A few examples will illustrate differences of this kind, which also have to be classified as differences of syntagmatic structure. Phoneme frequency does not affect the phonemic paradigm of a language. But it affects considerably the phonemic make up — the expression form — of syntagms. It therefore constitutes an important part of the structural description of a language.

Already in his descriptive analysis of Swedish dating from the beginning of this century ADOLF NOREEN gives some figures for the frequency of Swedish vowels and consonants in a text. Short *a* is e.g.

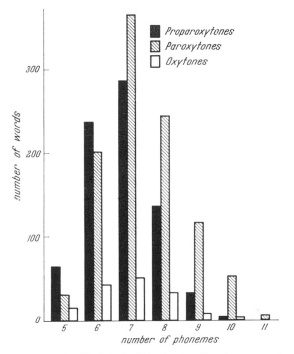

Fig. 71. C.-G. SÖDERBERG's graph of English trisyllables (number of words versus number of phonemes). The most productive type of word is the paroxytone of seven phonemes (only initially vocalic types). The most productive trisyllable according to SÖDERBERG is the paroxytone of the type V2V1V1, next comes the proparoxytone V1V1V1

the most frequent phoneme, followed by the consonants *t*, *r*, and *s*. Stenographers early became interested in phoneme (or rather letter) frequency, and the same interest is nowadays shared by speech transmission engineers and other technicians.

A pioneer work within the study of phoneme and word frequency was carried out by the American G. K. ZIPF who was the first to discover the relationship between the complexity of the phonemes and their frequency. The more complex a phoneme, the less frequent. Voiceless phonemes, in languages where they are opposed to voiced, are twice as frequent as the voiced ones. This is an interesting fact which has importance also for the problem discussed in Chap. VI (p. 118) concerning the concept of distinctive feature. If ZIPF's law, in this respect, is correct, this gives objective, linguistic evidence for the assumption that phonemes are of different complexity, that some phonemes are more composed than others, that, consequently, the concept of mark is justified, and that it is feasible to interpret a phoneme as a complex made up of a varying number of smaller elements (e.g. to say that $/b/$ is $/p/$ + voice, etc.). Other investigations have revealed a similar correlation between audibility and frequency (the more audible, the more frequent). These figures indicate a principle for the phonemic structuration of language which is known from other systems of communication, the principle of economy. The more complicated a linguistic signal (as articulation, as acoustic structure or as perception), the less economic it is as a means of communication and the lower its frequency in existing linguistic structures.

The same is true for the number of phonemes in words. The shortest words are normally the most frequent ones. The very long words are rare (cp. MENZERATH's graph quoted above).

Some members of the Prague group were pioneers in the field of phoneme statistics. B. TRNKA analysed English monosyllables and set up the form types utilized in English. Other writers have followed suit, and comparisons between syntagmatical structures begin to be possible on a larger scale.

In some cases, distribution may help to solve problems of phonemic interpretation (see Chap. IV). If, e.g., in a given position a language lacks a certain type of combination except for one single case and if this case depends on a certain controversial phonemic interpretation, there is a strong argument in favour of another interpretation which does not create the anomaly in question. The argument has been used in many discussions about the phonemic status of English affricates ($[tʃ]$, $[dʒ]$). The case will not be treated in detail here, but it is an interesting example of the part played by distributional facts in the scientific description of languages.

The example in Fig. 72 is taken from ZIPF's figures for tenues and mediae (voiceless and voiced stops) in some languages and will serve to illustrate his law. "This result is indeed startling", says ZIPF himself, "surely it is clear that the tenues tend to be more frequent than the mediae".

If we make once more a reservation concerning the abuse of terms such as "word" and "sentence" (cf. p. 137) we can look in this context also more closely at word distribution in the longer units which make up the linguistic message, i.e. what some linguists call the text (cf.

p.68), although we have not yet discussed the problems of content analysis and although by doing so we no longer limit our description to the expression level. The structure of longer units is conditioned by the distribution of the signs (morphemes, words). W o r d f r e q u e n c y has attracted particular attention because of its practical implications (e.g. for language teaching, the establishment of a basic vocabulary, etc.). Its role in the perception process will be treated later.

PIERRE GUIRAUD has summed up the results obtained in the field of word frequency statistics (from the pioneer F. W. KÄDING up till

	t %	d %	k %	g %	p %	b %
Bulgarian	7.54	3.55	2.98	1.46	2.82	1.32
English	7.13	4.31	2.71	0.74	2.04	1.81
Russian	7.49	3.42	3.49	1.10	2.19	1.76
Italian	7.02	4.74	3.63	0.41	2.78	0.89
Swedish	7.64	5.48	3.52	2.50	1.20	1.32
Hungarian	7.18	3.30	5.72	2.45	1.04	1.71
German	6.42	3.75	2.24	1.84	1.30	1.34
French.	6.28	3.55	4.81	0.76	3.54	1.39
Czech	5.60	3.73	3.93	0.15	3.52	1.86
Spanish	4.27	5.20	3.82	0.07	2.64	2.05
Sanskrit	6.65	2.85	1.99	0.82	2.46	0.46
Greek	7.58	2.87	4.07	1.74	3.38	0.49
Latin	7.72	3.41	3.71	0.96	2.01	1.40
Average	6.81	3.84	3.58	1.15	2.38	1.37

Fig. 72. ZIPF's figures for the distribution of tenues and mediae in a series of languages

now) in the following statements: 1. in a given text a very small number of words make up the essential part of the text; 2. a very small number of words, appropriately chosen, cover most of any text whatsoever (e.g. the 100 most common words cover 60% of any text, the 1000 most common ones cover 85% of any text, and the 4000 most common ones cover 97,5% of any text, and the whole rest of the vocabulary only 2,5% of the words of any text). We know thanks to ZIPF that the product of a word's frequency (the number of times it is to be found in a text) and its rank (the most frequent word has No.1, etc.) is constant: $fr =$ constant. Two tendencies may be supposed to be balanced against each other. The receiver's need for a maximum of information demands precise, concrete — and consequently rare — words, whereas the sender's desire to economise his effort results in a predilection for general, abstract and frequent words (pronouns like *he, it*, words like *thing, object* for the exact terms). The more general a word is, the more frequent. Most frequent of all are the grammatical auxiliaries (articles, pronouns, etc.) which convey very little information. Their probability is very high and their quantity of information consequently very small. They are in most cases predictable from the context and have a high degree of redundancy. The concrete, precise terms are rare, their predictability small and their amount of information large. ZIPF's equation illustrates the balance between the two tendencies.

But if frequent words are shorter than rare words, if complex phonemes are rarer than simple phonemes and complex groups less common than simple — and consequently the whole language mechanism built on the principle of least effort — this implies extremely far-going limitations on the probability of occurrence of the individual phonemes and of the phoneme groups (clusters, syllables, groups, periods, etc.). These units therefore admit considerable simplification and even suppression of certain parts of their phonemic substance — in the speech production (articulation) as well as in speech perception. They may be guessed at with a high probability of correctness. On the other hand, their information value is restricted. The rare units

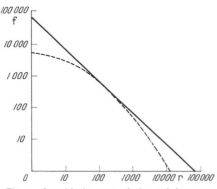

Fig. 73. Logarithmic curve of the rank-frequency distribution (straight line = theoretical curve; dotted line = real curve). According to GUIRAUD

have to be sent and received with a higher degree of exactness since their probability is small and their information value considerable — most often decisive for the message. Completely improbable units — e. g. names, and particularly names with a foreign phonemic structure, very often technical terms etc. — are not identified even under ideal conditions. They demand an abnormal degree of redundancy (have to be both spoken and written, spelled, etc.). More about this in Chap. XI.

A dictionary such as the French "Petit Larousse" contains (according to GUIRAUD) about 50,000 words and about 20,000 names. GUIRAUD has calculated that the actual vocabulary at the disposition of a speaker at a given moment is not very much above 20,000 words. A lexicon is defined by its extension (number of words contained in it) and its structure, or the distribution of these words expressed through the slope of the curve in Fig. 73.

ZIPF's law has been confirmed by recent studies on communication and transmission of messages (SHANNON, MANDELBROT). There exists for any system of signs an optimal distribution which permits the transfer of a maximum of information with a minimum of energy. The cost of transmission is inversely proportional to the frequency of the sign.

If text is understood here as a linguistically structured message of indifferent length (in time or space), we mean by lexicon the number of potential signs which a speaker (author, etc.) has at his disposal and a listener (reader, etc.) can refer to. We may talk of the lexicon of an individual, of a language, a dialect, a certain literary text (Hamlet, the Bible, etc.). No individual has at his disposal all the words listed in a dictionary of his language. And yet such a dictionary is never complete. (More about this in Chap. IX.) The word as an item in a dictionary has no frequency but a probability which for evident reasons is the counterpart, on the potential level, of the frequency on the level of an actualised linguistic message; thus, if p is the probability and r the rank, we get the corresponding equation $pr =$ constant, which means that the probability of the first word (p_1) is twice that of the second, three times that of the third, etc., the sum of probabilities of the whole vocabulary contained in the lexicon (L) being $= 1$, whence the equation (taken from GUIRAUD):

$$p_1\left(1 + \frac{1}{2} + \frac{1}{3} + \frac{1}{4} \cdots \frac{1}{L}\right) = 1,$$

in graphic presentation (linear vertical scale) (Fig. 74), or in (dyadic) logarithmic values (Fig. 75):

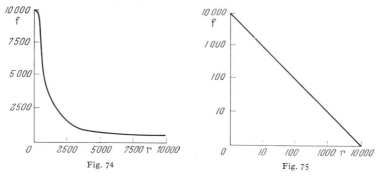

Fig. 74   Fig. 75

HERDAN's attempt to give a statistical interpretation of SAUSSURE's langue-parole distinction (Chap. I) is interesting. For HERDAN "la langue" is the total of linguistic habits, roughly the lexicon of the language (including grammatical forms). "La parole" is the individual utterance. The former consequently comprises the engrams of the language, the latter the words of actual speech. But the stability of the relative frequencies, HERDAN goes on, leads to the conclusion that "la langue" is these engrams plus their statistical probabilities of occurrence. Thus "la langue" has the essential characteristic of a statistical population. "La parole" is thus supposed to be a term for statistical samples withdrawn from "la langue" (the population). This is no doubt partly correct. But the peculiarity of human language is not exhaustively described in statistical terms. Language sets up absolute rules for what is possible and what is not. A Frenchman can oppose a final /e/ to a final /ɛ/ even if he only rarely makes use of this possibility of opposition. The statistical approach has implied a precious contribution to linguistic methods. Language has a quantitative and a frequency aspect which is part of its structure and which traditional linguistics neglected. We must, however, not go too far in the opposite direction and reduce everything in language to probabilities of occurrence.

The difference in "functional load" to which we referred in Chap. IV (Italian examples) is of course in a way a reflex of the probability of occurrence though no statistics will be able to tell us if, to a speaking individual, e.g. a given phonetic quality has a phonemic value or not (in our example, if an open Italian /ɛ/ occurring in a speech chain is felt as opposed to /e/, or as a mere variant of it). No linguistic material (text), however extensive, only the behaviour of the speakers, can give us information on this point which is essential for the linguist.

We stop this survey here, restricting ourselves to a final remark on the fact that the structure of the lexicon seems to be determined essentially by the same economy factor which also governs the structure and functioning of the expression system of language in both its aspects (as paradigms and as syntagms). The lexicon, on the content level, is a repertory of semantic units present in a speaker's brain in the same way as the phoneme system is (cp. with respect to expression units Chap. III, p. 31). The structural principle they both have in common cannot be due to chance. It confirms the glossematic idea of a parallel structuration of content and expression. Cp. hereto the quotation from LIBERMAN, p. 27.

What is valid for paradigmatic structures (see p. 96) is valid also for the syntagm. A more complex structure always supposes a simpler one. This is particularly evident in the structure of the syllable but it is not limited to this particular unit. Many languages have a reduced repertory of phonemes in unstressed syllables. No language uses more distinctions in this position than in stressed syllables. Some languages are monosyllabic. No language has words of two or more syllables without having at the same time monosyllables, and so on. Both structures — the paradigmatic and the syntagmatic — are governed by the same basic principle.

Chapter VIII
Content Analysis

A preliminary analysis of the content level of a short text was given by way of illustration in Chap. IV. The content is built up from discrete elements which, in exactly the same way as phonemes and prosodemes, have to be classified into paradigms of invariants. The procedure for establishing invariants is commutation. There is opposition between content invariants in the paradigm, and there is contrast between content units in the chain. Both the number of units and their relations are conventional and arbitrary. There are no *a priori* valid categories of content, though the particular functioning of the human mind may be supposed to restrict the possibilities to some extent, just as the acoustic and articulatory alternatives and variables do so on the expression level. Nor are there any sub-levels of analysis of the kind found in traditional grammar (no division into morphology, syntax, word-formation, semantics, etc.). The validity of such concepts has to be proved *a posteriori* for any language separately. Nothing makes their existence a necessity. All grouping of content units into functional classes or semantic fields consequently has to be looked upon as the result of an analysis of a given language system and must not *a priori* be supposed to exist in the same or a similar form in a language which has not yet been structurally described. It should be stressed that, as a consequence, terms like word, ending, prefix, suffix, parataxis, hypotaxis, substantive, verb, conjunction, tense, case, voice — all familiar to us from traditional grammar — have no raison d'être in the description unless they have proved to be appropriate denominations for structurally defined linguistic categories in the language in question. A very large number of older descriptions of exotic languages — often made by missionaries without any linguistic training — are useless scientifically because they are made on the model of classical (Greek, Latin) or traditional European grammar (English, Spanish). No grammatical structure is universal. Nor has any semantic categorisation general validity. Universal is only the basic structural principle, which remains identically the same whatever the particular linguistic structure[1].

A few examples of successive stages of analysis — passing from the most complex content units, i.e. the complete utterances, down to the

---

[1] Linguistic categories have nothing to do with logical concepts and must not be confused with them. No logical considerations, only linguistic evidence, can support a linguistic interpretation. Logical categories such as "subject" and "predicate" have nothing to do with the grammatical functions for which the same terms have sometimes been used. A general mistake in traditional linguistic description was to confuse logical and linguistic concepts.

minimal signs, and from those to the minimal expression elements —
may illustrate the general principle of how function determines, and
must necessarily determine, the definition of a given segment on both
levels of description. In the German utterances 'gehe mit mir' and
'komm mit mir', the first level of analysis becomes as follows:

$$\begin{array}{ccc} 1. & 2. & 3. \end{array} \qquad \begin{array}{ccc} 1. & 2. & 3. \end{array}$$
1. *gehe| mit| mir* and *komm| mit| mir*;

i. e. a division into three semantic units. The division may be continued,
thus[1]:

2. *gehe = geh- + e* and *komm = komm + 0*;

the verb form is consequently a complex one and may be broken down
into a stem plus an ending, which in the second of our examples is
manifested by 0 (thus *komm* is structurally complex, though formally
unmarked). The third stage of analysis must be one of expression, since
the content analysis is finished (the units arrived at being minimal
content units, or minimal signs), thus:

3. *geh-* and *-e* = /g/ + /e:/ + /ə/; *komm* = /k/ + /ɔ/ + /m/.

It should be noticed that the content unit *-e* and the expression unit
/ə/ are not identical, since the monophonemic character of the latter
unit is due to chance. There are other verb endings which contain
more than one phoneme (i.e. the imperative plural in *red-et*). The zero
morpheme of *komm* is analysed on the expression level as composed
of (a) zero phoneme(s).

If we take two corresponding Latin examples, *i mecum* and *veni
mecum* (same meaning as the German examples above), we get the
following analysis:

$$\begin{array}{ccc} 1. & 2. & 3. \end{array} \qquad \begin{array}{ccc} 1. & 2. & 3. \end{array}$$
1. *i| me-| cum   veni| me-| cum*
2. *i + 0* (cp. plur. *i| te*); *veni + 0* (cp. plur. *veni| te*)
3. /i/ (cp. /i/ + /t/ + /e/); /v/ + /ĕ/ + /n/ + /i/ (cp. /v/ + /e/ + /n/ + /i/ + /t/ + /e/).

The *i* on the three levels are, as may be seen, very different units, on
the first a complex morpheme (stem + a zero ending), on the second
a minimal morphemic unit (a stem), on the third a phoneme (opposed
to, and structurally parallel to phoneme sequences, e.g. /i/ ∼ /ite/).

---

[1] We do not take into consideration on the two following stages of the analysis
the two other semantic units, which, of course may be analysed in the same way.
Nor do we try any segmentation of the content below the sign level (into content
figurae).

Our third example is partly different, though in principle comparable. Let us imagine an emphatically pronounced answer *no!*. It is on the first level of analysis a complete syntagm:

1. *no!* (as opposed to 'yes!' or to any other "answer", emphatic or not).

This syntagm has a content and an expression. The content contains two basic elements: *negation* and *emphasis*[1], thus:

2. *no* (negation) + emphasis.

On the expression level, these two units are manifested phonemically as respectively a phoneme sequence (segmental phonemes) and a supra-segmental intonation contour, thus:

3. $/n/ + /o\widehat{u}/$ and ⟍.

The sentence *no* and the phoneme sequence $/no\widehat{u}/$, though superficially identical, are very different units structurally. The material shortness of a sequence — more apparent than real, since numerous signals may be manifested simultaneously in the spoken chain — is no indication of structural simplicity[2].

Content structure is for evident reasons more complicated than expression structure. The linguistic content is in fact the form given to the experience and to the needs of a whole speaking community, since no experience — at least if it is of some complexity — can be transmitted, no needs and no feelings expressed otherwise than in some particular linguistic form, which is the way in which the so-called reality outside us is perceived, experienced, and interpreted. Perception, experience, and interpretation are consequently identical with this linguistic form. For any perception implies an interpretation and a categorization of a continuum which can be transformed into discrete units only thanks to a procedure of linguistic quantization (already discussed in Chap. II).

When a witness reports that eight boys, three girls, two dogs, a cat, a bicycle, and a motor-cycle were to be seen in the street, this report is the result of a linguistic pattern applied on a series of "things" of which no two are absolutely identical and the grouping of which into classes (boys, dogs, bicycles, etc.) is due to linguistic convention. When talking about one of the girls he uses the sign *she* as opposed to *he* he conforms his categorization to English convention which prescribes

---

[1] These phenomena will be treated in more detail in Chap. IX.

[2] Cp. e.g. the analysis of so-called strong verb forms in Germanic languages (Engl. *brought* as 'bring' + past tense; or German *ging* as 'gehen' + past tense, *hätte* as 'hatte' + subjunctive, 'hatte' in turn as 'haben' + past tense). Cp. also the phonemic analysis of tone languages (Chap. IV, p. 91) where the result of the segmentation is no longer, as in other cases, a linear sequence of units. Nobody can tell us where, within a given word, the word tone is to be found.

a distinction, between 'masculine' and 'feminine' among "personal pronouns". That this is pure convention, not conditioned by the facts spoken of, is easily proved by e.g. Finnish, which would use the same pronoun (*hän*) for both genders. In English, both boys and girls would be spoken of in the plural by *they*, whereas in French (and in many other languages) they would be categorized even here into *ils* (masculine) and *elles* (feminine). It is not necessary *a priori* that the grouping into *boys* and *girls* would satisfy all speakers, since other categorizations, according to age or other qualities, might well seem more important to members of certain language communities. An exhaustive survey of content structures is out of the question here and therefore we must limit ourselves to a few further examples of different structuration. We start with a few so-called grammatical categories.

We have mentioned that traditional grammar is largely based on the structure of Greek and Latin. Even such a basic distinction in our grammar as that between "noun" and "verb" is far from being common to all languages[1]. There are e.g. languages which do not make any distinction between, say, 'the man is working' and 'the man's work', 'I love' and 'my love', etc.

Let us consider time dimensions as a verbal category. English and the other Germanic languages make a grammatical distinction between an action belonging to the past and one that takes place in present time: Engl. *I loved ∼ I love*. But we know that in the Romance languages, as well as in Latin, there is a more developed system with a distinction, in the past, between a limited and an unlimited action (French *je chantais ∼ je chantai*, Spanish *cantaba ∼ canté*, etc.), a system difference which may be illustrated diagrammatically as:

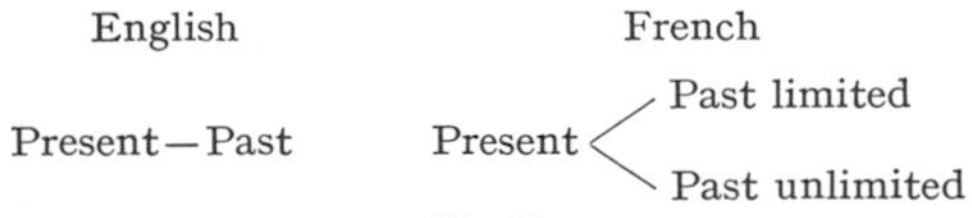

Fig. 76

On the other hand, English makes a distinction between progressive and non-progressive form which is often without any counterpart in French, i.e. the difference between *I sing* and *I am singing*, which is not found in French but is well-established in Spanish (*estoy cantando* 'I am singing', *estaba cantando* 'I was singing'). It is important to notice that these differences of structure do not imply that other languages, which do not have the categories in question, would necessarily be without any possibility of expressing the ideas in question. But they have

---

[1] Where it exists (in all languages belonging to Western civilisation), its validity has to be proved by means of formal criteria, not on the basis of any logical prejudice.

to use other, more analytic structures for this purpose, i.e. they have to compensate for the restrictions in the paradigm by extending the chain of lexical items (Engl. *I was singing*, French *j'étais en train de chanter*)[1]. Certain languages have elaborate systems of aspects (the way in which an action is considered, as finished, as going on, as repeated, etc.) but no real system of tenses (of time relations).

Some languages lack grammatical "persons" (*I ∼ you*, etc.). In Ainou — a language which, according to a recent theory put forward by PIERRE NAERT, is possibly related to the Indo-European stock — there is a "personal" pronoun which is indifferent as to grammatical "person" (meaning 'I', 'you', 'he' etc. indifferently). On the other hand, there are languages which make more distinctions than we do. Guaraní, the native language of Paraguay and adjacent regions of Brazil and Argentina, has as the plural of 'I' two pronouns, one meaning 'I and you', the other 'I and he', or schematized:

English		Guaraní	
Sing.	Plur.	Sing.	Plur.
'I' — 'we'		'I' < 'I and you' / 'I and he' (etc.)	

Fig. 77

English lost the distinction between singular and plural in the second person, when the old singular forms *thou, thee, thy* etc. became obsolete (modern *you* being indifferent as to number). Nor does English make the distinction common to a whole series of other modern European languages[2] between intimate and formal (respectful) address (French *tu ∼ vous*, Germ. *du ∼ Sie*, Spanish *tú ∼ usted*, etc.), which does not, as anybody knows, mean that English-speaking people cannot make any difference between a respectful and a familiar way of addressing people, only that there is no special linguistic form category reserved for such functions. What a German expresses by using respectively *du* and *Sie*, may be expressed in English for instance by adding or not adding *sir*, or by the use of *Mr, Mrs* or some other title as opposed to the mere name (the family name or the first name, etc.). But even in languages which have this distinction of address, the linguistic form

---

[1] In the same way, languages without grammatical tense can of course express differences of time by saying that an action took place yesterday, last year, or that it will take place tomorrow, next year, etc. The use of corresponding expressions even in languages which have tenses often implies extensive redundancy and in reality considerably restricts the communicative importance of the categories in question, in exactly the same way as redundancy, on the expression level, reduces the operative importance of the distinctive features.

[2] In certain non-European languages there are much more complicated systems of address.

mostly has an opposition between just two types: 'intimate' versus 'respectful', whereas the differences of relationship between people (i.e. the content substance) constitute an endless continuum of innumerable variations and nuances.

The series of numbers, to take another example, is equally unlimited: 1, 2, 3, 4, ... The grammatical categories referring to number are in most languages restricted to two: 'singular' ~'plural' ('one' ~'more than one', Engl., *boy* ~ *boys*). Some languages, however, distinguish between 'one' ~'two' ~'more than two' ('singular' ~'dual' ~'plural'), and a few have one or two further categories. To the unlimited continuum of extralinguistic "facts" correspond a restricted number of discrete conventional, linguistically patterned categories.

If we say that gender is irrelevant in Finnish but not in German or in French this only implies that differences of that kind are not reflected in the linguistic categorisation of the Finnish language as they are (in different ways) in French and in German. Indications of gender consequently are distinctive in the latter languages (Germ. *der See* ~ *die See*, French *le livre* ~ *la livre*). Morphologically rich languages such as Latin or German often give instances of extreme redundancy, in traditional grammar called c o n g r u e n c y (Latin *mei boni veteris patris*, but Engl. *my good old father's*, with only one indication of the genitive case where Latin has four; or Germ. *gute Bücher*, French *de bons livres* as compared with Engl. *good books*). Morphemic richness is a condition for the free word order found in Latin. Where Latin could have indifferently (though with nuances of style) *Petrus amat Paulum* or *Paulum amat Petrus* with the functions of the words implied in their form, French has only *Pierre aime Paul*. A change into *Paul aime Pierre* results in a different meaning, the same change as is brought about in Latin by an exchange of endings (*Petrum* and *Paulus*). If English words were put together in the order the corresponding words have in a literary Latin period, the result in most cases would become complete nonsense, because of the lack of indications of the relations between the units expressed by the Latin endings, which consequently, though they are redundant in such isolated groups as the one quoted above, may become strong cues to identification of the meaning in longer utterances. It is instructive to make a comparison with redundant e x p r e s s i o n phenomena and their role in perception (Chap. III and V). The mechanism of content form consequently functions in roughly the same way as the expression mechanism.

A few examples taken from the sphere of family relationships will afford sufficient evidence for the statement that not only grammatical forms but also our vocabulary are due to social conventions and consequently reflect the world as we experience it. No system is more natural, or more logical, than any other. The choice between possibilities and combinations is free and arbitrary (at least from the point of view of the language, but certainly not from the point of view of the social structure of which language is a part).

In Indo-European languages there is mostly one single concept 'brother' and consequently one word (Engl. *brother*, Germ. *Bruder*, Latin *frater*, French *frère*, etc., all of which are genetically related). This is so in many other languages belonging to other linguistic families (Finnish *veli*, Turkish *kardaş*, 'brother'). But most languages of the Far East (Tibetan, Japanese, Korean, Malay, Tamil, etc.) use entirely different words for 'elder brother' and for 'younger brother' and consequently do not know any category 'brother' independently of the distinction of (relative) age. It may even happen that the distinction of age seems more important than that of sex. Malay does not make any distinction between 'brother' and 'sister' but differentiates according to age. The existence in German and Scandinavian of a word meaning 'brothers and sisters' (Germ. *Geschwister*, Swedish *syskon*) and formed on the same root as the word for 'sister' (Germ. *Schwester*, Swedish *syster*) is supposed to be due to the important social status of women in ancient times, whereas the use of the indifferent Spanish *padres* (plural of *padre* 'father') for 'parents', *hermanos* for 'brothers and sisters', *hijos* for 'children' and even *reyes* for 'the King and the Queen' (*los Reyes Católicos* = Ferdinand and Isabelle) indicates a masculine dominance in the social hierarchy in question (still perceptible). In Russian, the 'son-in-law' and the 'sister's husband' belong to the same class (constitute one concept), whereas the 'husband's brother' is a different concept. The word 'brother-in-law' in English cannot be translated into Russian without a change of meaning. The Russian translation will not give the same information as the English original. Similar differences, but on a partly different level (distinctions of politeness), are reported in descriptions of Japanese, where two sets of family words have to be used according to their relation to the speaker or the interlocutor. 'Father' is said to be *chichi* in Japanese when the speaker's own father is being referred to, but *otōsama* when the other person's father is being spoken of. In the same way, *musume* is said to be 'my daughter' and *ojōsan* 'your daughter'. The last few examples thus illustrate a basic difference of language structure. Both English and Japanese can express the same differences of meaning, but they do it differently — English by using compounds made up of independent elements ('my' + 'daughter', i. e. a morphological element + a semantic unit). Japanese by using two unanalysable units ("words")[1]. The natives of the South

---

[1] I do not take into account here the possible analysis of the Japanese words into smaller elements of a different character.

Sea island of Ponape are reported to have five words for 'brother' but none for 'father', a situation which evidently reflects a matriarchal social structure in which the identity of the father is unimportant.

Colour denominations are often quoted as typical examples of the arbitrariness of the content form. A West-African language (Ewe) is said to have one concept (word) *amã*, covering a field of the colour spectrum which in our languages is split up into 'blue' and 'green'. The same Hebrew word (*šāhōr*) is said to "mean" 'black' and 'brown'. Swedish 'violet' was originally a variant of 'brown' — a system still noticeable in the names of violet flowers. The introduction of the new (borrowed) word implied a restructuration of the semantic paradigm (cp. Chap. XII). Another example of the same kind has been given in Fig. 78. See also Fig. 79.

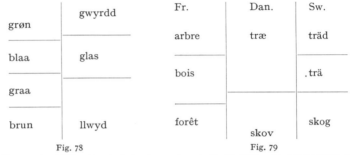

Fig. 78   Fig. 79

Fig. 78. An example of different content structure: colours in Danish (*left*) and in Cymric (*right*). The field covered in Danish, as in English, by four categories (green—blue—grey—brown) is covered in Cymric only by three which consequently partly overlap with the Danish ones

Fig. 79. Different semantic structures: (*left*) the French system (identical with the English system) with three; (*right*) the Swedish system with three, one of which overlaps with the French concept; (*in the middle*) the Danish system with two concepts, one of which covers two Swedish units, the other the third Swedish concept

The examples given above have illustrated the concept of content form. Such categories as tense, number, case, gender, different family relations or colour denominations (cp. Fig. 78) reflect different possibilities of forming the continuum of the "reality". The meanings covered by these different concepts have to be looked upon as content substance. This is one of the principles of glossematic theory. The meaning, on the content level, corresponds to the sounds on the expression level. Not everyone has found it easy to accept the glossematic principle of independence between form and substance on the content level, and, to the present author at least, the content substance seems to be of importance for the description of content form. We must refrain from discussing this problem any further in this context.

We also have to take into consideration, when analysing the content substance (the meaning), the very important distinction established between denotative meaning and connotative meaning, or connotations. The latter are intimately connected with the extra-linguistic context and with the experience of the interlocutors (cp. Chap. II). The connotations are of extreme importance for the choice between so called synonyms, which is one of the essential procedures of style. The words *bicycle* and *bike* have the "same meaning" if only the denotative function is taken into consideration. But they evoke different reactions in the listener and reflect different attitudes in the speaker[1]. One is colloquial, the other technical, literary, or even archaic. If a boy is talking about his *dad* or about his *father*, he means the same person. His attitude towards his father, or towards his listener or the social surrounding in which he is speaking, may, however, be very different, if he chooses one or the other of the two "synonyms". In the language system (in this case the vocabulary) there is an opposition between *father* and *dad* (just as there is one between *father* and *mother*). But whereas the distinction[2] between *father* and *mother* is one of deno-tation, the content substance consequently belonging to the symbolic level or language, the distinction between the former terms is one of connotation. The content substance forms part of the symptom level of linguistic communication. The choice of one or the other of the two words under discussion does not tell us very much about the "thing meant" (the father), but a lot about the speaker and his relations to his "social context". The opposition between *father* and *dad* is a counterpart, on the content level, to the opposition between French /epuvãtabl/ and /ep:uvãtabl/ on the expression level (see Chap. IX, p. 160).

As two persons never have exactly the same experience and their social context differs in at least some respects, it follows that the con-notative meaning of a word is never exactly the same for two speakers. This difference was symbolized by the two circles, only partly covering each other, in Fig. 3 (the communication process) in Chap. II.

In the same way as the independence of the minimal expression units was proved by examples from linguistic interference (see the ex-amples quoted in Chaps. V and VI), it is possible to give evidence for the same interpretation on the content level. Even completely naive speakers (children etc.) seem to be quite aware of the complexity of the chains they use and analyse them into their minimal constituents. It may be of some interest to quote a few examples from the author's

---

[1] The denotative meaning consequently belongs to the symbolic function of language (in BÜHLER's sense) whereas the connotations function as signals or as symptoms.

[2] Cp. for the terminology, Chap. IV.

own experience of a four year old Finnish girl gradually learning to speak Swedish in a completely Swedish-speaking milieu[1]. The least astonishing of the phenomena in her first attempts to imitate the language of her surrounding was her lack of feeling for the extension of the semantic field of a word (a sofa was called a bench, etc.). That she made a real analysis into morphemes (stems and endings) of the chains heard and imitated was proved by numerous examples of which I quote a few. Finnish is a typical case-language (15 cases) without prepositions, but with a series of "postpositions" governing the preceding substantive in the genitive (*isän kanssa* 'with father', *isän* gen. of *isä*). The Finnish girl during a long period used Finnish postpositions governing Swedish words in the genitive (the Swedish genitive-ending -*s*!), e.g. *pappas kanssa* 'with papa'. Later she could replace the Finnish postposition by the corresponding Swedish preposition but retain the Finnish construction: *vagnens under* 'under the wagon' (Swedish *under vagnen*, Finnish *vaunun alla*; Fin. *vaunu*- 'wagon', Sw. *vagnen* 'the wagon'). The construction is Finnish content form manifested through Swedish morphemes. Without a strong feeling for the morphemic independency of both the Finnish and the Swedish genitive-ending, the girl would not have been able to identify them and to create this hybrid construction (which can be understood only by people acquainted with both languages). Interference of content structures is often referred to as calque. It may be due to a substratum or to a superstratum language. Lapps or Finns in the North of Sweden often use *han* (Sw. 'he') indifferently for 'he' and 'she' in their Swedish (a calque on the Finnish undifferentiated *hän* or its Lapp counterpart).

The diversity of content structure on the form level, and the distinctions of connotative meaning on the substance level examined here may seem at first sight to be mere theoretical curiosities without any really serious consequences for human communication. And in so far as phenomena like Finnish *hän* for both masculine and feminine, or the distinction between elder and younger brothers in the Far East are concerned, this judgement may be justified. But if we examine thouroughly all the implications of the fact that any concept, within any sphere of human activity, is to the same extent conventional and, as such, arbitrary, we shall immediately understand that they must have rather serious consequences for international, or interlinguistic, contacts. The most important of these consequences is that people do not think in the same way in different languages. For if thinking means a particular way of handling concepts and ideas, pronouncing judgements about

[1] She was one of the numerous Finnish children who during the last war were brought over to Sweden from Finland.

them, interpreting reactions towards them, drawing conclusions from them, and so on, it follows that two different sets of concepts necessarily also imply two different ways of thinking (of feeling, and so on). Translation from one language to another becomes, in principle, impossible. The English *morning* can be translated literally into French *matin* but not into Swedish, which makes a distinction between the earlier hours (*morgon*) and the later hours of the time from six to twelve (*förmiddag*). Any choice between the two Swedish terms implies a specification of the information which is foreign to the original text. A French "imperfect" (imparfait, say *il lisait le journal*), when translated into a Germanic language, has to be rendered by a form which is not opposed, as in French, to a "perfect" tense and consequently covers a larger semantic field[1]. The mere fact that certain sciences (mathematics, logic) have created a special language of formulae proves the incapacity of ordinary linguistic signs to cover the special abstract concepts with which these sciences — independently of particular linguistic structures — operate. The reason why French was for centuries the international diplomatic language and why Latin still is the language of the Roman Catholic Church, is to be found in the need for a definitely fixed set of concepts. It should be added that the existence, in the languages belonging to Western civilisation, of a series of terms and concepts mostly taken over from Greek or Latin — abstract ideas, technical, and scientific terms, denominations for new inventions — strongly diminishes the disadvantages of this diversity of content structure within the Western hemisphere. The existence of such a super-structure of content is an important factor in linguistic communication. This is so not only because it makes foreign language learning easier within this larger unit. It also facilitates translation and reduces the difficulty of adapting a given content substance to different semantic forms. The whole width of the semantic problem becomes evident only when comparisons are established between languages belonging to different civilisations (Western and Chinese, etc.). The negative consequences for human communication of these discrepancies can hardly be underestimated. Long ago WILHELM VON HUMBOLDT — the great German humanist (who died in 1835) — warned his readers against the popular conception of words as mere labels put arbitrarily on pre-existing things. Word formation is identical with concept formation, when seen in the light of SAUSSURE's description of the linguistic sign.

---

[1] As we said above, this of course does not imply that the "poorer" language is incapable of expressing the "idea" wanted, only that it has to use other, more complicated procedures (the Swedish *förmiddag* may of course be translated into English by *the later part of the morning*, the French "unlimited tense" by a periphrastic expression, etc.).

Differences of religious or political ideology also have consequences for communication. What does 'democracy' mean? We know how differently this concept is understood within different areas of the modern world. Linguistically the "correct" meaning can of course not be defined[1]. One interpretation of the concept is as right or as wrong as any other. This may serve as a final illustration of the fact that a message is not transferred in its entirety only by a literal rendering of the "words" contained in it. There is no doubt that numerous difficulties in human intercourse — on the personal as well as on the political, the religious, the scientific and other levels — are due only to lack of insight into the peculiarities of linguistic structure and semantic analysis. A psychiatrical movement has been based on the assumption — no doubt correct in principle — that certain psychological difficulties might be overcome if people could get rid of certain connotations which they personally attach to the words of their language. LOUIS HJELMSLEV has expressed the opinion that the so-called iron curtain is a semantic frontier with different content substance attached to the words on either side. The increasing discrepancy of content substance on both sides of this ideological and political frontier has been studied recently in the German language as used in East and in West Germany.

It seems evident to the present author that the different levels of abstraction distinguished in the expression analysis in Chap. V are valid also on the content level and that, consequently, the role of substance (i.e. of meaning) becomes the more reduced, the higher the degree of abstraction chosen by the investigator. It might be theoretically possible to establish content units without any reference to meaning, that is in the last instance without referring to our extra-linguistic experience at all. In most cases the procedure — if possible — would probably not be very convenient. EINAR HAUGEN has been right in pointing out the importance of our non-linguistic experience for the identification of content units.

It should be added that, even if it is true that the so-called reality inside or outside ourselves is perceived and interpreted only thanks to some pattern superimposed on it and in the form this pattern gives to it, we must not forget, on the other hand, that linguistic structures are not the only possible structures we can stick to. There are other categories which may be taken into use for our interpretation and which, for certain purposes, are more convenient. Let us first mention as an example the controversy that may arise between a scientific classification (and nomenclature) and current every-day categories as reflected

---

[1] It is evident that reference to the "original", etymological meaning does not help. This meaning is very often completely obscured.

in the ordinary language system. A Swedish fisherman makes a clear-cut distinction between 'fish' and 'herring' as two independent groups and would never dream of calling a herring a fish. Not so the zoologist. Such examples can be multiplied. Specialized scientific and technical terminology has become a necessity, since every-day classifications are dependent on language conventions and as such are inconvenient to the specialist. The fact that, in so many cases, we are aware of differences and distinctions which are not reflected in our linguistic content structure, is easily explained by our acquaintance with other structures and other principles of categorisation than the linguistic one. This, however, does not prevent linguistic conventions from playing a primordial part in human thinking, from which they can be eliminated only by means of a conscious intellectual effort to replace them by other sets of patterns. It is doubtful if man is ever completely successful in this effort.

Chapter IX

The Functions of Language

The schematic representation of the communicative process set up in Chap. II implied a considerable simplification on one important point, which we shall have to discuss further in this chapter. It concerns the relations between sender and receiver on the one hand, and the so-called extra-linguistic phenomena to be communicated on the other. It is a popular and simplified idea of a linguistic situation that this implies just a transfer of information about something (a thing, an event, a "fact") from a sender to a receiver. *A* says this about that (*C*) to *B*, or *B* is informed about *C* by *A*. This conception of linguistic communication is not only a simplification. It may be misleading, since it is far from certain that this simplified process, on all levels of human language — synchronic and diachronic —, expresses the primary, dominating, or most general function of human language at the different stages of its development, and since, under such conditions, the scientific approach to the analysis of linguistic communication may in some respects be incorrectly biased.

When a child begins to utter its first intentional sounds (not phonemes!), it either wants to express its own feelings (of discontent, satisfaction, etc.), or to obtain a reaction from somebody else (to take it up, to give it food, etc.). The utterance is a symptom of something within the speaking individual, or a signal to a listener. Only at a later stage does the child use its sounds as symbols of things or events. In fact, any message from individual to individual — independently of its form — has a triadic relation 1. to the "thing meant" (the phenomenon outside the speaker which is communicated from A to B), 2. to the speaker (sender), and 3. to the listener (receiver). We can say with KARL BÜHLER that the message is at the same time a symbol of something outside the two interlocutors, a symptom of something within the sender, and a signal to the receiver. These three functions as defined by BÜHLER have nothing to do with the question of whether the message is intentional or unintentional, i.e. whether it is meant as a symptom, or meant as a signal. Nor has it anything to do with the effects resulting from the message, i.e. whether a signal is followed by an intended, or unintended reaction, or whether the receiver is actually informed about the state

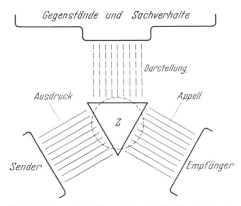

of the speaker as reflected in the symptom, etc. Even a zero-function is in this context a function.

BÜHLER's triadic schematization of the linguistic functions is illustrated by the graph seen in Fig. 80.

As a complete description, from a psychological point of view, of the communicative functions involved in a speech or other communicative situation, BÜHLER's scheme is probably too simplified, and

Fig. 80. BÜHLER's triadic model: *on top* the "facts" referred to; *to the left* the sender; *to the right* the receiver. Darstellung = symbol, Ausdruck = symptom, Appell = signal

other writers (KAINZ, UNGE-HEUER, etc.) have proposed important modifications which, however, have to be neglected here for reasons of space. And it is a matter of fact that, in its original form, BÜHLER's system has proved extremely useful as a tool in linguistic analysis. We shall give a few examples by way of illustration.

When the linguistic content, as defined above (Chaps. I and IV), is analysed, or when the relation between expression and content is used in order to define linguistic units in the commutation test, "content" and "change in the content" are normally used only with reference to BÜHLER's symbol function. Engl. $/b/$ and $/m/$ are two phonemes because they support a distinction of meaning in e.g. *bad ~ mad*. This is a difference in the symbolic function (sometimes called "lexical meaning") of the item. But if in the French word *épouvantable* the normal, short $/p/$ ($/epuvãtabl/$) is replaced by a long $[p:]$, the "lexical meaning" remains unaltered. The symbolic function remains the same. But the utterance becomes the symptom of an emotional state in the speaker and may have a particular effect on the receiver. The $[p:]$ becomes distinctive on this level, and the distinction /p/ ∼ /p:/ may be looked upon as phonemic for the symptom and signal functions of language (early emphasized by J. von Laziczius who proposed the term "emphaticum" for that kind of "phonemes").

We must, however, make an important distinction which may have seemed irrelevant to Bühler and actually is so from a purely psychological point of view, but which is fundamental if our approach to human communication is a linguistic one. The symptom and signal effects may be due either to conventional, linguistically determined means of expression (i.e. the length of the /p/ in our French example) and consequently be conditioned by a linguistic pattern, or they may be due to non-linguistic, non-conventional modes of expression of general validity.

Instances of the latter case are certain voice characteristics which, independently of the language used, indicate a state or a quality in the speaker. We can, at least to a certain extent, hear whether a speaker is happy or unhappy, sane or sick, angry or kind, etc., even if we do not understand his language[1]. In other cases, however, we may be mistaken and interpret for instance certain intonation patterns according to our own habits. Misunderstandings of this kind are numerous between people speaking different dialects of the same language (English and American), or closely related languages, such as Swedish and Norwegian. If we call such dialects or languages "mutually understandable" this often means just that the symbolic function is understood, whereas the signal and symptom functions — so important for the personal relations between speakers — are partly or totally misinterpreted. We have a tendency to ascribe to those non-symbolic means of expression a more general validity than they actually have. The same is true e.g. for gestures and mimicry. On the other hand it is a fact that numerous so-called stylistic features may be common to different — even historically unrelated — languages and consequently not necessarily be bound to a given code. It is e.g. well-known that classical and biblical patterns have to a large extent determined the literary style of most European languages, and also that these languages have influenced each other. Such phenomena as predilection for long or short periods, for parataxis or hypotaxis, for verbal or nominal expressions (cf. Chap. II, p. 19) are to a large extent independent of the grammatical structure and may be classed as super-linguistic (as opposed to the purely extra-linguistic means of content referred to above).

To the non-symbolic level of communication consequently belongs all that which is generally called style, with its corresponding scientific

---

[1] A systematic analysis of such non-linguistic means of expression and their physiological basis have been carried out by Felix Trojan who has given striking examples of their general validity.

analysis stylistics. Style has been defined as the use that a speaker or writer makes of the resources put at his disposal by the language system taken in its widest sense. An individual style may be determined as a particular variation of these resources and consequently be expressed in terms of frequency and distribution, i.e. in a statistical form. Much research work has been carried out in later years along these lines in order to determine the characteristics of the style of famous authors or literary works. The methods referred to in Chap. VII have been applied with much success for such purposes. The curve in Fig. 74 is an objective measure of one particular aspect of the "style" of an author (his vocabulary). The style and the stylistic particularities — of an individual or of a group of speakers (writers) — may concern the expression level or the content level of the sign or sign complexes. In the first case, it may consist in a particular, intentional choice of phonemes (for sound symbolism etc. in poetry), of prosodic patterns or variations of them, of syntagmatic structures (long or short groups, linking, etc.), or in a particular way of manifesting phonetically the different units (slow or rapid, distinct or slurred articulation, small or wide ranges of pitch and loudness, a peculiar pronounciation of certain phonemes, e.g. apical or velar r, etc.). In the second case, there may be variation of forms, of syntax, and of word formation (e.g. between colloquial and refined modes of expression, archaisms, vulgarisms, dialectalisms, etc.) and, particularly, in the choice of vocabulary, which is, of course, one of the essential means of stylistic variation. But as the choice of words is at the same time, and necessarily, a choice of concepts and ideas, this part of stylistics leads us into fields of analysis and research which are not, according to traditional views, exclusively the concern of linguistics. We refer to Chap. VIII and to the Introduction, p. 2.

It must be stressed that there are important structural differences between the symbolic level of language and the other levels. Human communication relies to a much larger extent on extra-linguistic means of contact for the latter functions than for the symbolic function, where an extreme degree of arbitrariness almost excludes any other association between content and expression than the one which is due to convention (except for some, relatively very few, sound-imitating words). This means that the limit between linguistic (conventionally structured) and extra-linguistic communication here becomes clear-cut. The signal and symptom functions rely on less strictly structured means of communication, in which the limit between arbitrariness (convention) and motivation (sound imitation, etc.) is vague or inexistent.

When some writers (JAKOBSON-HALLE, etc.) hold that expressive features are not discrete, this seems, at least to the present author, a definite exaggeration. Their degree of discreteness, of course, depends to a certain extent on their degree of arbitrariness, i.e. on the extent to which they are conventional. For discreteness is a method of securing arbitrariness (as was pointed out in Chap. I) and of excluding sound imitation. The conventional character of expressive and sound imitating features of language, however, has often been underestimated. We only need to think of how arbitrary even definitely onomatopoeic formations actually are in our languages (Engl. *cockedoodledo*, Germ. *Kirikiki*, or French *cocou*, Finnish *käki*, etc.). Most of the instances of continuity quoted from this level of human communication are undoubtedly due to a lack of exhaustive description and to the investigator's negligence to make a strict separation between the different linguistic functions as defined and distinguished by Bühler. A good example of a continuous sound symbol of an extremely conventionalized character is the repetition of apicodental click-sounds which are used in Argentina in order to attract the attention of restaurant waiters or tram conductors and which are understood only by members of the linguistic group in question. This sound-symbol is not at all linguistically structured.

One of the most difficult fields of phonetic analysis is the one concerned with sentence intonation, where the lack of exhaustiveness, in the description, on account of confusion of functions and levels, has often been particularly apparent. The reason for this is that all the varying attitudes of the speaker — which appear physically manifested in the same fundamental frequency curve containing not only the normal symbolic linguistic oppositions of statement versus question, etc. but sometimes also grammatical and semantic oppositions of word accent — are expressed partly by conventional melodic patterns on the symptom level, partly by intonation contours of an extra-linguistic or super-linguistic character. Only by means of careful analytic, synthetic, and perceptional methods is it possible to arrive at acceptable results within this field. Without the tool offered by Bühler's distinction of linguistic functions, this task would be impossible. A methodologically important investigation along these lines has recently been carried out by Kerstin Hadding-Koch (on Swedish material).

Versification and, more generally, poetic patterns (rhyme, number of syllables or stresses, alternation of stress or of length, etc.) give us extreme instances of (artificial) stylistic patterning. The metric form reduces the choice of expressions but at the same time provides the poet with expressive, emotional, and signalling effects which are never used in the same systematic way in normal conversation. But it is important to underline that these effects are always, and necessarily, based on phonemic procedures which are relevant in the normal phoneme system of the language. Allophonic sound differences are not utilized for metrical purposes. Rhyme and alliteration imply identity between phonemes, not between allophones. Only in languages with a phonemic length do we meet a metrical system based on quantitative variations (Greek, Latin). When the classical meters have been applied to modern languages, length has had to be replaced by stress. Word-tones are used metrically in languages which use word-tones, but only there, which means that contextual melody variations cannot be used in verse[1,2].

Poetry may be looked upon as a kind of reminiscence of an early, primitive function of human language. Its rhythmical, sound-imitating and sound-symbolizing character — indicating the prevalence of emotion and expressivity — reminds us of the relationship of language with religious rites and usages and of its role as a social factor in collective work and joint efforts. Ethnologists have given us numerous examples of the preservation of these primitive functions, in which language, poetry and song form an indivisible unity. Rhythm, duration, sound symbolism, melodic and dynamic effects are still the chosen medium of poets. They are also the most important expression variables for the functions of language which BÜHLER called signal and symptom. This can hardly be due to chance[3].

Chapter X

Perception and Linguistic Interpretation[4]

Perception is based on a whole chain of physiological events, from the peripheric organ which registers the stimulus to the centre in the brain where it is identified and interpreted as this or that sensation (of heat, of taste, of sight, or of audition). Although we take into consideration only auditory stimuli in this context and, in principle, limit our interest to such auditory stimuli as are connected in some way or other

[1] Word-tones are not necessarily used metrically in languages where they exist. In Scandinavian, words with different word accents are allowed to rhyme though good poets often seem to avoid it. In African poetry, word tones are often used as a basis for versification.

[2] There are of course instances of metrical systems based on an earlier phonemic system and now retained as an archaism. This is for instance the case in French.

[3] It should be added that there is no absolute limit between poetry and prose and that certain writers, even when writing prose, use a very personal rhythm (E. SIEVER's so-called "Schallanalyse" was based on this assumption). During certain epochs, "rhythmical prose" was a literary mode (late Latin).

[4] This chapter is only intended as a brief survey and summary of the problems in question. The essential facts have already been treated in the preceding chapters (particularly Chap. III).

with organized human communication, or more precisely with linguistically formed messages, we can formulate a generally valid statement
about perception by saying that in no case is this activity a purely
physiological one, nor even neurophysiological. Any act of perception
is intimately tied up with the perceiver's background, i.e. his anterior
experiences, his memory, and his attitudes. "Perception involves an
act of categorization. Put in terms of the antecedent and subsequent
conditions from which we make our inference, we stimulate an organism
with some appropriate input and he responds by inferring the input
to some class of things or events" (BRUNER). What we want to stress
here first of all is the concept of categorization.

The segmentation of the continuous sound-wave described in connection with the communicative process, and the scheme in Chap. II,
implied a quantization and supposed a discrete character of the elements
of which the linguistic message is built up. If this quantization is not
carried out by the listener, the linguistic, and therefore also the informative, character of the message is lost, and the continuous sound-wave
is heard as the complex of tones and noises which, physically speaking,
it is. If at certain points, this quantization is wrongly made, the receiver
is mistaken, partly or completely. Consequently, a perfect reception
mechanism is a first and necessary condition for auditory and linguistic
perception, but it is not the only one, and if the remaining conditions
fail, no reception mechanism, however perfect it may be, can secure a
satisfactory perception.

Certain measurements have been made recently in order to measure
the information capacity of the human ear, by computing the number
of discriminable sound patterns per second under application of the
Shannon theory (cp. Chap. III). For it is important to observe that the
ear can make out only a finite number of distinguishable stimuli per
unit of time. In an article by HOMER JACOBSON, a maximum rate of
10^4 bits/sec transmission is reported (for bits, cp. Chap. III, p.32). The
author also shows that the brain can utilize less than 1 per cent of
the information transmitted by the ear. Listening is to an astonishingly
large extent a selective activity.

Interpretation, which is the second stage in the perception process,
equals identification of the registered stimuli with one of the units in
the paradigm which the listener has at his disposal. The effect of the
stimulus is consequently due to a pattern. The expression level of language is a very rigidly categorized field of human behaviour. So are the
morphological and syntactical levels on the content level too, the purely
semantic level far less. We have pointed out above (Chap. IX) that the
symbolic function supposes a more strictly structured message than
the other (signal and symptom) functions of language. This explains

why the form of the pattern is much more decisive for the final effect
of perception — i.e. for identification and understanding — on the
phonemic level than outside this particular sphere, and that perception
as such becomes the more "physiological", the less conventionalized
the perceived object is linguistically or socially. The perception of a
flowering meadow will obviously be much more dependent on conventional structuration and classification in the brain of a botanist than
in a scientifically naive observer. With the systematic grouping into
classes and species, some of the richness of the continuous variation gets
lost. Cp. hereto the reaction of aphasics to colours (Chap. XI). We shall

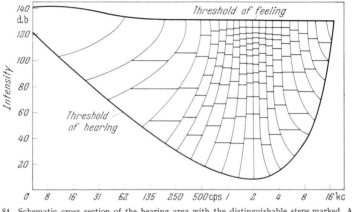

Fig. 81. Schematic cross section of the hearing area with the distinguishable steps marked. According to
JACOBSON

limit ourselves to a few remarks on the perception and identification
of strictly linguistic stimuli.

We have to consider the role of the following factors in the perception process:

1. The physiological reaction of the human ear, i.e. the audible
area (as shown in Chap. III, Fig. 42), and the possible discriminatory
steps (as shown in the data given in Fig. 81).

2. The structure of the expression pattern imposed on
the continuous sound-wave, i.e. the number of alternative units present
in the receiver's mind, thanks to which certain "points in the pattern"
are registered, others passed over (note that structure here refers to
paradigmatic as well as to syntagmatic relations, to oppositions and to
distribution [or expression context]).

3. The content context, i.e. the implications of word-form, of
sentence form (morphological and syntactic structure), and of "meaning"
in the widest sense of the word, i.e. the non-linguistic situation in which
the message is sent (reference to logic, to psychology, to the social

situation, to the experiences of sender and receiver). Factor no.1 is responsible for the auditory reaction of the receiver in the sense that the stimulus gives rise to a listening (discriminatory) attitude and thereby creates a communicative situation. If this situation is completely lacking (complete deafness or complete lack of mechanical transmission), no linguistic communication (on an auditory basis) will

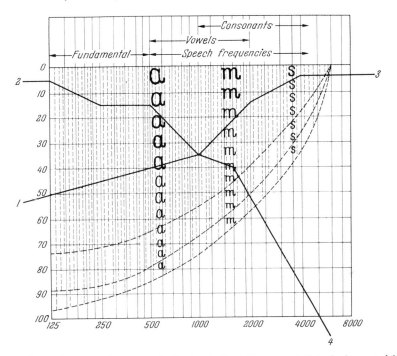

Fig. 82. The audible area and speech sounds. The lines indicate different types of hearing loss: 1–3, defective conduction (resulting in strongly reduced hearing capacity for low frequencies, almost normal for high tones); 2–4, nerve defect with strong reduction of the high frequencies (particularly typical of the consonant noises) but almost normal hearing of the fundamental frequencies (speech melody and low vowel formants). The latter type of defect has much more desastrous effects on speech perception, since consonants are more important than vowels for the identification of speech units. This implies that for hard of hearing persons of the latter category formant transitions may become an important cue to consonant distinctions and thus to the perception of speech. The so-called *auditory training* is based on these facts. Cp. Chap. III

take place. Factor no.2 is decisive for the linguistic reaction of the receiver, who, if the correct code is used, will identify the sound-wave as a specimen of a known language. It implies segmentation and categorization. Finally factor no.3 is responsible for the adequacy of the receiver's reaction. It decides whether he will "understand" the message or not, i.e. if the message received will be identical with the message sent — or, say, as identical as it is possible in view of the differences illustrated in Fig. 3, Chap. II.

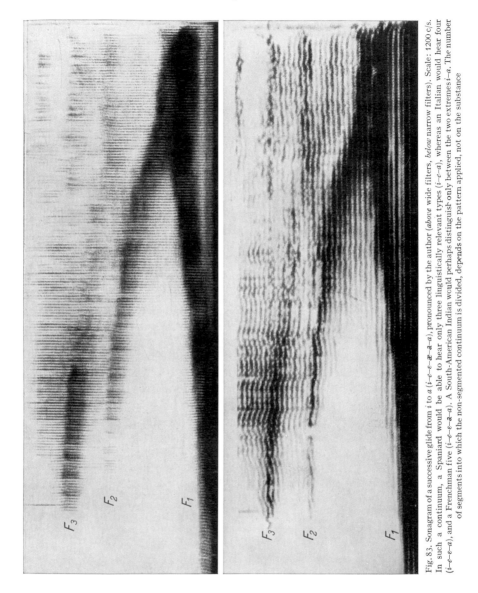

Fig. 83. Sonagram of a successive glide from *i* to *a* (*i–ι–ɛ–æ–a–ɑ*), pronounced by the author (*above* wide filters, *below* narrow filters). Scale: 1200 c/s. In such a continuum, a Spaniard would be able to hear only three linguistically relevant types (*i–ɛ–a*), whereas an Italian would hear four (*i–ɛ–ɛ–a*), and a Frenchman five (*i–ɛ–ɛ–æ–a*). A South-American Indian would perhaps distinguish only between the two extremes *i–a*. The number of segments into which the non-segmented continuum is divided, depends on the pattern applied, not on the substance

An experiment illustrating the role of factors 2 and 3 will be quoted as an instance, out of numerous others, of a perception test undertaken to examine the role of these parameters for the identification process. A listening test was undertaken with three series of phoneme combinations (here called "words"), the first containing existing English words, the second phoneme combinations which are possible but non-existant in English (English "not-words"), and the third combinations which are impossible in English ("non-English syllables"). The results were in general the following (according to ROGER W. BROWN and DONALD C. HILDUM): identification of English words was easier than that of English "not-words" and easier for these than for "non-English syllables" (mean values of identification from almost 70 per cent for the first type down to 9 per cent for the last type, with untrained listeners; linguistically trained listeners in that case had much better results: about 40 per cent, evidently because they were acquainted with other codes and could identify a number of combinations as existing phonemic combinations in languages they had studied).

i — y — ɯ — u	
Spanish	2 units
French	3 units
Swedish	4 units

Fig. 84. Within a continuous series of increasing flatting (see Fig. 63) of the vowel colour — here indicated arbitrarily by means of four steps — different languages distinguish a different number of categories (vowel phonemes). For the four Swedish phonemes, cp. Fig. 30 (Chap. III)

People's reaction to foreign speech sounds gives another kind of evidence for the role played by the pattern in the perception process. We have already given a few examples of this kind of "incorrect"

1. *Japanese:*	club > kurabu
	film > hirumu
	Christ > Kirisuto
2. *Finnish:*	strand > ranta
	skola — koulo
	Stockholm > Tukholma
3. *Sirkka:*	flicka > licka
	snäll > näll
	pɪata > pata
4. *Swedish childish language·*	klocka > kolocka
	blomma > belomma
	vrida > verida

Fig. 85. A few examples to illustrate to what extent "hearing" is an interpretation, determined by pre-existing patterns. 1. Japanese modifications (*to the right*) of three European loan-words; 2. Finnish words borrowed from Swedish and adapted to Finnish phonemic structure; 3. the way in which my Finnish girl at 4 years of age "heard" the Swedish words of her surrounding; 4. three Swedish words as pronounced by children before they have arrived at full mastery of consonant clusters. The "foreigner" interprets incorrectly because his pattern is different, the child because its mastery of syntagmatic structures is not yet fully acquired

interpretation of unfamiliar stimuli (Chap. VI)[1]. Nobody hears speech sounds independently of any pattern.

No listening can be "objective" or "exact" in the sense that it gives physically adequate information about what "is said". It was the mistake

---

[1] Another experience of my own concerns a Swede established in Argentina and speaking Spanish fluently though with a strong Swedish "accent". I once happened to mention to him the Spanish distinction between simple and double r (*pero* ~ *perro*). He could not see the point and pretended the difference between such words was one of vowel length (since in Swedish a short vowel is followed by a long consonant or a cluster and since an orthographically double consonant is used to indicate short vowels).

of traditional "ear phonetics" to imagine that this was possible. Classical dialectological field work has, at least partly, been based on this mis-understanding. If the trained phonetician hears "better" than the naive listener it is because he disposes of a larger set of patterns to apply on the varying continua, not because his attitude is different in prin-ciple.

The synthetic experiments on speech sound perception carried out during the last ten years or so (particularly at the Haskins Laboratories in New York, at Massachusetts Institute of Technology, in the Bell Laboratories, and in the department of speech transmission in the Royal Institute of Technology in Stockholm) have all pointed in the same direction in the sense that perceptual parameters are much less numerous than the corresponding physical parameters, and that the identification of speech units is made on the basis of combinations of some rather few, perceptually simple stimuli. To the spectrographic complexity of vowels corresponds an astonishing simplicity of perceptual elements. The close front vowels have two "distinctive" high formants on the spectrograms (F 2 and F 3). Synthesis has reduced these two formants to one by showing that an intermediate frequency band is enough to produce the vowel in question. The two formants (F 1 and F 2) in the back close vowels (type [u]) may be replaced in synthetic speech by a single intermediate formant (thus confirming HELMHOLTZ's idea that back vowels had only one formant). Under such conditions, the vocalic distinction of graveness (see Fig. 63), i.e. the series [i], [y], [u], may be described in terms of one single frequency domain (F 2) varying along the frequency scale approximately between 600 and 2500 c/s.

Within the domain of consonants we meet at first the same difficulty to reconcile the physical complexity with the relative simplicity of perceived distinctions. The identification which is made by listeners from among stimuli of noise burst frequency and formant transitions is partly a purely perceptual identification of physically different events, partly a question of linguistic interpretation on the basis of well-known phonemic patterns. Further experiments are needed in order to give a definite answer about where one kind of selective listening stops and the other begins, whether there is any limit between them, and what is the effect of training[1] on the capacity of identifying stimuli. LIBERMAN is

---

[1] LIBERMAN stresses the fact that for the capacity of identifying one-dimensional stimuli (frequencies, degrees of loudness) training does not seem to play any im-portant part. What we can train ourselves to do is to increase our discriminatory capacity by matching stimuli against some standard stimulus. In speech, we have a certain number of reference points in the sound already heard and identified. Cp. LADEFOGED's and BROADBENT's experiments quoted in Chap. V (p. 116).

probably right — and his view is confirmed by his own and other scholars' experimental material — when he ascribes the essential role in the identification process to the phonemic pattern. His own experiments prove for instance that, in a series of steps from /b/ through /d/ to /g/ (synthetic stimuli), the naive American listener hears the stimuli in such a way as to divide the acoustic continuum into three sharply defined categories, i.e. his three phonemes. Another experiment on the same material, aiming at discovering the discriminatory capacity between any two of these stimuli, showed that listeners discriminated more easily near the phoneme boundaries than in the middle of the phoneme categories, which proves that differences which are not tied up with any phonemic distinction are less easily identified than those which are.

One more problem of interest in this context remains to be discussed. We have already pointed out the absence of one-to-one correspondence between physical and perceptual phenomena on the one hand, and physiological on the other. This seems to be admitted by all modern phoneticians. Opinions seem to differ, however, as soon as the role of articulatory patterns for identification of phonemic units is discussed. Some phoneticians are inclined to look upon our muscular movements, and our memory of muscular movements, as important cues to identification, whereas others deny the importance of this cue and look upon the acoustic stimulus and the phonemic pattern as the only essential factors. LIBERMAN has explained the fact that (American) listeners identify a range of considerably different synthetic k-(g-)stimuli as /k/ (/g/), although there are important spectral differences (of the transition phase), by the identical articulatory (dorso-palatal) movements through which they are formed in live speech (see Fig. 34, DURAND). As soon as there is discrepancy between acoustics and physiology (as here acoustic difference but physiological quasi-identity), perceptions goes with physiology. This seems doubtful. The identification of the different k-stimuli is due to the phonemic pattern, which in English happens to have just one unit. The result may be supposed to be quite different if the listeners are speakers with a phonemic opposition between palatal and velar k.

The basic role played by the pattern in any perceptual process — even outside linguistic communication — is illustrated by an example reported by MANDELBROT.

An explorer wanted to bring home from a remote region of Africa a native melody but did not know how to write it down. He tried to learn it by heart by imitating it from morning to night, and finally found a European musician who wrote it down for him. On his return home he found the European specialists astonished at the degree of influence from modern European melodies on African music, even among such isolated tribes. This influence may seem less astonishing to those who know that the musician who had helped him was a cabaret singer. This, however, was hardly essential. The essential thing was that the explorer himself, and after him the musician, had interpreted the African melody according to European patterns and, consequently, had recognized in it patterns which are characteristic of our music but foreign to the native music of Africa. This is an excellent illustration of the important fact that what we hear is not a mere question of physiological response. Perception is a result of the joint action of physiology and conventional patterning.

Chapter XI

Primitive Structures and Defective Language

It was pointed out already in Chap. III and IV that certain solid[1] distinctions (within the vowel systems the extreme values $i - u - a$) have to be looked upon as basic in the sense that all languages have at least those oppositions. The distinction stop consonant $\sim$ vowel is the most extreme of all phonemic distinction, whereas fricatives, nasals, laterals etc. are to be regarded as intermediate types and therefore also, in fact, are less general than stops. Some of these contoids may, on account of this, be used as consonants or as vowels. Phonemic fricatives presuppose stops but not inversely. On the syntagmatic level we have pointed out that the open syllable is the most general one and has to be looked upon as more primitive then the closed syllable. Closed syllables suppose open syllables but not inversely. We have also stressed that the primitive (most simple) structures, on both levels, are those which appear first in the child's linguistic development and those which are the most resistant ones in aphasia. These facts, which were for the first time systematically described, and utilized for linguistic theory, by ROMAN JAKOBSON, reflect a basic principle in language structure. There may hardly be any doubt that this principle has also been at work in the gradual development of human language, even if the various stages of this development can no longer be traced by means of any historical method. No languages today, even the least developed ones, are primitive enough to serve as examples of any pre-linguistic or quasi-

---

[1] It is important for the fundamental problem of the relations between form and substance (see Chap. IV) that the solidity of oppositions is based on differences of substance (of acoustic structure, of audibility, and of articulations). When only a few functional units are needed, these always tend to be manifested through the most extreme differences. This is an aspect of the principle of economy.

linguistic structure, such as must have preceeded the birth of a fully-fledged language. Several primitive structures existing today are without doubt reductions of earlier, more developed systems.

There is, however, another way of finding traces of primitive linguistic structures. If human history is too short to have preserved any traces of those very old stages of language, the human mind itself, besides highly developed patterns of communication and of behaviour, also contains instances of extreme primitivity and of defective capacity. It is important to remember that the mastery of a linguistic system demands a certain intellectual capacity. We have seen above (particularly Chaps. III and X) that man's possibility of identifying stimuli is very much more restricted than the number of discriminatory steps he can actually hear. It may seem natural to suppose that there is an upper limit to the possible number of phonemes in a language, though no absolute figures have been established so far. No language described hitherto has more than 64 phonemes. The most common numbers are to be found between 20 and 40. This seems to indicate that at least a considerably higher number of phonemic units could not be mastered by a human brain with a satisfactory degree of accuracy.

It is important to remember that phonemic simplicity — i.e. a small inventory of units (cp. Chap. IV, p. 87) and reduced possibilities of combination — does not necessarily imply phonetic monotony. On the contrary, a poor phonemic paradigm may permit variations in the manifestation of the phonemes which can hardly be reconciled with a richer paradigm because of the risk of confusion. It is a general principle in information theory that the contrasts have to be worked out the more scrupulously, the more numerous the units of the repertory are ("... zwar müssen ihre Gestalten sich um so *kontrastreicher* [underlined here] ausprägen, je mehr Elemente das Reservoir M umfaßt"; UNGEHEUER).

What I propose to call JAKOBSON's law -- according to which there is a parallelism between the order in which the child learns to master the phonemes of its language and the order in which distinctions get lost in aphasia on the one hand, and on the other the degree of generality of phonemic distinctions — is in fact reflected in an interesting way on other levels of linguistic activity than the ones originally studied by JAKOBSON. It is not only aphasic disturbances that show the greater stability of extreme distinctions. Any peripheric handicap — physiological as well as auditory — may have exactly the same consequences. People who are hard of hearing cease to use subtle distinctions, not because they cannot perceive them, but because the differences seem too small to be fully mastered. In a word, it is too difficult to rely on them in communication. The training of anatomically or neurologically handicapped individuals (spastic children, etc.) has to start from the extreme phonemic differences. Under the influence of intoxication (alcohol etc.) or in a state of bodily or mental exhaustion the more subtle phonemic distinctions are often lost in an order which corresponds to that of aphasia. Drunk people have for instance difficulty in distinguishing between voiced and voiceless consonants. They make all consonants voiced. An experiment demonstrated in the International Congress of Linguists in Oslo 1957 by a group of Edinburgh phoneticians proved that if, in a synthetic speech chain, all consonants are made "voiced", the speech gives the illusion of a drunken person. Many people may have experienced the tendency to give up phonemic distinctions and complicated syntagmatic structures in states of illness or of exhaustion.

MERINGER and KAINZ have given systematic surveys of "slips of the tongue" on different language levels (phonemic, morphological, syntactical, semantic). These "slips" never take place in a random way but according to certain "laws" which, as far as the linguistic expression is concerned, show great affinity with JAKOBSON's law. The tendency towards simplified syllabic structures makes itself felt very distinctly in such sporadic mistakes of pronunciation. It is also perceptible in the simplified syntagmatic structures which are met with in individuals who never manage to realize fully the system of their speech community[1].

Another possibility of analysing primitive structures is given by the precious linguistic material contained in nursery words and rhymes, pet names, sound imitating expressions, etc. ROMAN JAKOBSON has treated the problem of nursery words in a study on 'papa' and 'mama'. All words of this category, in all languages, have a syllabic structure which is simpler than that of the language system as a whole. An extensive use is often made of reduplication — a very frequent primitive pattern where, originally, the number of syllables (or phonemes; cp. p.129) may have been indifferent. Consonant clusters are mostly avoided, etc. The vowels are only the basic ones, to the exclusion of the intermediate, more subtle distinctions (examples such as Swed. *piff-paff-puff, ding-dong, tick-tack, Bobo* [for *Bo*], Engl. *Bob* [for *Robert*], *dad, Betty* [for *Elisabeth*], Span. *Pepe* [for *José(pe)*]).

If language mastering and linguistic capacity, as was pointed out in preceding chapters, implies categorization, and consequently is a

[1] Even if Swedish, in contradistinction to Spanish (cp. Chap. V), uses all nasal oppositions even at the end of a syllable, there are numerous Swedish-speaking people who do not make these distinctions, assimilating automatically the nasal to a following consonant in respect of its place of articulation. Children make these simplifications to a very large extent. This is a typical instance of a kind of individual incapacity which is very common, though not great enough to be classified as a real speech defect. Most listeners do not notice such anomalies.

faculty of interpreting stimuli and complexes of stimuli as variants of familiar invariants on both levels of language, it would follow that the loss or weakening of linguistic capacity would result not only in phonemic confusion but also in a blurring of content boundaries and content contrasts. In fact, this is so.

We often comprise under the heading aphasia such language disturbances as have no apparently organic character. Some specialists make a distinction between nominal aphasia, where the referential function is lost or disturbed, and syntactical aphasia, or agrammatism, where the mastery of the grammatical structure — the bringing together of the separate discrete units into larger complexes, in other words the syntagms — is defective. In the former case, the patient cannot master his vocabulary, he forgets words, uses them in wrong contexts, etc. In the latter, the grammatical rules of the language are violated, or left unconsidered altogether (uninflected words enumerated as isolated elements, etc.). This is not the place to go further into the complicated problems of aphasia. Let us just underline one fact which is intimately connected with the problems discussed in other chapters in this book. The aphasic has lost his faculty of categorization — the fundamental condition for linguistic communication ("perte de l'attitude catégorielle"; OMBREDANE). We have seen that not only the content categories — semantic as well as grammatical — but also the expression units (phonemes, etc.) are due to an arbitrary categorization (segmentation) of an extra-linguistic continuum (the "reality" around us, the sound-wave).

Seen from this angle it is natural that word confusion, form confusion, and phoneme confusion (and of course also graphic confusions) should be due to the same kind of incapacity. The aphasic hears infinitely many sounds, not a limited number of phonemes, and consequently cannot realize the phonemic distinctions. The distinctiveness does not mean anything to him, or at least the most subtle differences do not. In the same way, an aphasic may notice the innumerable nuances of colour but be incapable of grouping them into colour categories. An aphasic, who saw a series of different bottles and who was asked what that was, answered that they were just different things. The common denominator — the word and the concept bottle — was lacking. He was incapable of seeing the identity between the items. And he could therefore not oppose them as a group to other groups (glasses, etc.). Which came first, the word or the concept? The question is useless, because the two are identical. The concept is created through the sign — through the arbitrary delimitation of two continuous phenomena and the combination of the segments (content and expression) into one indissoluble unit which SAUSSURE called sign.

The same incapacity is found on the syntagmatic level. The aphasic has a tendency, as has the child, to reduce the contrasts, and he tends to simplify phonemic complexes as much as possible. We meet tendencies towards vowel and consonant harmony and towards simplified (open) syllables; OMBREDANE mentions "l'impossibilité d'émettre les consonnes en fin de syllable". The famous Danish specialist MOGENS FOG talks in the same way about a general "primitivisation" of the linguistic functions which may thus characterize both aspects of the linguistic structure.

The origin of human language is not a historical problem, it is psychological and structural. The most primitive stages of human communication are still to be found in any man, though mostly covered by more recent and more refined structures. The savage within us is not dead. It is easy to bring him up from the bottom of our subconsciousness. Sometimes, a glass of alcohol, or two, is enough. We find these structures more easily on those levels of communication which BÜHLER called signal and symptom functions and where a lesser degree of arbitrariness — which is of course also a feature of primitivity — gives more scope to sound imitation. It is also interesting to note that sound imitations — which might perhaps be suspected *a priori* to be particularly rich in sound distinctions, since the reality to be imitated contains an innumerable variety of nuances — in fact show an extremely restricted phonemic variation. The phonemic make up of such words is not determined by the acoustic variety of the models but by the simplicity of the language structure — a simplicity which is likely to be maximal on the levels of communication where such words are used.

The structural approach to language study, particularly in its application on children's language and on aphasia, has for the first time in the history of our science given linguistics a method for unveiling the secrets of the origin and prehistory of human language. ROMAN JAKOBSON's discovery implied the first and most important step in this direction. There is no longer any reason for any society of linguists to forbid[1] their members to occupy themselves with the origin and early development of a function thanks to which man is man.

It has sometimes been said that the means of communication used by animals can be looked upon as stages of primitive linguistic communication. We often talk about the language of birds, the language of bees, and so on. It is, however, important to remember that this is a metaphorical use of the word language, if we define the concept as has been done in this survey. A few remarks will be devoted to this problem here, though in fact it is far too complicated, and the field still

---

[1] This was the case with the famous Société de linguistique de Paris.

far too unexplored, to admit of any definitive conclusions and any generally valid definitions.

We have defined language as a set of arbitrary, socially conventional signs. There seems to be no doubt that this definition may be applied also to the communication of some animals. Their signals are often definitely arbitrary, and the manifestation of them socially determined. Birds are said to sing differently in different regions, and are often reported to imitate each other. Bird song is consequently not exclusively physiologically founded. If the "talk" of animals is essentially composed of signals[1], this is in itself no argument against its having a linguistic character. Any communication has, as we have pointed out above, in addition to the symbol and symptom functions also a signal aspect, and the differences between man and animals — as between man in different stages of mental development — is only a difference of degree, not one of principle. The formation of symbols undoubtedly forms part of the communicative behaviour of animals. But symbols do not necessarily mean concept formation. It is at least doubtful whether the faculty of abstraction underlying the concept, as opposed to the individual item, is to be found in animals. Further there is no reason to deny that animals' signals are discrete elements. If a dog for different purposes uses different kinds of barking, this implies discreteness, since one type is effectively opposed to the others without any possibility of gradual passage from one to the other. Nor can we deny the complexity of certain messages sent by animals. The communicative behaviour of bees — used in order to give information about where food is to be found[2] — is no doubt built up by means of rather complex signals. Their language is said to have a real syntax. It is consequently articulated in our sense of the word.

One feature remains to be mentioned, which is proper of all human language but which has not been found, as far as the author of this book is aware, in the communication system of any animal. That is the articulated character of the expression level of the sign, i.e. its being built up by *figurae* (phonemes, cenemes, prosodemes, etc.). The invention of such empty units without any content of their own and with purely distinctive function made the creation of a fully-fledged language system possible, since it implied the possibility of extending enormously the number of signs and thereby, *ad libitum*, the number of messages. Even if this limit is not absolutely sharp — owing to the existence of restrictions in the arbitrariness and in the *figura* principle even in normal human language, and still more in its reduced forms (sound imitation, reduced syntagmatic structures, and so on) — it is

---

[1] In BÜHLER's sense; see Chap. IX.

[2] Essentially a system of movements.

important enough to be said to constitute the border-line between human speech and any other kinds of communication invented by living beings. It also excludes from the category of languages all systems of human communication which are not articulate language (signal systems, flag signals, sailor's codes, etc.), and of course also picture script and any script system of an ideographic or conceptual character. Only if the limit is drawn in this way, is it possible to make a self-consistent definition of what we call human language, as opposed to any other communication, or transference of messages, used by animals, or by men. No other criterion will permit us to establish any difference of principle. It is evident that this criterion is just as arbitrary as any other we could choose. But in contradistinction to any other, it is appropriate.

Chapter XII

Linguistic Change

If language is defined as a code, or more accurately, as a set of codes, applied on different levels of human communication and intercourse, linguistic change may be called a code-shift. If a thorough knowledge of the code on the part of sender and receiver is one of the indispensible conditions for language to function, another condition must be that the code remains identical with itself from one moment to another. This is in principle undeniable. A conclusion to be drawn from these premises is that a changing language is a contradictio in adiecto. Only thanks to the fact that language does not change are we able to use it as our principle means of communication. E pure si muove.

If we go back to our model in Chap. II and take into consideration the relation of the sender and the receiver to the code(s), we easily understand that there is never absolute identity between the code present in the sender's brain and the one stored in the receiver's and that our first condition is never absolutely fulfilled. One person may have a poorer mastery of his system than the other. One may have articulatory or auditory difficulties, the other not. And in no case is there complete identity between the different idiolects (cp. Chap. II) of which the system ("la langue") is the common denominator. This of course becomes particularly evident on the semantic level, as was pointed out in Chap. VIII. That linguistic communication under such circumstances functions to the extent it actually does is due, to a large extent, to redundancy. We do not need to pick out from the sound-wave all the theoretically necessary cues for identifying the phoneme sequence, because the context strongly delimits the possibilities among which we can choose. We do not always need to hear the suffixes, because our knowledge of the language enables us to predict or guess the missing items[1]. Under such conditions, the identity of the code — from time to time and in different individuals — is no absolute condition for linguistic communication. Quasi-identity is enough. Even a considerable amount of so-called semantic noise (cp. Chap. II) is perfectly tolerable.

It may accordingly be said that a certain alteration of the code — on any level — is acceptable without any serious consequences for communication. The loss of a phonemic distinction — say $/\tilde{\varepsilon}/ \sim /\tilde{\alpha}/$ in French, $/e/ \sim /\varepsilon/$ in central Swedish or in certain parts of Germany — is usually tolerated and can, in the few cases where comprehension requires it, be compensated for e.g. by the choice of another term. Classical examples from dialectology are well-known (e.g. the famous homophony between 'the cat' and 'the coq' in Gascon, both $= gat$[2], from Lat. *cattu-* and *gallu* respectively). If we add that in most cases linguistic change is slow and often affects only one or two minor features of the language at a time, we understand more easily why the theoretical contradistinction between the idea of a linguistic code and the fact that language does change implies no considerable practical difficulty.

If, however, we consider a language as an expression of a particular social (etc.) structure and as one of a set of social habits, it becomes possible to look upon linguistic change from a somewhat different point of view. The idea of the unchanged linguistic system as a condition for communication evidently implies that the relations between language and other social conditions — in a word the material to be communicated and the situation in which the communication takes place — remains unaltered. But if the social background changed while language remained identically the same, this would imply a break in the sociolinguistic relations and prevent communication. Thus it is not linguistic change as such, but a change in the relations of language to the rest of the social habits that would make communication difficult or impossible. It is consequently normal and natural that language changes together with its social background. A problem arises only when these relations are disturbed or modified (as may become the case in contacts between different generations and in the interpretations of old literature).

Since FERDINAND DE SAUSSURE established his distinction between synchronic (also improperly called descriptive) and diachronic

---

[1] This should not be confused with cases where we can predict an utterance because we know the speaker and the stimuli affecting him.

[2] The confusion is due to two phonemic reductions: the loss of a distinction of palatality in final position, i.e. $t < t' <$ Lat. *-ll-*, in Spanish $/\lambda/$ in intervocalic position, otherwise $/-l/$; and the loss of distinction between (initial) voiced and voiceless stops.

(historical) linguistics and, in opposition to the Neogrammarian tradition of his epoch, stressed the importance of the former, the relations between those two aspects of linguistic description and the possible priority of one over the other have been a subject of much discussion. HERMANN PAUL had been of the opinion that any explanation in linguistics must be historical and any synchronic description remain a mere accumulation of facts. Modern structural linguistics has often gone to the opposite extreme by neglecting completely the fact that languages do change. From a structural point of view, language change is a change of systems, of codes, not of isolated elements. Structural linguistics consequently looks upon the synchronic description of linguistic stages as a first, necessary condition for diachronic analysis. Without a solid knowledge of the previous system within which the change took place, no really linguistic description of the change itself is possible, since any change of language is a change of structural relations. If diachrony is regarded as a stage of description secondary to synchrony this is just a question of appropriateness. In principle, the two stages of analysis are strictly separated. In concrete cases, they may be carried out simultaneously under the condition that the investigator knows which is which. The constant mixture of both which is recommended for instance by W. VON WARTBURG ("das Ineinandergreifen von deskriptiver und historischer Sprachforschung") is not theoretically satisfactory.

Another confusion often met with in recent discussions about structural methods is that between description and explanation. Even if HERMANN PAUL's view that any explanation must be historical had been correct — which for evident reasons it is not —, it does not necessarily follow that the inversed statement would be correct, i.e. that any historical fact *eo ipso* provides an explanation. In fact, most of the material presented in linguistic history is just as purely descriptive as the synchronic material collected from old or modern sources. If we find, in surviving texts or on the basis of comparative analysis, that Latin /u/ has become /y/ in French, or that Old Swedish long /a/ has become /o/ in Modern Swedish these facts do not explain anything. We can find out that a certain evolution has taken place, determine the conditions under which it has occurred etc., but these facts as such in no way explain why the changes have taken place. Most of the phonetic explanations given in traditional historical linguistics of sound shifts — palatalisation, labialisation, nasalisation, etc. — are at the most pseudo-explanations. In fact they are purely descriptive. For we know, to take an example, that a non-palatal phoneme followed by a palatal one is only sometimes palatalised, not always. Consequently the existence of a palatal in a given phonetic context is a possible condition for a palatalisation to take place but does not explain why a change has occurred at a given moment. To say that French (*je*) *viens* has a diphthong, but not (*nous*) *venons*, because Latin short *o* was diphthongized in a stressed but[1] not in an unstressed syllable does not explain more than if we say that St. Paul's cathedral stands where it does because it was built there.

There is no doubt the structural approach has given a more solid basis also for historical linguistics. Even if it might be questioned whether the structural explanations put forward recently by several writers — the theory of which has been stated most succinctly by MARTINET — are explanations in the strict sense of the word, there can hardly be any doubt that structuralism has at least made one important contribution to the problem of language change. It has given us a more exact picture than we had before of the phenomenon that is changed. The principle of economy referred to above is at least one of the factors of which any linguistic change (any "sound law" or any "semantic law") is in some way or other the effect. The panchronic laws established by JAKOBSON have given a partly new content to the concepts of regularity, of exceptionlessness, and of law. False analogies from the natural sciences have been replaced by references to the psychological and sociological complexes of structures and relations within which language is a kind of subsystem.

In discussing briefly the different aspects of linguistic change, limiting ourselves for the moment to the expression level, we must consider them in terms of the levels of abstraction which were established in Chap. V. A change may affect 1. one, or several, of the physical manifestations of an expression unit without implying any modification either of its place within the paradigm or of its distinctive feature(s) (e.g. when the aspiration of *p*, *t*, *k* is lost in the pronunciation of the Swedish dialects spoken in Finland)[2]; 2. the distinctive feature(s) of phonemes without effecting the form of the paradigm and, consequently, the expression possibilities of the language (e.g. when the distinction between the series /*p*, *t*, *k*/ and /*b*, *d*, *g*/ is changed in Danish from being

---

[1] This answer does not even give us any complete historical information, since other questions immediately come up, e.g. why we do not have the vocalic alternation in French (*je*) *lève*, (*nous*) *levons* where Latin had the same short *e*. The answer given by the historians of the language that *lève* is due to the analogy of *levons* with unstressed *e* results in a third question why this analogy has not worked in *viens* — *venons*, and in a fourth why it worked in favour of the monophthong alternation, since in *j'aime* — *nous aimons* the quality of the s t r e s s e d vowel has supplanted that of the unstressed one (Old French *amer* < Latin *amare*, *aime* < *amat*), and so on. Any of these "explanations" is equally descriptive.

[2] According to what was said in Chap. IX, any perceivable sound factor, and consequently any perceivable sound change, may be utilized on some level of linguistic communication (as signal, symptom, etc.).

a distinction of voice to one of aspiration while preserving intact the phonemic system of oppositions); 3. the set of phonemes and the relations between them, i.e. a re-structuration of the phonemic system of the language (i.e. when Castilian Spanish loses the distinction between voiceless and voiced fricatives towards the end of the Middle Ages, /s/ ∼ /z/, etc. and, a little earlier, its distinction between voiced stops and voiced fricatives, /b/ ∼ /v/, etc.).

A few examples will be given. Fig. 86 shows a sub-system within the Castilian consonant system at the beginning of the literary period (10th century).

p	− t − k
b	− d − g
ƀ (v)	− ð − γ
f (φ)	− −

Fig. 86

p	− t − k
b	− d − g
ƀ (v)	− ð − γ
	＼ h ／

Fig. 87

The phoneme /f/ (probably a bilabial, [φ]) was isolated in the system. It was sufficiently differentiated from the other phonemes by being just a voiceless fricative. Its labial character was redundant and was lost, with the system seen in Fig. 87 as a result.

Though important in principle the distinction between substance change and form change on the expression level is not always easy to make, since there is constant interaction between substance and form. A distinction which is based on a solid articulatory and auditory difference is e.g. more easily maintained than one which is based on subtle differences. Traditional phonetics tended to explain most sound changes by articulatory facts (e.g. slight gradual modifications of the place of articulation). Modern phonetics seems more inclined to consider auditory relationship and confusion as a starting point for phonemic change. In both cases the explanation is only a partial one. It never answers the question why such gradual modifications and such auditory confusions take place in certain regions and at certain epochs but not always when analogous conditions seem to be at hand. Explanations of this kind are only descriptions of what goes on when such changes take place. The problem of the causality remains unsolved.

This is a problem which, in fact, has been attacked from many different points of view. A few remarks must be enough here. On the expression level, it is for instance important to distinguish between external and internal causes of phonemic change. The essential factor among the external causes is interference between linguistic systems (equally important on the content level). Interference supposes bilingualism, regional, social, and individual. The bilingual individual does not succeed in keeping the two systems apart. He applies the wrong code on the substance used. The effect may be phonemic simplification — which is the most common result —, or just re-structuration (re-interpretation). Interference in the individual is what is popularly called a foreign accent. When it is extended to a group and becomes the norm of a speaking community it implies what is called sound change. Interference is mostly the phenomenon behind the so-called substratum effect, which implies an influence from a previously spoken language on one later introduced (through conquests, foreign dominance, or cultural superiority). Of the same kind are the corresponding superstratum and adstratum influences, i.e. the modifications caused by an imported language on the one already spoken in a region, and by one neighbouring language on another. As long as such influences are restricted to the phonetic substance, they do not imply any structural change, though even so they may prepare a structural modification.

Another way of explaining the substratum effect and similar phenomena, particularly the extension of phonetic-phonemic peculiarities over regions speaking historically unrelated languages, is the assumption of genetic factors as the cause of linguistic modifications, in other words an extreme case of external influence on a language. A predilection for a given phonetic type is supposed to be due to a particular combination of genes statistically predominant within a "mating group", and a change in pronunciation as a change in this genetic dominance (brought about by migrations, etc.). The recent contributions to this question by C. D. DARLINGTON and L. F. BROSNAHAN have given a good survey of the genetic theory and the genetic conditions for such a biological factor in linguistic evolution but have not, so far, been successful in presenting the linguistic facts which would support this assumption. The maps illustrating the extension of phonetic characteristics published by BROSNAHAN do not stand up to detailed criticism. They do not, for instance, take into account dialect differences within the speaking communities under discussion, nor do they consider the age of a given phonetic factor in a region, or differences of stability and of tendencies. No clear-cut distinction is established between phonetic and phonemic facts, etc. We have better so far leave biological factors out of consideration in the discussion of phonetic change.

As internal factors we have to consider in the first place the so-called system (paradigmatic) pressure — particularly the role of the so-called holes in the pattern ("cases vides") — the idea of economy as worked out in MARTINET's brilliant study, and the role of syntagmatic pressure brought about by the statistical predominance of certain distributional patterns over other, less frequent ones. Two examples will be given to illustrate these principles.

If we leave out of consideration liquids and nasals which have remained unaltered since the early Middle Ages and /h/ (< Lat. f-) which disappeared without any consequences for the rest of the system, the phonemes of Old Castilian could be arranged in the following way:

stops	/p/	/t/	/k/[1]
	/b/	/d/	/g/
	/b̃/[2]	/ð/	/γ/[3]
	/f/	—	—
fricatives	/s/	/z/	
	/ʃ/	/ȷ̃/	
affricates	/t͡s/	/d͡z/	
	/t͡ʃ/	/d͡ʒ/.	

During the period of Old and Middle Spanish three of the distinctions in this paradigm tend to be given up: 1. the distinction between the stop series /b/ etc. and the corresponding fricative series /b̃/ etc., a tendency which had made itself felt very early (already in Latin inscriptions in certain "weak" positions, and later in the early texts); 2. the distinction between voiced and voiceless /s/ ∼ /z/ and /t͡ʃ/ ∼ /d͡ʒ/; and 3. the distinction between /ts/ and /s/ (and the disappearance of the stop element in /d͡ʒ/). The first change might possibly be explained by the isolated character of this distinction in the system (the lack of a parallel voiceless series of fricatives), reflected already in Latin ("betacism", as far as the labial is concerned). The second and the third changes have no indisputable structural explanation but seem to be, just as the first, a consequence of the general destruction of the Castilian consonantal system, which was a result of the "Reconquista" and of the colonisation of new territories (in the rest of Spain, later also in the new world). We are interested particularly in the consequences. The loss of the voiced — voiceless distinction was accepted. The disappearance of the /t͡s/ was accepted roughly in the South of the Peninsula and in Latin America, whereas another sound, the interdental /θ/, was substituted for it in the central regions and became standard in European Spanish. /θ/ became opposed to /s/ (from /s/ and /z/); /dʒ/ after the loss of its stop element had become the counterpart of /ʃ/ and shared its evolution). /ȷ̃/ was adapted to the system of alternation between stop and fricative which was created on the basis of the lost opposition /b/ ∼ /b̃/ etc., i.e. fricative [ĵ] or affricate [d͡ĵ] according to the context. Consequently the system had acquired a new series of three fricative phonemes: /θ/, /s/, and /ʃ/ besides the two series /p/, /t/, /k/ and /b/, /d/,

---

[1] I shall not discuss the possible phonemic status of the labio-velars.

[2] In phonetic manifestation either [b̃] or [v], a question we need not discuss here.

[3] The existence of a phonemic [γ] may seem doubtful but is at least probable.

/g/. There was no fricative in the back (velar, grave) series, but three degrees of more or less front (acute) distinctions. The least front (acute) of them, the /ʃ/, was pushed backwards (in traditional articulatory terminology) and became /x/, thus the modern system[1]

$$\begin{array}{cccc} /p/ & /t/ & /\widehat{t\!\int}/ & /k/ \\ /b/ & /d/ & /\widehat{d\!j}/ & /g/ \\ /f/ & /\theta/ & /s/ & /x/ \end{array}$$

Traditional evolutive phonetics did not consider duly the important difference between purely phonetic (substance) change and phonemic restructuration (form change). A fairly common case is that where a phonetic (combinatory) change precedes and conditions the phonemic one. Old Icelandic — as all Germanic languages — was rich in meta-phonic phenomena (umlaut). At an early stage the language must have had a system where an -u in the ending did not affect the vowel of the stem; we call this stage no. 1, e.g. (Icelandic)

sing. land — plur. landu.

The influence of the ending changed the vowel of the stem into a labialized vowel written ǫ, thus stage no. 2

sing. land — plur. lǫndu.

At this stage, the linguistic form is unaltered, though the sound sub-stance has been modified. The phoneme /a/ has got a new allophone due to a following -u. A third stage is the disappearance of the ending -u, whence stage no. 3

sing. land — plur. lǫnd,

where the new phoneme /ǫ/ has taken over the function of the lost ending. /ǫ/ is no longer dependent on a given context, no longer pre-dictable, but has become a carrier of information, in this particular case of an important morphological function.

MARTINET has systematized the evolution of primitive Celtic con-sonantism — where any consonant in intervocalic position, even at word boundaries, must have been weakened as compared with its initial and postconsonantal counterpart — in the following way:

/-oko- -osko- -so ko- -sos ko-/

a stage where the /k/ phoneme had weaker allophones after vowel than after consonants with, after a spirantisation of the weaker variants, phonetically

[-oxo- -osko- -so xo- -sos ko-].

A third stage implies a phonemicisation of the weak allophones through the disappearance of the unstressed /o/, thus

/-ox- -osk- -s xo- s ko-/.

---

[1] Still without counting the labio-velars.

The new opposition $/k/ \sim /x/$ takes over a distinctive function which
was earlier filled by the lost vowel. It is a very common phenomenon
in phonetic evolution that a reduction of syntagms, e.g. by the loss
of weak (unstressed etc.) elements leads to a phonemisication of allophonic differences. What is gained through syntagmatic simplification
is consequently lost through paradigmatic complication — shorter
morphemes but more phonemes to master. This is an instance of a
tendency — very natural in a system of communication and far
from restricted to human language — towards b a l a n c e, expressed
in this case through an inverse quasi-proportion between the number
of distinctive features and the length of the expression part of the
sign.

   We know from statistical phonemics that the least complex phonemes
are relatively the most frequent ones. Their so called "rendement
fonctionnel" may to a large extent be measured by this relative frequency. It has therefore been proposed (by REBECCA R. POSNER) to
look upon this frequency as the "phonemic strength" of the phoneme
and to replace the traditional concept of (physiological) strength as
manipulated e.g. by GRAMMONT in his diachronic explanations by
another type of phonemic, statistically based f r e q u e n c y s t r e n g t h.
POSNER postulates in her study on dissimilation that a) the relatively
less frequent phoneme will be more likely to be dissimilated than the
more frequent; b) the dissimilated phoneme will be replaced by a
relatively more frequent one. Thus, the statistically determined syntagmatic structure may be a factor of importance in linguistic change.
She warns, however, against a danger of generalisation. An infrequent
phoneme may have a high emotive content which modifies the process
outlined for "normal" cases.

   That high frequency is not the only factor behind the supposed
"strength" of a phoneme is also proved by a reference to syllabic structure where we have seen that the initial position is "stronger" in all
respects (articulatory, acoustic, auditory, psychological) than the final
and that consequently an initial phoneme, in spite of its low frequency,
may be less subject to modifications than even a frequent but syllable-
final one. The strongest position in a phonetic group is the absolutely
initial one. A study of evolutionary phonetics also teaches us that
consonants in this position are often retained to an extent which is
rare in other positions (intervocalic, final). And when even an initial
consonant is modified this is sometimes a case of secondary generalisation from e.g. intervocalic positions, or of further changes. The so-called
Celtic lenition just referred to is an instance of this kind. The initial
consonants in Latin are normally preserved in the Romance languages,
whereas intervocalic as well as syllable-final and other consonants are

to a large extent modified or dropped. The reason might be found in
the decisive part played by the initial position from the point of view
of information. Any following phonetic unit is, at least to a certain
extent, predictable from the first element and this is consequently
the one which contains the incomparably largest amount of information.
Any weakening of its distinctive features may threaten its communicative value.

A Spanish example will illustrate some questions of general interest
within the field of evolutionary phonetics. In Old Spanish a group -*dl*-
tended to be reversed (> -*ld*-). This change is responsible for the structure of a series of (half-learned)[1] Spanish words, such as *tilde* < Lat.
tǐtǔlu, *molde* < Lat. mǒdǔlu, *cabildo* < Lat. capǐtǔlu, *espalda* <
Lat. spatǔla. A group -*ld*- must consequently have seemed more in
accordance with the syllabic structure of the language because of the
sonorous, vocalic character of the liquid. This "phonetic law" did not
respect the morpheme boundary, for in imperative forms like *dadlos*
('give them'), *dezidles* ('say to them') the same interversion took place,
forms such as *daldos, dezildos, valelde, cantalda* being current during
the Middle Ages and still in the Classical period. A corresponding
change, phonemically identical, took place with -*dn*- (*dandos* for *dadnos*
'give us' etc.). Those forms disappeared earlier. In both cases, however,
the later evolution proves that such forms must have seemed shocking
in some way because of the absence of parallelism between expression
and content, the liquid and the nasal belonging to the second morpheme
(the pronoun *lo, los, nos*, etc.), the dental to the verb-form (imperative-
ending). The primitive, analytic forms were re-established, and modern
Spanish has *decidlo, dadnos*, etc. Morpheme analysis has beaten syllabic
structure. The example also shows us that on the one hand content
and expression (in accordance with glossematic theory) may be independent of each other, on the other that language prefers a parallelism
between the two levels. It also exemplifies the part played by both
syntagmatic (syllabic) and morphemic structure in phonetic change.

Since structural analysis as such is more complicated on the content
level, and particularly the semantic structure is often difficult to determine (for reasons explained in Chap. VIII), it follows that changes
of content structure become less easy to classify. We can, however,
make a few distinctions, partly in accordance with traditional rhetorical
categories. But let us have a look at purely grammatical functions first.

---

[1] Half-learned implies that their phonetic treatment is not in accordance
with the one reflected in the original stock of purely popular word material. This
is irrelevant for our problem.

It is evident that e.g. a modification of forms which is only a consequence of some phonetic and/or phonemic modification, is no morphological change at all. Whether in Spanish the plural *casas* 'houses' is
pronounced ['kasas] or ['kasah] has nothing to do with the grammatical
system, only with the physical manifestation of the phoneme /s/. Nor
does the middle Swedish pronunciation of a plural like *fäder* (from
sing. *fader* 'father') with an /e/-phoneme for the original and "correct"
/ɛ/ as umlaut-vowel of /a/ imply any morphological modification of the
Swedish system. Another, rather more strictly morphological change
can be said to have taken place in a case like Italian *-iamo* as the ending
of the first person plural of all verbs instead of the etymologically in-
herited endings which were lost (*-iamo* was originally only a subjunctive
form). In such a case the verbal paradigm is retained, though manifested
differently (and with confusion of indicative and subjunctive in the
first person plural: syncretism). Italian and Spanish have identical
paradigms as far as the number of units and their relations is concerned,
namely [of the verb *cantar(e)* 'I sing']

It.	Sp.
cant-*o*	cant-*o*
cant-*i*	cant-*as*
cant-*a*	cant-*a*
cant-*iamo*	cant-*amos*
cant-*ate*	cant-*ais*
cant-*ano*	cant-*an*

though on two points (second person singular and first person plural)
Italian presents innovations historically speaking, the endings in question
being due to a replacement of the original Latin endings, preserved in
Spanish (only with the modifications caused by sound changes).

But a look at the paradigm does not give all necessary information
about what has been changed and what has been preserved. If we compare again Italian with Spanish, one of the Italian forms (*-iamo*) is
becoming rare, and is now restricted to the written language and high
style, having been replaced by a reflexive construction (*si canta*) in
colloquial style. The frequency of the *-iamo* form has been strongly
reduced and it has assumed at the same time a stylistic value which
the Spanish form *-amos* does not possess.

We may finally have to do with a linguistic change which is caused
by a phonetic or phonemic alteration. If final consonants tend to be
dropped, morphological distinctions may be difficult to maintain, and
the traditional form system breaks down. This is, according to a widespread opinion, what happened in numerous Indo-European languages

(Old Germanic, Vulgar Latin, etc.). When the final vowels in prehistoric Gallo-Romance were dropped (except -*a*), the Latin paradigm

	Sing.	Plur.
nom.	*servus*	*servi*
gen.	*servi*	*servorum*
dat.-abl.	*servo*	*servis*
acc.	*servum*	*servos*

was no longer possible[1]. Old French, which preserved till rather late, the Latin final -*s*, could use a two-case paradigm[2] of the following structure:

	Sing.	Plur.
nom.	*sers*[3]	*serf*
gen. acc.	*serf*	*sers*

unknown in Italian, where final -*s* had disappeared before the earliest texts in vulgar language.

The rest of the development of this French system is of a purely grammatical character and implies the loss of case-distinction in nouns. The most frequent gen. acc. form is retained and the nominative disappears (with a few exceptions, personal names, etc.), with the curious consequence that final -*s*, from having been a case-mark, becomes a mark of plural. This is a real content change (form change). Such a change implies a modification of the grammatical or semantic categories of the system. Other examples of such changes are on the one hand the disappearance of the dual in most Indo-European languages, the loss of the middle voice found e.g. in Old Greek, or the disappearance of gender[4] in English (a reduction of the number of categories), on the other the introduction of a progressive verb category in English, of a fourth Swedish gender in modern times, of a new passive voice in languages which had lost the original one, and so on (examples of an extension of the system). In all these examples we have to do with a modification of the number of categories and/or of their mutual relations.

----

[1] It is interesting to note that the only form which had a stressed ending (-*orum*) was retained till after the disappearance of the others, namely the form in -*or*, -*our* in Old French in a whole series of expressions and with a particular meaning, in use even after the two-case system had begun to break down (*la gent paienour* etc. in the "Roland" poem).

[2] The unmarked genitive-dative is not taken into account here. It was replaced by the prepositional expression with *de*.

[3] The loss of -*f* before *s* is purely phonetic.

[4] Retained only through the use of *he*, *she* with reference to persons (and certain animals).

Whether such a development implies a reduction of the number of distinctions or categories, or an increase, or just a re-structuration, the effect of the change is a new form. The "reality" to be communicated has been structured in a new way.

As can be seen from the examples given above the parallelism between expression change and content change is not complete, and hardly could be. On the other hand, it is striking enough, in principle, for our survey to indicate very clearly that the similarity between the different structural levels distinguished within both expression and content may be said to be well reflected even in the dynamics of human language.

A content parallel to our first instance on the expression level (change only of substance) may be seen in cases where new or modified meanings are grouped under traditional headings. A 'car' covers a semantic field very different from what it did a few centuries ago. As long as no new signs are introduced into the semantic paradigm of which 'car' is an element, no change of structure has, however, taken place[1]. Very often a language hesitates between the introduction of a new sign and a re-structuration of the system, and an extension of the semantic field of the word(s) with the preservation of the form. So, in our example, there has often been hesitation between new concepts like *motor-car*, *automobile*, Germ. *Kraftwagen*, *Auto*, and an extension of the field of the old one (Engl. *car*, French *voiture*, etc.).

Far-going restriction of the semantic field is a rather common phenomenon in languages. Latin *ponere* 'to lay' has survived in French in the verb *pondre* which is a regular development of it but which has got the very limited sense of 'lay eggs'. In the same way, Latin *trahere* (or rather the vulgar form *tragere*) 'to draw' is the etymon of French *traire* with the meaning of 'to milk [a cow]'. In both cases, the general abstract concept is expressed by a new verb (in both our instances other Latin verbs with a partly changed meaning: *mittere* > Fr. *mettre*; *tirare* > Fr. *tirer*). Latin *caput* 'head' has survived in French (as *chef*) only in a figurative sense ('chief' etc.), whereas the concept 'head' has got another expression, originally a metaphoric, popular and perhaps humoristic term (Lat. *testa* 'pot', Fr. *tête*). Other instances of content change can be explained by social re-structuration. The French *maréchal* has nowadays the highest rank in the military hierarchy of the country. But the word has developed out of a Medieval Latin *mariscalcus* the Germanic etymon of which means 'groom', 'horse-servant'.

---

[1] The Swedish paradigm of colour denominations was extended when 'violet' was introduced by means of contact with other languages and together with the foreign word. This nuance had earlier been classified as a variety of brown, as was pointed out in Chap. VIII.

A change of content structure of this type is illustrated by W. VON WARTBURG by the Latin system of kinship, reflecting differences in the social position between the father's and the mother's relations:

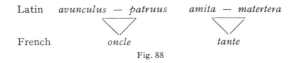

Latin   *avunculus — patruus*   *amita — matertera*

French   *oncle*   *tante*

Fig. 88

With the loss of this old system the denominations have changed too and are now reduced to an opposition between masculine and feminine only. It should, however, be noticed that in Swedish, where the old Germanic system of kinship is also lost, the linguistic structure remains unaltered, with an opposition still existing between 'the father's brother' and 'the mother's brother' (sister, parents). This is a point in linguistic structure where the interdependence between language and other social conventions, classifications, distinctions, and traditions makes itself most clearly felt and is most easily demonstrated.

Without taking into consideration the place of language within a larger system of human behaviour, linguistic change must necessarily seem enigmatic and, in fact, is so. An ordinary code — a structure *sui generis* — is by definition static. But incorporated into the more general structure of human social intercourse — necessarily dynamic — the changes of language become an unavoidable consequence of the modifications of this intercourse which have taken place during the centuries and millionaires of the existence of man.

The structural approach to language change is not in any way in contradistinction to the traditional neo-grammarian concept of s o u n d l a w, nor to the idea of t e n d e n c y which the French phoneticians particularly during the first thirty years or so of this century, wanted to substitute for it. On the contrary, if a language is a system in which any element depends on all other elements, the effect of any change in such a structure must be strictly determined by the linguistic form itself. And if this form is subject to hierarchic laws regulating its oppositions and contrasts, no linguistic change can ever be a random phenomenon. In fact, all the famous phonetic laws or sound-shifts, well-known from traditional comparative linguistics, are excellent instances of unconscious structural thinking. Neither the Germanic nor the High-German shift affected isolated elements but correlative series of phonemes. The sonorisation of Latin intervocalic $p — t — k$ to $b — d — g$ (with further changes in several dialects) is another good instance of the same kind. When Latin short o was diphthongized to uo (ue, etc.) this change also happened to the corresponding half-closed front vowel e ($> ie$), etc.

The contribution of modern structuralism to diachronic linguistics is to have stressed more than before the role of the paradigmatic relations in the final result of expression changes. Though hitherto less applied, there is no doubt that the structural approach to content change may offer corresponding advantages and contribute to a greater stringency of method in linguistic history. In any case, thanks to structuralism the old atomistic methods, applied particularly often in Romance languages (of the type "Latin intervocalic -*p*- in Gaul"), now belong to history. Thanks to structural principles, the traditional dialect monographs on a historical basis have almost completely disappeared, scientifically unsatisfactory and practically useless as they were.

If the fascinating problem of the origin and early stages of human language was touched upon already in the preceding chapter, and not here, the reason is that the oldest stages of linguistic structures that are historically ascertainable are not more primitive than the languages of today. History is too short a period in the development of man to show any noticeable traces of a passage from any proto-linguistic or pre-linguistic to a strictly linguistic period. We must find primitivity else-where. And, as we have already seen, we do find it. On the other hand, it is evident that the more primitive structures of which we find examples in certain layers of language and which are always present as structural tendencies towards simplification constitute in any system a factor of importance in linguistic change. The primitive patterns may reappear under unfavourable conditions. We know for instance that they may result from linguistic interference, from bilingualism, or other social conditions which weaken social norms and linguistic standards. We know from dialect geography that they are often to be found in the peri-phery of a linguistic area. So we come back again to the interdependence of language and society and to the conclusion that linguistic change is not in the last instance a linguistic but a social phenomenon.

Bibliographical Notes

Introduction. For some of the general, basic ideas of structural linguistic theory and analysis, see among others L. HJELMSLEV, "Prolegomena to a Theory of Language", 2nd revised ed., transl. (from the Danish original "Omkring Sprogteoriens Grundlæggelse", 1943) by FRANCIS J. WHITFIELD, University of Wisconsin Press, Madison, 1961, and H. J. ULDALL, "Outline of Glossematics; a Study in the Methodology of the Humanities with Special Reference to Linguistics, part I: General Theory" /Travaux du Cercle linguistique de Copenhague X, 1957/. B. SIERTSEMA has given a critical survey of the fundamental concepts of glossematics in "A study of Glossematics", 1955. Cf. also HJELMSLEV's "Principes de grammaire générale", 1928, and other of his works (e.g. "Structural Analysis of Language", in "Studia linguistica" II, 1948, pp. 69—78; together with other of the author's articles re-edited in "Essais linguistiques", /Travaux du Cercle linguistique de Copenhague XII, 1959/. An important modern orientation has been given by H. A. GLEASON, "An Introduction to descriptive Linguistics", 2nd revised ed., 1961. Cp. also P. HARTMANN, "Allgemeine Strukturgesetze in Sprache und Grammatik", 1961; "Zur Theorie der Sprachwissenschaft", 1961. A critical analysis of linguistic form was given by G. F. MEIER, "Das Zéro-Problem in der Linguistik; kritische Untersuchungen zur strukturalistischen Analyse sprachlicher Form", 1961. The philosophical and logical background to glossematics can be found in RUDOLF CARNAP (e.g. "The Logical Syntax of Language", 2nd ed., 1949). A tendency similar to that of structuralism and of glossematics may be found not only in philosophy (ÉMILE MEYERSON) but also in aesthetic and literary criticism (e.g. in WOLFGANG KAYSER, "Das sprachliche Kunstwerk", 3rd ed., 1954) and within natural sciences. Cf. e.g. E. SCHRÖDINGER: "... the ultimate particles are — *pure shape*, nothing but shape", and further: "identity arises out of form or organization. — The identity of the *material*, if there is any, plays a subordinate role" ... "Form, he says, not substance /is/ the fundamental concept" ("Science and Humanism: Physics in our time", 1951; cp. the same author's "Mind and Matter", 1958). See also L. HEILMANN in "Quaderni dell' Istituto di glottologia di Bologna" II, 1957, particularly p. 16. A survey of the use of the term "structure" has been given by different writers in R. BASTIDE, "Sens et usages du terme structure dans les sciences humaines et sociales", 1962. — Some of the ideas exposed here may be traced as far back as WILHELM VON HUMBOLDT (e.g. in "Über die Verschiedenheit des menschlichen Sprachbaus", ed. from 1949). — General problems of communication are treated by G. A. MILLER, "Language and Communications", 1951; by C. CHERRY, "On Human Communication", 1957; by NORBERT WIENER, "The Human Use of Human Beings", 1950, etc. The concept itself and various definitions given of it are discussed by A. J. AYER in "Studies in Communication" /Communication Research Centre, University College/, London, 1955, pp. 11—28. A short survey of the problems and their practical implications for human intercourse was given by the author in "Linguistic Barriers to Communication in the Modern World", Ibadan University Press 1960. — A general survey with numerous references is also given in the author's work "Nya vägar inom språkforskningen" (2nd ed. 1962); English translation "New Trends in Linguistics" (1964). References to works on communication, sound transmission, pedagogical applications, semantics, sociology and social anthropology are given in later chapters. The quotation from H. GLINZ ("Denkform") is to be found in

"Die innere Form des Deutschen" /Bibliotheca Germanica IV, 1952, p. 19/ (with reference to L. WEISGERBER, etc.). For the quotation from QUINE, see his book "Word and Object", 1959. — RASMUS RASK has been treated in recent years by L. HJELMSLEV, "Rasmus Rask" (in "Store danske personligheder" II, 1949, pp. 174—185), and by PAUL DIDERICHSEN, "Rasmus Rask og den grammatiske tradition", 1960. — A survey of the discussion about the Neogrammarian doctrine and sound-laws is given in my book "New Trends" (pp. 12—15, 20—22, 69—73) with further references. — For FERDINAND DE SAUSSURE and his theories, see in the first place "Cours de linguistique générale" (1916, and following editions; English translation by WADE BASKIN, "Course in General Linguistics", 1960; German translation by H. LOMMEL, "Grundfragen der allgemeinen Sprachwissenschaft", 1931; Spanish translation, with an important introduction and numerous notes, by AMADO ALONSO, 1945), and also R. GODEL, "Les sources manuscrites du Cours de linguistique générale de F. SAUSSURE", 1957; A. SECHEHAYE, "Les trois linguistiques saussuriennes", 1940; B. MALMBERG, "F. SAUSSURE et la phonétique moderne" /Cahiers F. DE SAUSSURE, XII, 1954, pp. 9—28/, etc. — TRUBETZKOY's system is exposed in "Grundzüge der Phonologie" /Travaux du Cercle linguistique de Prague VI, 1939; French translation "Principes de phonologie", by G. HAUDRICOURT, 1949/. — BLOOMFIELD's doctrine is exposed in "Language", 1933; JAKOBSON's in, among numerous other works, "Fundamentals of Language", 1956, and "Selected Writings" I, 1962; MARTINET's in e.g. "Phonology as Functional Phonetics", 2nd ed. 1955, "Éléments de linguistique générale", 1960, "La description phonologique", 1956; "Économie des changements phonétiques", 1955, and "A Functional View of Language", 1962. Cf. also ZELLIG S. HARRIS, "Methods in Structural Linguistics", 1951; A. MARTINET and U. WEINREICH, "Linguistics Today", 1954; MARTIN JOOS, "Readings in Linguistics", 1957; SOL SAPORTA, "Psycholinguistics", 1961. — NOREEN's mode of linguistic description and his great descriptive work on Swedish "Vårt språk" (= Our language), Vol. I—V, VII, IX, 1903—23, has been described by J. LOTZ in "Studia linguistica" VIII, 1954; a selection of his studies was translated into German and published by HANS POLLACK, "Einführung in die wissenschaftliche Betrachtung der Sprache", in 1923. — BUYSSEN's notes on SAUSSURE were published in "Cahiers F. DE SAUSSURE" XVIII, 1961, pp. 17—33. The quotation from MARTINET is to be found in "Économie", p. 13. Cp. hereto MALMBERG, in "Studia neophilologica" XXXI, 1959, pp. 298—306. — For the general problem of opposition versus identity, see also my article "Opposition et identité" in "Journal français de phoniatrie et d'oto-rhino-laryngologie" I (Bull. de la Société française de phoniatrie VIII) 1959, pp. 65—83.

Chapter I. S. ULLMAN has treated the concepts of sign and symbol in his recent book "Semantics. An Introduction into the Science of Meaning", 1962. ULLMAN does not himself make any distinction between them. — For the general ideas about the linguistic sign before SAUSSURE, see in the first place the works of WILHELM VON HUMBOLDT ("Über die Verschiedenheit", quoted in the Introduction; id., "Sprachphilosophische Werke", published by H. STEINTHAL, 1884, and his famous "Über die Kawi-Sprache der Insel Java", I—III, 1836—39). In a recent paper ("Les origines du structuralisme", 1962), B. COLLINDER has questioned the originality of SAUSSURE's ideas which he traces as far back as the Sanskrit grammarian Panini. Sir ALAN GARDINER has exposed his theories in "Theory of Speech and Language" (2nd ed., 1960). See also R. JAKOBSON, "Linguistics and Communication Theory" /Proceedings of Symposia in Applied Mathematical Aspects; American Mathematical Society, 1961; pp. 245—262/. HERDAN's book will be referred to in following chapters (particularly in Chap. III). The quotation from HJELMSLEV is taken from "Prolegomena", p. 58. Most American linguists, from BLOOMFIELD onwards, have regarded language as one hierarchy. Later scholars, however, have adopted an attitude more similar to that of SAUSSURE and HJELMSLEV (cp. HOCKETT, "A Course in Modern Linguistics", 1958, etc., and RULON S. WELLS, "Proceedings of the VIIIth International Congress of Linguistics", Oslo 1958, pp.654—666; cf. also J. GREENBERG, "Essays in Linguistics", 1957). The quotations from "Cours" are to be found on pp.164, 151, and 167 respectively. Cf. also the works of the Swiss ANTON MARTY (publ. by OTTO FUNKE, e.g. "Psyche und Sprachstruktur, A.M.'s nachgelassene Schriften", 1940; and "Innere Sprachform, eine Einführung in A.M.'s Sprachphilosophie", 1924). For onomatopoeic word creation and its possible role for the development of language, see e.g. G. RÉVESZ, "Ursprung und Vorgeschichte der Sprache", 1946 (who believes it must have been minimal and rejects more or less the so-called "wow-wow"-theory); B. COLLINDER in "Studia linguistica" III, 1949, pp.118—123, and the recent works of B. ROSENKRANZ, "Der Ursprung der Sprache", 1961, particularly pp.15ff., and E. ROSSI, "Die Entstehung der Sprache und des menschlichen Geistes", 1962. Instances of primitive sound imitation are given in my book "Die Quantität als phonetisch-phonologischer Begriff", 1944 (e.g. p.58), with references. — For the concepts of "signe motivé" and "signe arbitraire", see "Cours", pp.100—101 and 181. — A similar approach to the problem of sign and "meaning" is to be found in L. WEISGERBER's works (e.g. "Vom Weltbild der deutschen Sprache", I—III, 1953—54; "Sprachwissenschaftliche Methodenlehre", 1950), and in H. GLINZ (the work quoted in the Introduction). — A work of fundamental importance is FR. KAINZ, "Psychologie der Sprache" (I—IV, 1941—1956). See for the linguistic sign particularly Vol.I, p.67ss. Other works of fundamental importance for our discussion are A. GARDINER's "The Theory of Speech and Language" (quoted above); OGDEN-RICHARDS, "The Meaning of Meaning", 1923 and following editions (with a different interpretation of the concepts); further H. SPANG-HANSSEN, "Recent Theories on the Nature of the Linguistic Sign", 1954; P. DIDERICHSEN, "Semantiske problemer i logik og lingvistik", 1953; PIERRE NAERT, "Arbitraire et nécessaire en linguistique" /Studia linguistica I, 1947, pp.5—10/; and NIELS EGE, "Le signe linguistique est arbitraire" /Travaux du Cercle linguistique de Copenhague V, 1949, pp.11—29/. — For HJELMSLEV's linguistic theory and glossematics, see his works quoted in the Introduction (passim). For correlation and relation, see "Prolegomena", p.38. — SAUSSURE's famous solution of the problem of Indo-European vowels and laryngeals was published under the heading "Mémoires sur le système primitif des voyelles indo-européennes", 1879. The quotations from "Cours" on p.13 are to be found on pp.151 and 167. — For the "phonological" doctrine, see TRUBETZKOY's and JAKOBSON's works, quoted in the Introduction. — For MARTINET's conception, see "Cahiers F. DE SAUSSURE" XV, 1957, pp.105—116; and also "Éléments", particularly p.17ss. — E. SAPIR was in a certain sense a fore-runner to American structuralism ("Introduction to the Study of Speech", 1921). Numerous contributions to the exegesy of the "Cours" have been given in the review "Cahiers F. DE SAUSSURE" (up to now 22 volumes, 1941 ff.). — The French sociologist ÉMILE DURKHEIM published for instance "De la division du travail social", 1893; and "Les formes élémentaires de la vie réligieuse", 1912. His countryman LUCIEN LÉVY-BRUHL has written among other works "La mentalité primitive", 1922, "L'âme primitive", 1927, and "L'expérience mystique et les symboles chez les primitifs", 1938.

Chapter II. The communication process and the conveying of linguistic messages has been treated from many different points of view and by numerous scholars, inside and outside linguistics. We give just a few references of particular interest from a linguistic and structural viewpoint. See e.g. G. MILLER, "Language and Communication", 1951; C. CHERRY, "On Human Communication", 1957; J. B. CARROLL, "The Study of Language", 1955; ABRAHAM MOLES, "Théorie de l'information et perception esthétique", 1958; NORBERT WIENER, "Cybernetics or Control and Communication in the Animal and the Machine", 1948; id., "The Human Use of Human Beings", 1950; L. BLOOMFIELD, "Language", 1933, pp. 21—41; K. BÜHLER, "Sprachtheorie", 1934, Chap. I; FR. KAINZ, "Psychologie der Sprache", Vol. III, particularly Chap. III—V; D. B. FRY, "Speech and Language" /The Journal of Laryngology and Otology, Vol. LXXI, 1957, pp. 434—452/, and id., "Perception and Recognition in Speech" /For ROMAN JAKOBSON, 1956, pp. 170 —173/. A short survey was given by G. UNGEHEUER, "Einführung in die Informationstheorie unter Berücksichtigung phonetischer Probleme" /Phonetica IV, 1959, pp. 96—106/. The quotation is from this article p. 96. The scheme of the communication process set up in Fig. 3 has on certain points been influenced by D. B. FRY's written and oral contributions to the question; see the articles quoted above. — For the problems of script and written language (alphabets), see in the first place M. COHEN's great work "La grande invention de l'écriture", 1958. The Egyptian and Chinese signs are taken over from respectively F. BLATT, "Alfabetets historia", 1945, and B. KARLGREN, "Kinesisk elementarbok", 1948. The Japanese syllabic types are quoted from PH. NOACK, "Lehrbuch der japanischen Sprache", 1886; for further details about Japanese syllables and script, see G. WENCK, "Japanische Phonetik" I, 1954. Graphemes have been described structurally by HENNING SPANG-HANSSEN in "Probability and Structural Classification in Language Description", 1959; and by PIERRE NAERT, in "Une définition et classification nonphonétique des graphèmes du vieil-islandais" /Studia linguistica XV, 1961, pp. 29 —51/. — For semantic noise and similar phenomena, see CHERRY, "On Human Communication", p. 67. The quotation from S. S. STEVENS is taken over from CHERRY, op. cit., p. 6. Conceptualization (code formation, etc.) has been treated by A. KUHN in "Synthèse", No. 2, 1961, p. 130. For quantization, see in the first place CHERRY's "On Human Communication" (the example quoted is taken from pp. 46—47) and B. MANDELBROT, "Structure formelle des textes et communication" /"Word" X, 1954, pp. 1—27/. — The quotation from FRY is to be found in "For ROMAN JAKOBSON", p. 173. The schematic picture of a nerve impulse is taken from W. A. VAN BERGEIJK, J. R. PIERCE, and E. E. DAVID Jr., "Waves and the Ear" (Fig. 45). — Fundamental problems of linguistic communication are treated by JEAN-CLAUDE LAFON, "Message et phonetique", 1961 (cp. particularly his scheme of the communication process, p. 68).

Chapter III. The concepts of information, amount of information, and entropy are treated in numerous introductions to information and communication theory and in well-known handbooks. We refer in the first place to W. MEYER-EPPLER, "Grundlagen und Anwendungen der Informationstheorie", 1959; and also to G. HERDAN, "Language as Choice and Chance", 1956, "The Calculus of Linguistic Observations", 1962; to B. MANDELBROT and A. MORF, "Logique, langage et théorie de l'information", 1957; to C. F. SHANNON and W. WEAVER, "The Mathematical Theory of Communication", 1949; to "Information Theory", ed. by C. CHERRY, 1956; and particularly to B. MANDELBROT's important article "Structure formelle des textes et communication" (quoted in Chap. II). The example from HERDAN is to be found on p. 163 in the work quoted above. The formulae quoted are taken from the pp. 164—165. See also MOLES (the work quoted in Chap. II), further N. WIENER, the works quoted in Chap. II, and C. CHERRY, "On Human Communication", 1957 (concerning the beginning of information theory, p. 43). The survey of the principles of information theory given in this chapter is to a large extent based on CHERRY's book. TILLMAN's and ROSWELL RUSSELL's article "Information and Entropy" was published in "Synthèse" no. 3 1961, pp. 233—241. — For the general principles of human speech production, see G. FANT, "Acoustic Theory of Speech production", 1960; and T. CHIBA and M. KAJIYAMA, "The Vowel — its Nature and Structure", 1941; G. UNGEHEUER, "Elemente einer akustischen Theorie der Vokalartikulation", 1962; J. L. FLANAGAN, "Speech Analysis, Synthesis and Perception", 1965; elementary data e. g. in B. MALMBERG, "La phonétique" (Que sais-je ?, 6th ed., Paris 1966; English translation, "Phonetics", 1962); in P. LADEFOGED, "Elements of Acoustic Phonetics", 1962; further in O. VON ESSEN, "Allgemeine und angewandte Phonetik", 3. erweiterte Aufl., 1962; in HARVEY FLETCHER, "Speech and Hearing in Communication", 1953; in MARTIN JOOS, "Acoustic Phonetics", 1948; for the Sonagraph see R. K. POTTER — A. G. KOPP — H. C. GREEN, "Visible Speech", 1947; cf. also MALMBERG, "Le problème du classement des sons de langage et questions connexes" /Studia linguistica VI, 1952, pp. 1—56/; id., "Questions de méthode en phonétique synchronique" /ibid. X, 1956, pp. 1—44/; id., "Distinctive Features of Swedish Vowels, some Instrumental and Structural Data" /For ROMAN JAKOBSON, 1956 pp. 316—321/; and id., "Les voyelles suédoises et la notion de 'fermeture vocalique'" /Studia linguistica XIII, 1959, pp. 49—61/. — A. GEMELLI's spectra are taken over from "La strutturazione psicologica del linguaggio studiata mediante l'analisi elettroacustica" /Ex Aedibus Academicis in Civitate Vaticana/, 1950. ELI FISCHER-JØRGENSEN's criticism of GORDON PETERSON is to be found in "Proceedings of the VIII the International Congress of Linguists", 1958, pp. 447—448. Fig. 34 b is from MARGUERITE DURAND, Studia linguistica VIII, p. 112. — The terms diffuse ∼ compact — acute ∼ grave — plain ∼ flat etc. are taken from JAKOBSON—FANT—HALLE, "Preliminaries to Speech Analysis", 1952, and "Fundamentals", quoted in the Introduction. — For my own scheme of Swedish vowels, see "For ROMAN JAKOBSON", pp. 316—321, and "Studia linguistica" X, pp. 18—21. For vowel-consonant transitions, see B. MALMBERG, "Studia linguistica" X, p. 41, and the references made there (particularly to the publications of the Haskins Laboratories in New York), and, in the first place, the fundamental work of P. GREEN, "Consonant-vowel Transitions; a Spectrographic Study" /Travaux de l'Institut de phonétique de Lund, publiés par BERTIL MALMBERG, II, 1959; also in "Studia linguistica" XII, 1958/. — References to synthetic experiments will be given in Chap. IV. — The data on chest and falsetto register, and Fig. 38 are taken from CHIBA—KAJIYAMA, "The Vowel", p. 20. The glottis mechanism has been examined e.g. by SVEND SMITH, "Remarks on the Physiology of the Vibrations of the Vocal Cords" /Folia phoniatrica VI, 1954, pp. 166—178; cf. also ibid. IX, 1957, pp. 32—36/. Concerning the voice quality of the Lapps, see B. MALMBERG, "Système et méthode", 1945, p. II, and the references made there to B. COLLINDER, "Lautlehre des Waldlappischen Dialekts von Gällivare", 1958, p. 44; and M. A. CASTRÉN, "Nordiska resor och forskningar" I, 1852; for Spanish, see TOMÁS NAVARRO TOMÁS, "Manual de entonación española", 1944; also MALMBERG, "Études sur la phonétique de l'espagnol parlé en Argentine", 1950, p. 216; and P. HENRÍQUEZ UREÑA, "El español en Santo Domingo", 1940. — On the relation between acoustics (sounds) and physiology (articulation) in speech production, see the author's article quoted above "Le problème du classement des sons du langage" and the references made therein. A certain modification of my view on these questions, in the direction of stressing more than in the work quoted the role of articulation and of muscular sense and muscular patterns for speech recognition and phoneme identification may have taken place since the publication of this article, though I am still of the opinion that the identity of a sound — and consequently also of the physical manifestation of a phonemic unit — is to be found in the acoustic structure, not in the way of producing the sound, which may vary without any resulting acoustic change. A classification of speech sounds — as far as this is possible on a general (e. g. non-phonemic) basis — must primarily be made on the basis of their acoustic structure. FORCHHAMMER's articulatory classification is useless, since no unambiguously defined acoustic or auditory types correspond to these units. See for the discussion between the author and FORCHHAMMER particularly "Studia linguistica" VIII, 1954, pp. 34—61, and ibid. IX, 1955, pp. 88—101; FORCHHAMMER's own articulatory system may be studied e.g. in "Die Sprachlaute in Wort und Bild", 1942; in "Lautlehre oder Sprechkunde? (Phonetik oder Laletik?)", in "Zeitschrift für Phonetik" II, 1948, pp. 65—82; or in "Einführung in die allgemeine Sprechkunde (Laletik)", 1951.

Chapter IV. For the concept of glide as opposed to the stable or typical sound phases, see A. ELLIS, "On early English pronunciation", 1869; E. SIEVERS, "Grundzüge der Phonetik", 2nd ed., 1881, p. 107—108 (the first edition had the title "Grundzüge der Lautphysiologie", 1876); C. L. MERKEL, "Physiologie der menschlichen Sprache (physiologische Laletik)", 1866. The quotation from GEORGE MILLER is to be found in "For ROMAN JAKOBSON" (1956), p. 353; that from MARTIN Joos in "Journal of the Acoustical Society of America" XXII, 1950, p. 702. — The commutation test has been treated in detail by many specialists, e.g. by HJELMSLEV, "Prolegomena" (p. 74), who makes a logically important distinction between permutation, which is a shift within the chain (the syntagm), and commutation, which is a shift between units in the paradigm. A common term for both is mutation. It should be noted that in HJELMSLEV's terminology, substitution is the absence of mutation between members of a paradigm and is therefore the opposite of commutation. Certain entities consequently have neither commutation nor substitution (i.e. those which do not enter into the same paradigm, e.g. vowels and consonants, /h/ and /ŋ/ in English; see p. 73). — For the general debate concerning the phonemic principle we refer to the works quoted in the introduction and in Chap. I. An important theoretical analysis has also been given by A. JUILLAND, "Structural Relations", 1961. Phoneme definitions have been given e.g. by TRUBETZKOY in "Grundzüge", p. 34 (see also "Projet de terminologie phonologique standardisée" in "Travaux du Cercle linguistique de Prague" IV, 1931, p. 311); by W. FREEMAN TWADDELL in "On defining the phoneme", 1935; by ANDRÉ MARTINET, "Éléments de linguistique générale", 1960, p. 20 (cp. the same author's discussion in "Phonology as Functional Phonetics", Oxford 1955, pp. 1—10); by ZELLIG S. HARRIS in "Methods in Structural Linguistics", 1951, especially pp. 59 ff.; by KENNETH L. PIKE in "Phonemics. A Technique for Reducing Language to Writing", 1947; by ROMAN JAKOBSON, "On the Identification of Phonemic Entities" /Travaux du Cercle linguistique de Copenhague V, 1949/, pp. 205—213; by E. ALARCOS LLORACH, "Fonología española", 3rd ed., 1961; by AMADO ALONSO, "La identidad del fonema" /Revista de filología hispánica VI, 1944, pp. 280—283/, etc. Phonemic principles have been discussed in detail, and with numerous citations, by ELI FISCHER-JØRGENSEN in a series of articles and communications (for instance "On the Definition of Phoneme Categories" in "Acta linguistica" VII, 1952, p. 14 ff.; "The Commutation Test and its Application to Phonemic Analysis", in "For ROMAN JAKOBSON", pp. 141—151; "Remarques sur les principes de l'analyse phonémique", in "Recherches structurales", pp. 214—234). The quotation from JAKOBSON—FANT—HALLE is to be found in "Preliminaries", p. 6. For phonemic classification on the basis of complementary distribution, see e. g. MEYER-EPPLER, "Grundlagen", p. 279; H. SPANG-HANSSEN in "Proceedings of the VIIIth International Congress of Linguists", 1958, p. 182—194. Though DANIEL JONES' approach to the phoneme concept is rather different from that of the more definitely structural schools, we refer to his important book "The Phoneme", 2nd ed. 1962. — The phonemes of English have been treated by many scholars, e.g. A. COHEN, "The Phonemes of English", 1952; B. NORDHJEM, "The Phonemes of English. An Experiment in Structural Phonemics", 1960; for American English,

see particularly HARRIS, "Methods in Structural Linguistics", passim; cf. also CHARLES
F. HOCKETT, "A Manual of Phonology", 1955; G. L. TRAGER and H. LEE SMITH, "An
Outline of English Structure", 1957, etc. The French and Spanish problems quoted
in the footnote have been discussed by the author (MALMBERG, "Le système consonantique du français moderne", 1943), and by E. ALARCOS LLORACH, "Fonología
española", 3rd ed., 1961, §§ 96—100, respectively. For a more complete description of the French phonemic system, see my own recent article in "Orbis",
1962, where also Spanish and Italian are treated. — The alphabet of the International Association is to be found in several of its publications (the last edition
from 1949, last reprint from 1960). Instruments for acoustic analysis of speech
sounds have been described by G. FANT, "Modern Instruments and Methods for
Acoustic Studies of Speech" /Acta Polytechnica Scandinavica, Physics including
nucleonics, Series No.1, 1958; also published in the "Proceedings of the VIII International Congress of Linguists", Oslo University Press, 1958/. Synthetic methods
have also been described in the publications of the Haskins Laboratories; see for
instance F. S. COOPER, P. C. DELATTRE, A. M. LIBERMAN, J. M. BORST, L. J. GERST-
MAN, "Some experiments on the Perception of Synthetic Speech Sounds" /Journal
of the Acoustical Society of America XXIV, 1952, pp. 597—606/; LIBERMAN et al.,
"Tempo Frequency Change as a Cue for Distinguishing Classes of Speech Sounds"
/Journal of Experimental Psychology LII, 1956, pp.127—137/; id., "The Rôle
of Selected Stimulus-Variables in the Perception of the Unvoiced Stop Consonants"
/The American Journal of Psychology LXV, 1952, pp.497—516/; id., "Acoustic
Loci and Transitional Cues for Consonants" /Journal of the Acoustical Society
of America XXVII, 1955, pp. 769—733/; MARGUERITE DURAND, "La perception
des consonnes occlusives" /Studia linguistica VIII, 1954, pp. 110—122. — Neutralisation, syncretism and the concept of archiphoneme have been treated by
TRUBETZKOY, in "Grundzüge", pp. 206 ff, etc.; by HJELMSLEV, "Notes sur les oppositions supprimables" /Travaux du Cercle linguistique de Prague VIII, 1939, pp. 51—
57/, and in "Prolegomena", pp.87—93; and by MARTINET, "Neutralisation et
archiphonème" /Travaux du Cercle linguistique de Prague VI, 1936, pp.46—57/.
Cf. also ALONSO, in "Hispanic Review" XIII, 1945, pp.91—101. — The concept
of economy is due to MARTINET ("Économie des changements phonétiques",
Théorie générale, pp.1—195). Coarticulation has been examined instrumentally
by H. M. TRUBY, "Acoustico-Cineradiographic Analysis Considerations with
Especial Reference to Certain Consonantal Complexes" /Acta Radiologica, Suppl.
182, 1959; doctor's thesis, Lund 1959, printed in Stockholm/; on an articulatory
basis also by P. MENZERATH and A. DE LACERDA, "Koartikulation, Steuerung und
Lautabgrenzung" /Phonetische Studien, herausgeg. von PAUL MENZERATH, I,
1933/. Syllabation and phonemic interpretation of groups like mb, nd in African
languages (o-mba-nda) are discussed by OTTO VON ESSEN, "Die Silbe, ein phono-
logischer Begriff" /Zeitschrift für Phonetik V, 1951, pp.199—203/; "Über den Begriff der Silbe"/Wissenschaftliche Zeitschrift der Humboldt-Universität zu Berlin
V, 1955—56, pp.85—88/; see also for instance L. E. ARMSTRONG, "The Phonetic
and Tonal Structure of Kikuyu", 1940, pp.40ff. The reference to Gold is due to
JAKOBSON—FANT—HALLE, "Preliminaries", p.41; for the phonemic system of Guaraní, see for instance L. I. BRIDGEMAN in "International Journal of American
Linguistics" XXVII, 1961, pp.329—334; P. N. PRIEST, ANNE PRIEST and J. E.
GRIMES, ibid., pp.335—344, etc. — The particular problem of monophonemic
or biphonemic interpretation is the subject e.g. of articles by MARTINET, "Un
ou deux phonèmes?" in "Acta linguistica" I, 1939, pp.94—103, and by F. HINTZE
in "Studia linguistica" IV, 1950, pp.14—24. Harris' interpretation of Amer. Engl.
/ʃ/ is to be found in "Methods in Structural Linguistics", p.95; ELERT's study
on Swedish phonemics in "Arkiv för nordisk filologi" LXXII, 1957, pp.35—60.

C. E. Bazell has suggested that a phonemic unit exceptionally could be interpreted as monophonemic in opposition to one unit and as biphonemic as opposed to another (Engl. /tʃ/ monophonemic in opposition to /ts/ and biphonemic as opposed to stops). — For the phonemic interpretation of loan-words, see e.g. E. Polivanov, "La perception des sons d'une langue étrangère" /Travaux du Cercle linguistique de Prague IV, 1931, pp. 72—95/. For Fant's and Halle's hierarchic schemes of distinctive features, see e.g. G. Fant, "Structural Classification of Swedish Phonemes" /Speech Transmission Laboratory, Quarterly Progress and Status Report, 1961, pp. 10—15/. The examples of West-African tones are taken from Ida Ward (works quoted above), the Chinese example from B. Karlgren, "Kinesisk elementarbok", 1948, p. 11; the Vietnamese example from Lê Vǎn Ly, "Le parler vietnamien", 1948. For tone languages, see particularly K. L. Pike, "Tone Languages. A Technique for Determining the Number and Types of Pitch Contrasts in a Language", 1948. The Danish stød was instrumentally described by Svend Smith, "Bidrag til løsning af problemer vedrørende stødet i dansk rigssprog", 1944 (English summary: "Contribution to the Solution of Problems concerning the Danish Stød"). The example from Mende (West-African) is due to Trubetzkoy, "Grundzüge", p. 132. For the quotation from Leigh Lisker, see his article "Linguistic Segments, Acoustic Segments, and Synthetic Speech" /Language XXXIII, 1957, pp. 370—374/. Dwight D. Bolinger's work has the title "Generality, Gradience, and All-or-none", 1961. For Roman Jakobson's theory, see particularly "Kindersprache, Aphasie und allgemeine Lautgesetze" / Språkvetenskapliga Sällskapets i Uppsala förhandlingar 1940—1942/, and also Jakobson—Halle, "Fundamentals of Language", 1956, pp. 55—82. See also my own article "Om vår förmåga — och oförmåga — att behärska ett språksystem" /Nordisk Tidsskrift for Tale og Stemme, 1961, pp. 41—61/, and my reports to the IXth Intern. Congress of Linguists, Cambridge, USA, 1962, and to the Vth Intern. Congress of Phon. Sciences. Münster 1964.

Chapter V. Bühler's principle of "abstract relevancy" ("Prinzip der abstrakten Relevanz") is exposed in "Sprachtheorie", 1933, pp. 42—48. For the concepts relevant and irrelevant, see e.g. Trubetzkoy, "Grundzüge", particularly pp. 29 ff. For redundancy from the point of view of information theory, see e.g. Meyer-Eppler, "Grundlagen", pp. 60 ff. (Chapter "Informationsgehalt /Entropie/ und Redundanz"); Herdan, "Language as Choice and Chance", pp. 167—169. An extremely important contribution to the form-substance problem was given by E. Coseriu in "Forma y substancia en los sonidos del lenguage", 1954. My own analysis of French consonants was presented in "Le système consonantique du français moderne", 1943 (partly modified in my article in "Orbis", 1962). For Wang's and Fillmore's distinction between extrinsic and intrinsic cues, see their article in "Journal of Speech and Hearing Research" IV, 1961, No. 2, pp. 130—136; Jespersen's is to be found in "Lehrbuch der Phonetik", § 12.3; mine in "Die Quantität als phonetisch-phonologischer Begriff", 1944, p. 28—32. — The syllable has been treated recently by D. Jones in "Zeitschrift für Phonetik" IX, 1956, pp. 99—107; by A. Rosetti, "Sur la théorie de la syllabe", 1959; by A. Skaličkova in "Zeitschrift für Phonetik" XI, 1958, pp. 160—165; by B. Hála, "La syllabe, sa nature, son origine et ses transformations" /Orbis X, 1961, pp. 69—143/; and by the author of this book, particularly in "The Phonetic Basis for Syllable Division"/Studia linguistica IX, 1955, pp. 80—87; also ibid. X, 1956, pp. 35—37/; in "Remarks on a Recent Contribution to the Problem of the Syllable" /Studia linguistica XV, 1961, pp. 1—9/; and in "Juncture and Syllable Division" ("In Honour of Daniel Jones", 1964). Cf. also R. H. Stetson, "Motor Phonetics" 2nd ed. 1951. — The question of levels of abstraction in expression analysis has been treated in some more detail in my article "Levels of Abstraction in Phonetic and Phonemic Analysis" (Phonetica VIII, 1962, pp. 220—243). The

Swedish word accent was analysed instrumentally and structurally in the following publications of mine: "Recherches experimentales sur l'accent musical du mot en suédois" /Archives néerlandaises de phonétique expérimentale XVI, 1940, pp. 62—76/; "Sydsvensk ordaccent", 1953; "Observations on the Swedish Word Accent" /Haskins Laboratories, Report, 1955/; "Bemerkungen zum schwedischen Wortakzent" /Zeitschrift für Phonetik XII, 1959, Calzia-Festgabe, pp. 193—207/; and "Questions de méthode en phonétique synchronique" /Studia linguistica X, 1955, pp. 1—44/. A preliminary structural interpretation was proposed in my report to the 4th International Congress of Phonetic Sciences, Helsingfors 1961, and in my article "Levels of Abstraction" (quoted above). — For FRY's experiments, see "Duration and Intensity as Physical Correlates of Linguistic Stress" /Haskins Laboratories, Report, 1954/, and in "Experiments in the Perception of Stress" /Language and Speech I, 1958, pp. 126—152/. Similar problems were discussed by FISCHER-JØRGENSEN in "Die Bedeutung der funktionellen Sprachbeschreibung für die Phonetik" /Phonetica IV, 1959, pp. 7—27/, and in her report to the VIIIth International Congress of Linguists. Oslo 1958, pp. 433—478. For the Danish stød, see SMITH's work quoted in the preceding chapter. For Norwegian tones, see e. g. the numerous publications by E. W. SELMER in the series "Opuscula Phonetica", Oslo University. Tones in whispered Chinese have been studied by e. g. F. GIET, in "Lingua" V, 1956, pp. 372—381; cp. also MEYER-EPPLER, in "Journal of the Acoustical Society of America" XXIX, 1957, pp. 104—106, and my article in "Zeitschrift für Phonetik" XII, 1959, p. 207. LISKER's experiments concerning the American English voiced-voiceless distinction has been reported in "Language" XXX, No. 1, 1957, pp. 42—49. For Danish vowel phonemes, see e. g. POUL ANDERSEN, "Dansk fonetik" in "Nordisk lærebog for talepedagoger" I, 1954. LADEFOGED's and BROADBENT's experiments are reported in "Journal of the Acoustical Society of America" XXIX, 1957, pp. 98—104.

Chapter VI. The concept of distinctive feature was at the base already of the phonological program presented to the First International Congress of Linguistics in Amsterdam in 1928 ("Actes du premier congrès de linguistes", 1928, pp. 33—36) by JAKOBSON, KARCEVSKY, and TRUBETZKOY, and it was developed by TRUBETZKOY in "Grundzüge", pp. 29 ff. It was more expressly formulated in JAKOBSON—FANT—HALLE, "Preliminaries", 1952 (reprint 1955). For the following discussion about this basic concept and the binary principle we limit our references to a few notes: D. B. FRY in "For ROMAN JAKOBSON", pp. 169—173; MARTINET in "Économie", pp. 73 ff.; J. R. LICKLIDER in "Journal of the Acoustical Society of America" XXIV, 1952, p. 594; P. L. GARVIN, in "Language" XXIX, 1953, pp. 472—481 (the quotation on p. 479); H. MOL and E. M. UHLENBECK in "Lingua" IV, 1954, pp. 167—193; G. UNGEHEUER in "Studia linguistica" XIII, 1959, pp. 60—97. V. BRØNDAL's contribution is to be found in "Travaux du Cercle linguistique de Prague" VI, 1936, pp. 62—74 ("La structure des systèmes vocaliques"). For the articulatory orientation of the classical phoneticians, see e. g. O. RUSSELL, "The Vowel", 1928. WINTELER's scheme can be found in SIEVERS' "Grundzüge", 2nd ed., p. 70. WINTELER's most famous book is "Die Kerenzer Mundart des Kantons Glarus", 1876. He was one of the forerunners of phonemics. — SOL SAPORTA's and UNGEHEUER's works have been quoted above. GÖTE HANSON's investigation (from the Institute of Phonetics, Uppsala) is from 1962 ("Phoneme Perception. A Factorial Investigation" /Acta Universitatis Upsaliensis 1960/. The passage quoted from ULDALL is to be found in "Outline of Glossematics" p. 29. The quotation from A. LIBERMAN is taken from his article in SOL SAPORTA's "Psycholinguistics", mentioned in the notes to the Introduction. The reference to HERDAN concerns what he says in "Language as Choice and Chance", p. 162. For the problem of phonemic interpretation of foreign phonemes, see the reference

made in Chap. IV. — For the discussion about the binary principle, see M. HALLE,
"In the Defense of number two" /Studies presented to J. WHATMOUGH, 1957/,
and JAKOBSON's works quoted above; cp. also e.g. MEYER-EPPLER, "Grundlagen",
p. 319ff. The quotation on p. 126 is taken from p. 320 in his book.

Chapter VII. The idea of consonants as marginal units and of vowels as
central units is old, reflected e.g. already in the term "consonant" ("which sounds
with something"), or in the German terms "Selbstlaut" and "Mitlaut" (Swedish
"självljud", "medljud"). Traditional handbooks often define consonants as sounds
which cannot alone make up a syllable. — The idea that the syllable is just a phonological (structural) unit is due to OTTO VON ESSEN (works quoted in Chap. IV).
See also his chapter on the syllable in the 3rd edition of his "Allgemeine Phonetik"
(quoted above). Cf. my criticism in the articles quoted in Chap. VI. CARL HJ. BORG-
STRØM published his article in "Norsk Tidsskrift for Sprogvidenskap" XV, 1949,
pp. 137—187. I have published an article "Voyelle, consonne, syllabe, mot" in
"Miscelanea Homenaje a ÁNDRÉ MARTINET", part III, 1962. The generality of
open syllables has been pointed out by JAKOBSON (works quoted above). For the
primitive word type *mama* and *papa*, see JAKOBSON, "Why 'mama' and 'papa'?"
in "Perspectives in Psychology", 1961, pp. 124—134. For Japanese syllabic structure, see e. g. G. WENCK, "Japanische Phonetik" I, 1954, §§ 54—55. For SIGURD's
studies, see "Studia linguistica" XI, 1955, and XII, 1958; cf. his "Ponotactic
Structures" 1965; ELI FISCHER-JØRGENSEN's in "Acta linguistica" VII, 1952,
pp. 8—39. The mathematical theory behind SIGURD's analysis was exposed
by LARS GÅRDING in "Studia linguistica" XI, pp. 21—34 ("Relations and Order").
The syllabic structure of Spanish was treated by the author in "La structure
syllabique de l'espagnol" /Boletim de filologia IX, 1949, pp. 99—120/, and in
"Notes sur les groupes de consonnes en espagnol" /Zeitschrift für Phonetik II,
1948, pp. 239—255/; cf. also my "Linguistique ibérique et ibéro-romane" /Studia
linguistica XV, 1961, pp. 57—113/. The substitution of vowel length or vowel
quality for final -s in Spanish dialects was treated by T. NAVARRO TOMÁS, "Travaux
du Cercle linguistique de Prague" VIII, 1939, pp. 184—186; and E. ALARCOS
LLORACH, "Fonología y Fonética" /Archivum VIII, pp. 191—203, Universidad
de Oviedo, Facultad de Filosofía y letras, 1958/. Hottentot phonetics is described
by BEACH in "Phonetics of the Hottentot Language", 1938. The example given is
quoted from G. S. NIENABER in "Album EDGARD BLANQUAERT", 1958, pp. 113—
122. For the phonetics of Modern Greek, see J. T. PRINGS, "A Grammar of Modern
Greek on a Phonetic Basis", 1952. — The phonetic unity of the word was treated
by BJÖRN COLLINDER in "Das Wort als phonetische Einheit" /Språkvetenskapliga
sällskapets i Uppsala förhandlingar 1937—39, pp. 63ff./. The "word" was treated
by A. ROSETTI in "Linguistica", 1965. The French preference for open syllables
has been proved by GUNNAR VON PROSCHWITZ, "Étude sur la répartition des
syllabes ouvertes et fermées en français moderne", 1953. For the background of
consonant alternation in Celtic, see e.g. HOLGER PEDERSEN, "Vergleichende Grammatik der keltischen Sprachen" I, 1909, Chap. XIII, § 295ff.; and MARTINET,
"Économie", pp. 257ff. For FRANZ GIET's studies on Chinese tones, see his thesis
"Zur Tonität nordchinesischer Mundarten", 1949. MENZERATH's contributions to
the structure of German words were given in "Studia linguistica" IV, 1950, pp. 54
—93 (together with W. MEYER-EPPLER) and in his book "Die Architektonik des
deutschen Wortschatzes" /Phonetische Studien, herausgeg. von PAUL MENZERATH.
III, 1954/. ADOLF NOREEN's phoneme statistics for Swedish were published in
"Vårt språk" I, 1903, p. 542. G. K. ZIPF's fundamental works were "Relative Frequency as a Determinant of Phonetic Change" /Harvard Studies in Classical Philology XL, 1929/, and "Human Behavior and the Principle of Least Effort", 1949.
B. TRNKA's work on English has the title "A Phonological Analysis of Present-

Day Standard English", 1935. Cf. CARL-GUSTAF SÖDERBERG, "A Typological
Study on the Phonetic Structure of English Words with an Instrumental-Phonetic
Excursus on English Stress" /Travaux de l'Institut de phonétique de Lund, publiés
par BERTIL MALMBERG, I, 1959/. — Problems of linguistic statistics have been
treated by PIERRE GUIRAUD, particularly in "Les caractères statistiques du voca-
bulaire", 1954, and "Problèmes et méthodes de la statistique linguistique", 1960.
F. W. KÄDING's pioneer work had the title "Häufigkeitswörterbuch der deutschen
Sprache", 1898. Concerning LIBERMAN's opinion about the problem discussed in
this chapter, it is expressed in his article in SOL SAPORTA's "Psycholinguistics",
quoted above. — The general problem of the application and validity of statistics
in linguistic description was taken up recently by HANS KARLGREN in "Die Trag-
weite lexikalischer Statistik" /Språkvetenskapliga sällskapets i Uppsala förhandlingar 1958—60/. — The reference to HERDAN concerns "Language as Choice
and Chance", pp. 79—80.
    Chapter VIII. General problems of content and meaning have been treated
e. g. by GUSTAV STERN, "Meaning and Change of Meaning", 1931; by C. K. OGDEN
and I. A. RICHARDS, "The Meaning of Meaning", 1923 and following ed.; PAUL
DIDERICHSEN, "Semantiske problemer i logik og lingvistik", 1953; by CHARLES
MORRIS, "Foundations of the Theory of Signs", 1938, and "Signs, Language and
Behavior", 1946; by ERNST CASSIRER, "Philosophie der symbolischen Formen"
I—III, 1923—29; by STEPHEN ULLMAN, "Principles of Semantics", 2nd ed.,
1957, and "Semantics", 1962; by PIERRE GUIRAUD, "La sémantique", 1955;
by HANS REGNELL, "Symbolization and Fictional Reference", 1949, and "Semantik"
(a more general survey, written in Swedish), 1958. A short survey is also to be
found in my book "New Trends", pp. 123—139. A philosophical analysis of meaning
was given by N. E. CHRISTENSEN, "On the Nature of Meaning", 1961. — For the
more special problem of content analysis and content structure, see e. g. HJELMSLEV;
report to the VIIIth International Congress of Linguists, "Proceedings", pp. 636
—654 (answer to the question "Dans quelle mesure les significations des mots
peuvent-elles être considérées comme formant une structure?", and his more
popular article in Danish "Sprogets Indholdsform som Samfundsfaktor" /Det
danske Magasin II, No. 1, pp. 1—7/, translated into English, "The Content Form
of Language as a Social Factor", in "Essais linguistiques" /Travaux du Cercle
linguistique de Copenhague XII, 1959, pp. 89—95/; further JENS HOLT, "Rationel
Semantik (Pleremik)", 1946, and "Pleremics" /Proceedings of the University of
Durham Philosophical Society, Vol. I, 1959, pp. 49—53/; and RULON WELLS,
"Meaning and Use" /Linguistics Today, 1954, pp. 115—130; also Word X, 1954/.
Examples of different content structures (morphological as well as semantic)
have been given in my article "Opposition et identité", quoted in the Introduction.
For the Guaraní system of pronouns, see e. g. JUAN DE BIANCHETTI, "Gramática
guaraní", 1944. — The distinction between denotative and connotative meaning
has been worked out by several American linguists and is characteristic of the
semantic approach of the members of the so-called American semantic school.
We refer to S. J. HAYAKAWA, "Language in Thought and Reality", 1941; to Jo-
SEPH GREENBERG, "Essays in Linguistics", 1957; and to CHARLES FRIES, in "Lan-
guage" 1945. Important for the theory of content analysis is also B. LEE WHORF's
works (e. g. "Language, Thought, and Reality", selected writings, publ. by JOHN
B. CARROLL, 1956). — The semantic field theory has been worked out by JOST
TRIER, "Der deutsche Wortschatz im Sinnbezirk des Verstandes" I, 1831; by
WALTHER VON WARTBURG, "Begriffssystem als Grundlage für die Lexikographie",
1952. Cf. hereto also B. MALINOWSKI (e. g. "Culture", in "Encyclopaedia of the
Social Sciences" IV, 1935), who stresses the role of "the context of cultural reality",
"the context of situation", and "the context of speech"; and H. F. MULLER,

"Phénomènes sociaux et linguistiques" /Word I, 1945, pp. 121 – 131/. Important contributions to the field problems have been given by ELS OKSAARS, "Semantische Studien im Sinnbereich der Schnelligkeit" /Stockholmer Germanistische Forschungen, herausgeg. von G. KORLÉN, II, 1958/; and SUZANNE ÖHMAN, "Wortinhalt und Weltbild", 1951. Cf. also the works of WEISGERBER, GLINZ, etc. quoted in the Introduction and in Chap. I. – The author gave a short popular description of a Finnish girl's language learning in "Nordisk Tidskrift" XXI, 1945, pp. 170 – 181. Interference of content structure was treated by U. WEINREICH, "Languages in Contact", 1953. – Some of HUMBOLDT's works were quoted in the Introduction and above, Chap. I. HJELMSLEV's idea about the "iron curtain" was expressed in the article "Sprogets Indholdsform", quoted above. Cf. as to the final remarks in this chapter e. g. CASSIRER's article in "Word" I, 1945, pp. 99 – 120 ("Structuralism in Modern Linguistics"). Fundamental problems within the field of "sociological linguistics" have been treated by ALF SOMMERFELT in a series of articles (recently re-printed in "Diachronic and Synchronic Aspects of Language", 1962).

Chapter IX. This chapter is based entirely on KARL BÜHLER's so-called Organon-Modell. See in the first place "Sprachtheorie", 1934. We also refer to the works quoted above by GARDINER, KAINZ, and UNGEHEUER. My own personal ideas and conclusions have been presented in "Système et méthode", 1945 (particularly the chapter "Authour du problème langue – parole"). FELIX TROJAN's principal work is "Der Ausdruck der Sprechstimme; eine phonetische Lautstilistik", 2nd ed., 1952. LAZICZIUS' "emphaticum" is treated in "Proceedings of the 2nd Intern. Congress of Phonetic Sciences", p. 57, and in "Ungarische Jahrbücher" XV, 1935. The definition of style as the use made of the resources of a linguistic system is due to J. MAROUZEAU. A linguistic definition of style was given and applied by PIERRE NAERT, "Stilen i Vilhelm Ekelunds essäer och aforismer", 1949. JAKOBSON — FANT — HALLE's idea referred here is to be found in "Fundamentals of Language", p. 18. The problem of the linguistic analysis of sentence intonation was studied and demonstrated by KERSTIN HADDING-KOCH in her thesis "Acoustico-Phonetic Studies in the Intonation of Southern Swedish" /Travaux de l'Institut de phonétique de Lund, publiés par BERTIL MALMBERG, III, 1961/. – For classification as based on phonemic distinctions, see MEYER-EPPLER, "Grundlagen", quoted above. For tones in African poetry, see e. g. "Yoruba Poetry", collected and translated by BAKARE GBADAMOSI and ULLI BEIER, 1959 (Introduction). For SIEVER's "Schallanalyse", see e. g. O. GJERDMAN's critical survey "Die Schallanalyse" /Yearbook of the New Society of Letters at Lund, 1924, pp. 173 – 185/.

Chapter X. An article on the subject is the author's "Analyse linguistique et interprétation auditive" (Journal français d'oto-rhinolaryngologie XI, 1962, pp. 807 – 818). For the problem in general, see e. g. H. FLETCHER, "Speech and Hearing in communication", 2nd ed., 1953; and the works quoted in Chap. II (MILLER, CHERRY, CARROLL, and FRY). Cf. W. A. VON BERGEIJK, J. R. PIERCE, and E. E. DAVID Jr., "Waves and the Ear", 1960. – The quotation from BRUNER is to be found in the "Psychological Review" XLIV, 1957, pp. 123 – 152. H. JACOBSON's investigation is reported in "Journal of the Acoustical Society of America" XXIII, 1951, pp. 463 ff. (the scheme on p. 465). BROWN's and HILDUM's experiment is presented in "Language" XXXII, 1956, pp. 411 – 419 ("Expectancy and the Perception of Syllables"). For HELMHOLTZ's vowel theory, which is still the very starting-point even for modern acoustic analysis of vowels, see his "Die Lehre von den Tonempfindungen", 1863. For segmentation problems, see in the first place the numerous publications of the Haskins Group (some of which are quoted in Chap. IV); and G. FANT and B. LINDBLOM, in "Speech Transmission Laboratory, Quarterly Progress and Status Report", Royal Technical Institute, Stockholm,

July 1961, pp. 1—10. LIBERMAN's ideas about the role of articulation for identification of linguistic stimuli are expressed in his article in SOL SAPORTA's "Psycholinguistics" (quoted in the notes to the Introduction). MANDELBROT's article was
published in "Word" X, 1954, pp. 1—27 (the anecdote quoted is to be found on
p. 7).

   Chapter XI. The chapter is based on R. JAKOBSON's great theory of linguistic
(phonemic) hierarchy as expressed particularly in his "Kindersprache" (quoted
in Chap. IV). Cf. also my own article "Om vår förmåga" (quoted in the same
chapter), and my report to the IXth International Congress of Linguists, 1962.
For further examples of children's speech and nursery words, see JAKOBSON,
"Why 'mama' and 'papa'?" (quoted in Chap. VII), and the classical work by
R. MERINGER and K. MAYER, "Versprechen und Verlesen", 1895. — Some other
general works on children's speech and on aphasia: A. GRÉGOIRE, "L'apprentissage
du langage" I—II, 1937—1947; O. JESPERSEN, "Language", 1922 and ff. (particularly Chap. II "The Child"), and other works of the same author; E. FRÖSCHELS etc.,
"Psychological Elements in Speech", 1932; A. OMBREDANE, "L'aphasie et l'élabora-
tion de la pensée explicite", 1950; M. FOG and K. HERMANN, "Om afasi", 1941;
R. LUCHSINGER and G. E. ARNOLD, "Lehrbuch der Stimm- und Sprachheilkunde",
2nd ed., 1959; W. PENFIELD and L. ROBERTS, "Speech and Brain Mechanisms",
1959; M. JOOS, in "Language", XXXIII, 1957, pp. 408—415.

   Chapter XII. Linguistic change is discussed in old handbooks of general
linguistics of traditional orientation. The strictest application of structural principles made hitherto is MARTINET's "Économie". Cp. the important contribution
to the problem synchrony — diachrony made by E. COSERIU in "Sincronía, dia-
cronía e historia", 1958. Other important works on "historical phonemics" than
MARTINET's have been published by e.g. A. G. HAUDRICOURT and A. G. JUIL-
LAND, "Essai pour une histoire structurale du phonétisme français", 1949; by
H. WEINREICH, "Phonologische Studien zur romanischen Sprachgeschichte",
1958; by H. LÜDTKE, "Die strukturelle Entwicklung des romanischen Vokalismus",
1956; and by B. SIGURD, "The Code Shift in Old Norse" /Studia linguistica XV,
1961, pp. 10—21/. — The role of distribution in phonemic change was studied
by REBECCA R. POSNER in "Consonantal Dissimilation in the Romance languages",
1961. My results on Spanish phonetic change have been reported in several articles
(e.g. "Le passage castillan f > h — perte d'un trait redondant?" /Mélanges linguistiques offerts à EMIL PETROVICI par ses amis étrangers à l'occasion de son
soixantième anniversaire, 1958, pp. 337—343/; and "La structure phonétique de
quelques langues romanes" /Orbis XI, 1962, pp. 160—162/, etc.). An example
of a structural explication of sound shifts was given in my article "A propos d'un
fait de phonétique historique castillane" /Lingua XI, 1962, pp. 276—279 [also
Studia gratulatoria dedicated to ALBERT WILLEM DE GROOT in the year of his
seventieth birthday]/. — The problems of sound change and sound laws as well
as the numerous problems connected with them have been discussed in more
detail in my book "New Trends", Chap. I, with references. A general survey was
given by E. H. STURTEVANT in "Linguistic Change", 1942, and "An Introduction
to Linguistic Science", 1947; by W. P. LEHMANN in "Historical Linguistics",
1962, etc.

Author Index

The numbers in *italics* refer to the Bibliographical Notes

208 Author Index

Subject Index

Offsetdruck: Julius Beltz, Weinheim/Bergstr.